RECORDING AND ANALYZING
CHILD BEHAVIOR

RECORDING
AND ANALYZING
CHILD BEHAVIOR

with Ecological Data from an American Town

HERBERT F. WRIGHT

University of Kansas

From an Earlier Volume:
Midwest and Its Children

HARPER & ROW, PUBLISHERS
NEW YORK, EVANSTON, AND LONDON

Library of Congress Catalog Card Number: 66–17285

CONTENTS

PREFACE

Essentially, these chapters abridge and reassemble Chapters V-VIII and X-XII of *Midwest and Its Children* (Barker and Wright, 1955), which is now out of print.

This book sets apart and reintroduces a method for description of the naturally occurring situations and behavior of individuals. Conceptual grounds of the method are represented, and so are data from its application to children of Midwest, a town in the central part of the United States. It is hoped that the reintroduction may extend examining and testing of one way to study behavior in its natural habitat, that it also may extend the useful life of the data, and that it may complement reports of later studies in which modifications of the method or similar methods have been applied.

The research of *Midwest and Its Children* was done under the direction of Roger G. Barker and the present author. In the face of a many-sided task, we were obliged to work out a division of labor to implement joint planning. Continuous responsibility for the development of this part and the writing up of it fell to me. But the main ideas and research processes here and the particular formulations at many points owe much indeed to the creativity of Roger Barker, who first called what the book is about: the method of the *specimen record*. Concerning origins, I have thought it of general interest in connection with the method that, before Midwest, he and students of his classes had experimented, in the direction of this work, with the making and analysis of narrative behavior records.

Jack A. Nall and Phil H. Schoggen made special contributions by way of projects that are to be identified. Both participated additionally with Louise S. Barker, William A. Koppe, and Lorene N. Wright as research associates in the larger investigation; and others who took part in the work represented here are: Don Albert, Chris Argyris, Margery Baldwin, William A. Binns, Harold R. Dickman, William Dreese, Beverly Fox, Milton Horowitz, Lucille Johnson, Blaine Kinkaid, John Lubach, Louise Mason, Irene Nall, Howard V. Perlmutter, Robert Reiff, Mariana Remple, and Maxine Schoggen.

It is gratefully acknowledged that financial support of the research was provided throughout its course by PHS grant MH-6, from the National Institute of Mental Health, and that funds for special parts of the work were supplied by the University of Kansas, the Association for the Aid of Crippled Children, and the Carnegie Corporation of New York.

Great indebtedness of the investigators to many individuals for participation in the field and analytical tasks of the research and for teaching and counseling that helped us to lay its conceptual groundwork have been put on record in the source volume; and full thanks to all of these persons are renewed. The earlier book was dedicated to Kurt Lewin and the people of Midwest. So also is this one.

I am grateful to D. D. M. Ragle for a reading of the present manuscript and to Betty S. Allen for preparing it.

Code names are used, in protection of privacy, for the subject persons and communities.

H. F. W.

Lawrence, Kansas
October, 1966

RECORDING AND ANALYZING
CHILD BEHAVIOR

Chapter 1

THE DESCRIPTION AND THE ECOLOGY OF BEHAVIOR

BEHAVIOR IN LIFE AND THE LABORATORY

This book presents a way to describe the life situations and behavior of individuals and applies it to the behavior streams of children who lived in or near the American town of Midwest during the middle years of the twentieth century.

The application of the method is ecological in purpose. Ecological research in the biological sciences is concerned with the habitats or natural environments of plants and animals and with the related structures and functions of the living organism. We are here concerned analogously with the habitat of the Midwest child and with the related structural properties and content of his behavior.

The first psychological scientists worked in laboratories where, as new practitioners of the experimental method, they created special environments for their subjects. The experimenter supplied and arranged exterior conditions to suit his problem and then recorded the behavioral effects of these conditions. Until today, moreover, this model of manipulative control over the environmental determinants of behavior has largely ruled the scope as well as the procedures of psychological research (cf. Barker, 1965). Psychologists have not often ventured as scientists into naturally occurring environments. They have not often sought to record and examine the characteristics and the behavioral effects of exterior conditions that nature and society create. In short, for whatever reasons, which are here to be left to the sociology of science, psychology lacks a developed ecology of human behavior.

Consequent serious gaps in our knowledge of human behavior are apparent. Experiments can tell us what will happen if stated conditions of behavior occur. Drawing examples only from research with children, one can say that, *if* children are deprived, frustrated, praised, or blamed as in named experimental studies, *then*, they may tenably be expected to behave in specified ways. But these investigations have not disclosed, nor can studies like them be hoped to discover, the distributions and the manifestations and effects upon behavior of deprivation, frustration, praise, or blame in the daily lives of children. Knowledge of child behavior from psychological tests is similarly illustrative. It tells us what children are able or disposed to do under specified conditions. But we lack comparable information about the tests that families, playmates, organized groups, and, in short, whole communities give to children, and the performances of children in response to them. Scientific knowledge of what persons can or will do if their life situations are thus and so, notwithstanding its great importance, leaves an unfilled need for research to describe what persons actually do and have done to them in these situations.

Some beginnings have been made in psychological investigation of ecological significance. Examples are to be found in time-honored biographies of young children (inventoried in Dennis, 1936), in case studies (White, 1952), in assays of personal documents (Allport, 1942), in studies of work efficiency (Muse, 1946; Barnes, 1958), in self reports (Sorokin and Berger, 1939), in surveys of resources for behavior in communities (Koppe, 1954; Muchow and Muchow, 1935), and in primarily observational studies of behavior: at school (Anderson, 1939; Biber, *et al.*, 1942; Dawe, 1934), in therapeutic milieux (Raush, 1959; Raush, *et al.*, 1959a, 1959b, and 1960), and in communities at large (Barker and Wright, 1951; Barker, 1963; Wright, 1961, 1966). This is not the place for extended review of the pertinent research. Suffice it to say that contributions by psychologists to description of naturally occurring human behavior and its conditions stand out in comparative isolation.

Psychology differs here from other sciences. Natural history studies have long supplied basic data for the theories and applications of biology. Astronomy and the earth sciences are monuments to investigation that examines at first hand what it finds in nature. All of the social sciences but psychology owe most of their empirical accomplishments to direct recording of conditions and events in society. Even the predominantly experimental sciences of physics and chemistry have amassed and regularly call upon stores of information about the incidence in nature of their materials and subject processes. Psychology appears to stand alone as a science without a substantial descriptive, naturalistic, ecological side.

What is the territorial range of the child who lives in a metropolitan suburb? On a farm? In an American small town? How are the situations and resulting behavior of children altered by economic booms and busts? By holidays and family vacations? By wars and the threat of war? How may crucial psychological conditions of life differ across large and small families? Across national cultures? Across large and small communities? Such questions have been left as a rule to novelists, journalists, biographers, and other lay observers and interpreters of behavior, whose contributions to our psychological understanding, invaluable though they are, lack the advantages in positive knowledge that scientific field research can bring.

It can be added to this that ecological investigation in psychology offers more than faithful description as an end to be desired in itself. For one important thing, it stands also to extend the limits of our knowledge about the laws of behavior. Although the accomplishments of laboratory science foster belief that it can bring virtually anything under experimental control, this is more difficult in practice than in principle. Laws of rivers and whirlwinds can be investigated in laboratories, but it is necessary to go to natural settings to learn how and how much to allow for important complications in these uniformities; and it would seem reasonable to assume that a like necessity must hold indeed for the vastly more complex phenomena of human behavior. It is fortunate, therefore, that psychological experiments in nature are abundant everywhere and that we need only suitable methods to capitalize upon them. These experiments rarely if ever conform to the rule of one variable. But this stricture has anyhow become increasingly suspect in all sectors of psychological inquiry. Multivariable research designs are increasing as recognition of behavioral complexity grows and technical facilities for the transformation of phenomena into data are improved. Behavior in its natural habitat must require at last the ultimate in these designs and give the fullest opportunity to test them in explorations of basic psychological regularities.

The descriptive procedures here are based upon direct field observation of behavior and its environmental conditions. This alone, however, does not make them contribute to the ecology of behavior. Ecological investigation in psychology has to be defined by its objective rather than its means: by the purpose of revealing the naturally given habitat and behavior of the individual. Non-observational procedures, such as interviewing and projective testing, have been used to this end (Wright, 1961, 1966). Observational procedures, on the other hand, can be and have been used for purposes that are not ecological. A survey (Wright, 1960) of literature in child development has shown that, prior to 1960, 1409 empirical studies with children or adolescents as subjects had been reported in principal journals of the field. In the first place, only 110 or 8 percent of these studies were found to be observational in method; and, beyond this, a minority of the observational investigations proved to be ecological in aim.

Normative, idiographic, and *systematic* objectives respectively appeared in (1) studies in which children were classified as to age or some other variable and then observed directly for the purpose of disclosing central behavior tendencies in the distinguished populations: 2-year-olds, 5-year-olds, boys, girls, or the like, (2) studies of particular children as individual persons, and (3) studies of relationships between universal behavior variables that were singled out for attention in the absence of explicit regard for the contextual significance of habitat conditions.

Future nonecological uses of direct observation in psychological research with children seem variously promising. Normative applications can supply norms that describe the behavior of children with an authenticity and fullness beyond the hard numbers from psychological tests. Idiographic applications can enrich personality assessments, concerning which a critical point is that the diagnostic tools of clinical investigation are often cross-validated within a kind of closed system in the clinic setting. Observational techniques can extend the range of this system by validating projective instruments, play sessions, and similar devices against accounts of everyday behavior and its conditions. Systematic applications, as earlier suggested here, can at least be fairly expected to enlarge the scope of laboratory investigation in the face of behavior variables that defy experimental manipulation. (Cf. ibid.)

Both the recording and the analysis procedures of the observational method at hand would seem to be open, in principle if not always in detail, to testing for each of these purposes as well as for the ecological purpose to which they are here committed.

MIDWEST AND THE SUBJECT CHILDREN

Here is a sketch of Midwest from a writing that presents it essentially as the town stood in the 1950s.

Midwest has a population of 725. It is the seat of an agricultural county in the central part of the United States. It is surrounded by rolling, partly wooded farmlands and pastures that are cut by winding streams.

Although no railroad or transcontinental highway touches it, Midwest is not an isolated town. It is within an hour's automobile drive of five cities with populations varying from 10,000 to 500,000, and scheduled bus and truck service help to make these cities easily available. Fifteen randomly selected issues of the *Midwest Weekly* report 178 vacation or business trips by residents of Midwest. The destination on 64 of these trips was more than 500 miles away. The same issues of the *Weekly* report 160 visitors to Midwest. Over 90 percent of the families of the town receive a city newspaper daily. Practically every family has a radio. At almost any time there are four or five out-of-state automobiles on the streets. The currents of American life flow strongly through Midwest.

And there is a strong and full life within Midwest; it is a self-sufficient community. Near though it is to the five cities, the town is not a suburb to any larger place. Only 10 of its 338 gainfully employed adults commute daily to a city to work. Most of the necessities and many of the adornments of modern life can be secured within its borders. The vitality of the community is suggested by the existence in Midwest of more than 140 organized groups, including business and professional establishments, governmental and religious institutions, and civic and social clubs.

The economy of Midwest is dominated by three facts: it is a county seat; it is not on a railroad; it is surrounded by farms. The economic activity of the town is based upon the distribution and repair of goods, personal and professional services, and governmental work. Ninety percent of all businesses are locally owned and managed. Eighteen percent of the gainfully employed hold government jobs.

The town is neither wealthy nor poor. There are no rich families in Midwest. A number of families maintain a living standard that includes a new car once every two or three years, clothes of the latest fashion, a sizeable yearly vacation, a modernized home with the latest equipment, an education for the grownup children in a nearby college or university. At the other extreme, a few aged and infirm persons are receiving public assistance, although not a single employable resident of Midwest is on relief.

The social class differences in Midwest are small. There are no segregated residential districts in Midwest; no slum, no country club. Most of the social organizations of the town are open to citizens of all groups. The dim social class lines are honored as much in the breach as in the observance.

Midwest covers an area of 400 acres on a slightly elevated knoll. From the borders of the town one can see a mile or two in almost every direction. The town site includes 100 acres of land under cultivation. Two hundred and sixty-five houses, 54 business places, and 10 public buildings stand on the remaining 300 acres. The homes of Midwest are not crowded together. Few of the houses are on lots smaller than 100 by 200 feet. The architectural center of the town is a red brick courthouse, two stories high, which dignifies a tidy square. The business district surrounds the square and with it occupies about 10 acres. (Adapted, with minor omissions and paraphrasing, from Barker and Wright, 1951, pp. 2–4.)

These particulars reveal Midwest much as one might read about it if a guidebook were to be prepared for the tourists who sometimes reach it on side-trips. These sojourners, however, would see in some degree parts of the town to which the sketch only alludes, but in which, nevertheless, the citizens of the town selectively live and move around the clock every day. The visitor could not fail to see the Post Office, and he might easily note Cliffords Drugstore on a corner, Garnett's Grocery next door, the Variety Store next to it, and so on around the square. Continuing, he might see a duly scheduled occurrence of the Boys' Town Baseball Game or of the Midwest Garden Tour, the Chaco Service Station, the Office of Attorney Wolf, a Vacant Lot here and there, the Cemetery, and, stopping to talk or to glance through an issue of the local *Weekly,* he could learn of the Annual Rotary Club Football Banquet, the Women's Club I Regular Meeting, the Boy Scout Court of Honor Session, or the Last Day of School Dinner. These are *behavior settings* of Midwest, and their plain visibility extends from the tourist to the social scientist as well as to the people of the town. Conceptual properties, special criteria, measurable dimensions, and theoretical uses of behavior settings are elaborated in reports of earlier research (Barker and Wright, 1955; Barker, 1960; Barker and Barker, 1961; Barker and Gump, 1964), so that it is sufficient here only to note the essential marks of these ecological units.

A behavior setting is defined by two components: a stable part of the physical and social milieu of a community, and an attached standing pattern of human behavior. The milieu part invariably has distinguishing attributes of time, place, things, and inhabitants that fit the behavior pattern and supply it with behavior supports. Invariably, too, this pattern is extraindividual and invariant in that it stays fundamentally the same while different individuals enter the setting and leave it. Consider as an example the Methodist Regular Worship Service in Midwest.

Its time is 11 to 12 A.M. every Sunday, and its place the Methodist Sanctuary. Its things include hymn books, collection plates, and a pulpit. Ushers, congregation members, the choir, and a minister are its inhabitants. These elements form the milieu part. The behavior pattern includes ushering, sitting, standing for prayer, preaching and listening, gathering in the vestibule, conversing, and shaking hands, all of which change little Sunday after Sunday, year after year, no matter who goes to church. (Wright, 1956, p. 266.)

Behavior settings are by no means neutral scenes of action. They are the seats of forces that coerce behavior, as one can see by watching the behavior of Midwest children change rapidly from setting to setting through a day. Settings are also behaviorally all-embracing in a community; everything everyone does "in town" occurs within their boundaries.

For these and other reasons, behavior settings have been used for earlier description (Barker and Wright, 1955) of the larger habitat in which the children of Midwest behave. This description divides the town into elemental and yet comparatively gross environmental units in such a way as to present basic living resources of Midwest's citizens en masse. It does not bring into the foreground, however, the sights and sounds, the particular things and persons, the acts of persons, the invitations and denials, the commands, the problems, the rewards and punishments that make up the immediate situations and directly affect the behavior of individual Midwest persons. All such momentarily changing and directly effective conditions of behavior belong to what we shall call the *psychological habitat* of the individual; and it is principally these conditions and their behavior correlates that are to serve here for demonstration of one way to describe and analyze child behavior. Actions in sequence and the here-and-now ingredients of psychological habitat are mixed as interdependent parts of the individual behavior stream. That stream does not flow in an ecologically seamless channel; it winds across the boundaries and within the interior regions of behavior settings. We shall not reintroduce the earlier behavior setting survey. But it will be necessary to refer at various points to behavior settings of Midwest in tracing the behavior streams of Midwest children from part to part of the community.

It also will be necessary to refer at various points to *behavior objects* of Midwest. These community parts occur within settings. They include physical objects, or things, and social objects, or persons. Each is like a setting in that a milieu part and an attached standing behavior pattern define it. The critical mark of distinction here is that, in the case of an object, the pattern is circumjacent to the milieu part, whereas the reverse holds for a setting. The behavior of a child occurs around and about a mother, for example, but within a home; or around and about a school book, but within a school classroom. Midwest children will later be seen to transact behavior with diverse behavior objects in settings of the town.

We have chosen as main subjects of the demonstration Midwest children under 12 years of age and, for special comparative purposes, physically disabled children of the same age range in nearby communities. The children of different studies are designated in course and represented in the Appendix. Each sketch identifies the child minimally as to personal characteristics, presents the members of his family, and notes characteristics of his home or institutional setting. Most of the stated particulars are everyday facts that people of Midwest and the neighboring communities commonly note and understand.

As will be found, every child is placed as to social class or *group*. On the basis of the Warner participation criteria (Warner, *et al.*, 1949), three social classes appear in Midwest: groups I, II, and III, which correspond respectively to Warner's Upper Middle, Lower Middle, and Upper Lower categories. The class identifications are based upon the ratings of three resident staff members, whose judgments were checked independently with the Index of Status Characteristics (cf. *ibid.*) on a sample of 71 families, for 62 of which the two methods gave the same placements. The assignment by the criteria of participation was found to be justified in every case when the disagreements were carefully scrutinized, in view of which the original staff judgments were used throughout.

The reader might now wish to have the information about these children that skillful uses of ink blots, pictures, incomplete sentences, other testing materials, and carefully framed questions would give. The investigators, in any case, would value such information. But our goal was to see what could be learned to advantage about the behavior of the children and their conditions without pressing questions or anything else upon them. Midwest was the ink blot; and the various test items were, as anticipated above, the circumstances and things of its behavior settings, although this should not be taken to imply that efforts were made to probe into the personalities of the children. The observers went to the children to see what could be seen of their *behavior* and of the things and events in its context, to examine these phenomena, and to arrive at something of a picture that would show what it means for a child to live and behave in Midwest.

How was this to be done?

THE STEPS OF THE METHOD

The method has three parts: recording the stream of behavior, dividing it into units, and analyzing the units one by one. These stages of description are treated in the succeeding chapters.

How can one set down in retrievable form the ongoing behavior and moment-to-moment things, persons, and events in the life of a child? What procedures can achieve rich enough and sufficiently reliable specimens of these phenomena? Chapter 3 answers to these questions.

The stream of behavior has continuity. Yet it is in some respects less like a stream than a chain; it has links such that its continuity is continually one thing after the other. Then by what criteria can the integral parts of the continuum be recognized? This is a problem in unit formation and detection. What are the defining properties of basic, if not *the* basic, units of everyday behavior, and how may these be marked off from one another meaningfully, manageably, and reliably in the behavior record? This unitizing problem is dealt with in Chapter 4.

Consider *Objecting to Getting Picture Taken*, to look ahead to a behavior unit that the method has discriminated. Objecting by whom and to whom? Where? That is, in what behavior setting? Against how much social pressure, and at what advantage or disadvantage in relative power, with how much eventual resistance or submission, and with what degree of terminal satisfaction, dissatisfaction, failure or success? These questions exemplify what is meant by stepwise analysis of the separate behavior units. An instrument for one kind of behavior-unit analysis, within the limits set by phenomena of interpersonal action, is presented in Chapter 6.

Chapter 7 exhibits some behavior specimens, a unit at a time. These units have been found to sustain to one another various interpositional and temporal relationships that characterize the structure or anatomy of behavior. Results of a special inquiry into behavior structure as it occurs in the days of Midwest children and disabled children of nearby communities are set forth in Chapter 5, and Chapter 8 reports results from application of the interpersonal-action instrument, again to the behavior units of Midwest and nearby disabled children.

We are concerned throughout with behavior and psychological habitat as the all-inclusive objects of study. It is necessary, therefore, that each be examined in preparation for the reports of what has been done with both in the field; and this is the assignment for the next chapter.

Chapter 2

BEHAVIOR AND HABITAT AS DESCRIPTIVE TARGETS

LEVELS OF BEHAVIOR

One way of setting off the behavior to be described is to identify it as primarily molar rather than molecular.[1] Consider the following comparisons.

[1] Since they were used first in psychology by Tolman (1932) in the context of learning theory and data, these terms have acquired a somewhat bewildering variety of psychological meanings, as Littman and Rosen (1950) have shown. Yet we know of no better words for our purpose. Others who have dealt with this problem include Lewin (1936), Murray (1938), Muenzinger (1942), and McDougall (1923). Our view may differ most from other views of the problem in more concern here with direct observation of behavior.

Perspiration	*versus*	Hurrying to school
Salivation, chewing, swallowing, grasping	*versus*	Eating lunch at home or buying candy at Clifford's Drug Store
Elbow bending, extensor adjustments of the fingers, visual fixation	*versus*	Saluting the flag
Movements of the lips, tongue, vocal cords, arms, legs, trunk, and diaphragm	*versus*	Reciting at school

The units of behavior on the right necessarily engage a person; those on the left engage only subordinate and more or less independent parts or mechanisms of the person. A *child* never perspires in running to school or salivates in buying candy; and a child rarely bends his arm in saluting the flag or moves his tongue in reciting a lesson. He runs to school, buys the candy, salutes the flag, and recites the lesson while, cotemporaneously, lesser systems do the sweating, salivating, bending, and the like, with greater or lesser independence of the person as a superordinate whole.

It is true that in common speech the parts of persons are sometimes the subjects of sentences about behavior of the person as a whole. And the reverse also holds; persons are sometimes the subjects of sentences about behavior of their parts. "His hand shot up in answer to the question" and "Her eyes said, 'Yes' " are examples of the former construction. We recognize the elliptical nature of every such statement, however, and do not fail to find in a person the unit source of the behavior. On the other hand, when it is said of a person that "He sweat profusely" or that "He swept his eyes back and forth across the page while reading the book," we know again more or less explicitly that the statement leaves something out, and understand that the behavior is an event of a subordinate mechanism.

Examine again the parallel lists of behavior units. Those on the right occur in relation to parts of the world with some kind and degree of meaning for the person: school; the hum in the classroom; the candy, Mr. Clifford, and the drug store; and the flag. The units on the left have essentially different contexts. They go off in relation to thermal and chemical conditions, light waves, sound waves, and physical impacts that are not organized by cognitive processes of the organism into meaningful things and events.

The units on the right exemplify molar behavior or *actions* while those on the left exemplify molecular behavior or *actones* (cf. Murray, 1938). The molar units are molar in the sense that they occur in the context of the person as a whole and a molar environment. The molecular units are molecular in the sense that they occur in the context of subordinate parts or mechanisms of the person and a molecular environment. The size of a piece of behavior, as defined by how long it lasts or how much of the physical organism it uses, cannot be made a test for this distinction. Bodily massive and long extended patterns of behavior, like the movements in walking, swimming, or dancing, can be molecular whenever they only mediate action by the person; and, conversely, very small behaviors are often molar. A footstep can be molar in the context of crossing a muddy street, and so can a wink in the context of a love affair.

Molar behavior has two additional main distinguishing features, both implicit in the idea of action by a person. It is goal directed and it generally occurs within the cognitive field of the person.

As for the first of these ascriptions, an action is always a "getting to" or a "getting from" a part of the molar environment (cf. Tolman, 1932). It is, in the language of Lewin (1936), a locomotion or change in position of the person from a *starting region* to a terminal or subordinate *goal region* of the life space. Physical, social, and "intellectual" ("imaginal," "mental") locomotions are distinguished by Lewin: a child goes from home to school, from bidding for attention to getting it, from 9×43 to 387. Each of these behavior units is an action and, as such, each entails a particular directional change in position of the person.

To say that molar behavior generally occurs within the cognitive field of the person is only to recognize that characteristically a person knows, within limits, what he is doing. Nor can we believe that the most ardent devotee of the unconscious will doubt the truth of this, within limits. The action of the moment, simultaneously occurring or alternative and mutually exclusive actions, actions of the immediate and remote past, and future things to be done all may exist as cognitively separate units of a person's situation.

Molecular behavior, on the other hand, is not comparably structured. Turning a wheel is not generally perceived as a part of driving somewhere in a car. Neither are individual steps of the feet generally perceived as parts of walking to a store, nor oculomotor movements as parts of reading a book, nor laryngeal adjustments as parts of making a speech. There is no boundary line for the person between consecutive molecular units such as these.

It is true at the same time that units of molar behavior are not all differentiated cognitively with equal clarity.

At one extreme there are small molar parts of larger, including actions. These involve the person with minor subgoals within the whole configuration of an including action unit. They can virtually "go unnoticed," especially when they occur only as "means to an end" under circumstances such that their own ends are not sought in themselves. Opening a door on the way downtown, righting an easel in painting a picture, walking one block of three in catching a train, even scanning a paragraph in reading a book sometimes are examples. Like molecular units, actions on this level may lack discreteness as parts of an own behavior sequence.

There are at the other extreme inclusive units of molar behavior in pursuit of major long-range goals. These also tend to go unnoticed or to be only vaguely perceived. Persisting actions that unfold gradually over long periods of time have indeed been referred often to entirely unconscious processes.

Implications for behavior description in these minimal identifying characteristics of molar and molecular behavior are developed in the following sections and in Chapter 3.

DEPENDENCY BETWEEN BEHAVIOR ORDERS

Molar and molecular behavior units are by no means phenomena of completely foreign orbits. On the contrary, they are joined by links homologous to those between the whole of a person and the subordinate parts of this whole. While partially independent as events on different levels, they are also partially interdependent as events of a larger system. Goldstein (1939) has shown that the interdependence works both ways; that "part responses" of the organism depend upon the processes of the whole individual and vice versa.

As for the partial independence of actions, there is ample precedent in science for treating them as processes with some integrity. Precisely as the laws of wheels and levers, of planetary and trade winds, of ocean currents, and the classical laws for gases have been demonstrated without reference to subordinate arrangements and changes on the level of material particles, so uniform relationships may reasonably be expected to hold for molar behavior without reference to molecular behavior units. The biological version of this position has been expounded by Novikoff, who states that each stratum of biological organization, whether that of the cell, the tissue, the organ, the organ system, or the whole organism, ". . . possesses unique properties of structure and behavior which, though dependent on the properties of the constituent elements, appear only when these are combined in the new system." He adds that "the laws describing the unique properties of each level are qualitatively distinct, and their discovery requires methods of research and analysis appropriate to the particular level" (Novikoff, 1945, p. 209). The facts of biological research are in line with this view. Thus the biologist who studies the intact multicellular organism uses different techniques and a different set of explanatory concepts than the biologist who studies individual cells. Obviously, for example, the former would reap nothing but confusion if he applied the presently available methods of cytology to the problems of mammalian respiration.

There may be no real need to suppose that in the domain of any science the properties of a superordinate level are in some way "emergents" which, in theory, could never be revealed by study of relationships between the elements of subordinate orders. The question as to whether or not this is true can be left open. It holds either way in practice that, of the different orders in many event hierarchies, each shows unique properties and raises special questions which, up to the present time in the history of science, have required special methods. "Living cells present problems not to be encountered in the test tube or flask" (Novikoff, 1945, p. 210). Similarly the actions of persons present unique properties and problems not to be encountered in the behavior of their parts.

One may not discriminate both molar units, on the one hand, and molecular units, on the other, in observing a behavior sequence. The whole complex is often perceived as a more or less unified pattern, much as one hears a musical phrase without noticing its individual notes and measures. It may be observed only that the person as a unit is engaging in this or that action; that a child is reading a book, perhaps, or talking with a playmate. One may even perceive that a child is reading a book *eagerly* or talking *angrily* with a playmate without taking note of particular actones, although, to anticipate a point in our later discussion of behavior recording, actones are often highlighted by an interest in *how* a person does a thing. Since, in any case, actions do not occur apart from actones, molecular units of behavior are implicated at least implicitly in all that an observer can see in molar behavior. We need to ask more, therefore, about interdependence of the units on these two levels.

ACTONES AS MEDIA

Actones and actions are related as mediating to mediated processes. Atmospheric conditions mediate weather phenomena. Processes in conductive substances mediate electrical current. Light and sound waves mediate visual and auditory perception. Comparably, actone manifolds mediate actions of the person. Steps mediate walking to school, lip and tongue movements reciting a lesson, arm and finger movements saluting the flag.

General characteristics of the relationship between mediated and mediating events have been treated by Heider (1927) in a paper that states also the main ideas in the present suggestions relating to actones as media. Following Heider's analysis, we shall indicate some characteristics of a mediating process and consider wherein they fit molecular behavior in relation to actions as molar behavior units. Major points made by Heider and key examples will be paraphrased or quoted in italics.

1. *A mediating process is "conditioned externally"; its properties do not arise from within, but depend upon the properties of a mediated process.*

This holds for a configuration of sound waves that mediates between a source of sound and the ears. Let the source be a tuning fork. The vibrations that reach the ears are "forced vibrations." They are forced in the sense that their form depends upon the form of the vibrations of the fork. The form of the mediating wave configuration is not conditioned from within itself. It is determined instead by the form of an internally conditioned process, namely, the pattern of "free vibrations," which depends in turn upon the properties of the sounding body.

A manifold of actones evidently conforms in some degree to this first characteristic of a mediating process.

Consider the steps of a child when he walks somewhere. Whether his steps are high or low, slow or fast, constant or variable, to the right or the left depends in part upon properties of the action in progress. His steps, more precisely the steps of his locomotor apparatus, are high and fast when he is going to the circus. They are low and slow when he is going to see the principal to whose office he has been sent for misconduct. They bear to the left if his destination is to the left of him; or to the right if his destination is to his right. The form of the steps is not conditioned essentially from within, but from without; it depends upon the form of the mediated action.

The same is true for the actones of speech. The words of a vocabulary get organized into configurations only when they are "used" by an action; and the form of the word pattern depends upon the properties of the action. The language of a person may assume a primitive form, as when a scholar talks to a baby; or it may have a form that is very complex, as when the scholar talks to a colleague on a difficult subject. But the verbal actones themselves are not primary determinants. They can be used or not used; they can be used for any purpose and on any level of complexity up to the maximum of which the person is capable.

Not all media are perfect. In general, other things being equal, the less internally conditioned a mediatory process is the better the mediation it provides. Heider uses as an example of a mediator the pointer of a recording instrument. Like the column of mercury in a thermometer, it yields flexibly to external influence. Under ideal conditions, "the successive positions of the pointer are not connected in a way that is characteristic of the pointer itself, but they are externally conditioned" (Heider, 1927). The conditions are not always ideal, however, as Heider indicates. They are not, for example, if the shaft of the pointer is attached to a fulcrum in such a way that friction is created. The movements of the pointer in this case are in part internally conditioned; they are affected by processes of the lower order context that includes the fulcrum and the shaft.

A manifold of actones is never a perfect mediating process in the sense of being all externally conditioned. The steps of a child may be slow partly because his legs are tired. He may talk without communicating what he means partly because his mouth is dry or read a story without understanding it well because his vision is poor; actones have their own context that can be secondarily coercive. It is nonetheless true that changes in an actone medium apparently do not effect certain changes and no others in the mediated process. The child is not made to walk to a particular place, even to a bedroom, by the weariness of his legs. He is not made to say one thing or another by the dryness of his mouth or driven to read a story meeting certain specifications as to content or even size of print by the impairment of his vision. Actions like these depend essentially upon needs, goals, and other conditions of the action context; they are not selected and coerced by the context of the mediating molecular units.

2. *A mediating process consists of parts that are in a high degree mutually independent.*

A source from which a mediating configuration of light waves issues is a real unit. Yet the configuration itself is only a "composite." It is an atomistic manifold and, as such, a "spurious unit." The same holds for a manifold of sound waves. The individual vibrations of every such complex are "guided by the external cause in each small section." The elements are not themselves internally united.

There is good evidence for high mutual independence of the units in a manifold of actones. First, the same actones can combine readily in many different configurations. The vast numbers of combinations and permutations of the actones of language are instructive here. The formation of a letter is ordinarily an actone when a person writes something. The composition of a sentence is invariably an action. Multitudes of sentence-writing actions are mediated by different combinations and permutations of the 26 letter-forming actones. Heider develops the essentials of this example and points out that the letters can be combined in many different ways only because they are independent of each other.

Also, mediating actones do not of themselves invariably "require" one another. An abundance of evidence has been brought against the reflex chain construction in which each movement of a series unfailingly calls up the next; the tool systems of the person do not in themselves independently bring and keep actones together. Molecular behavior units could not be so readily recombined and they would more characteristically organize themselves independently of actions if they were strongly united internally. It appears, therefore, that the unity of an actone manifold is essentially spurious; it has the sham unity of a composite.

Heider shows that media are by no means all equally good insofar as their efficiency is determined by mutual independence of parts. Thus, as he mentions, pliable bodies, whose parts are relatively independent of one another, mediate certain processes better than solid bodies, whose parts are less mutually independent. An example of his is that a piece of cloth mediates better between the fingers and the contours of an object than a piece of equally thin but less flexible paper.

An actone manifold is never a perfect medium in this respect; its parts are not wholly independent of one another. Links in the chain of a "habit" are sometimes hard to separate, as Guthrie (1935) and others have shown. A learned motor configuration, like swimming a certain way, tends to be self-maintaining and may not be easily changed. Semantic studies have shown, too, that this can be equally true of word patterns. Yet all such composites are open enough to change that "relearning," formulated as reorganization of actone manifolds, is never impossible; even the oldest dogs *can* be taught new tricks. This is understandable when the great adaptability of molecular behavior mechanisms is considered. The system of the hand, with its separate and independently movable fingers, excels here, as Heider notes, and so does the vocal apparatus. All carriers of molecular behavior lend themselves in varying degrees to the formation of differing actone combinations; and the members of these combinations show commensurate mutual independence.

3. *A mediating process is an "offshoot" that generally constitutes a sign of the mediated process.*

"The light rays that meet the eyes are messengers from the object and represent it." These processes, however, like the vibrations from a source of sound, "spend themselves, so to speak, in the process of mediation." The same does not hold for all mediators. Thus, "The barometer that informs us of the air pressure appears in consciousness as something on its own account." So appearing, moreover, it stands for the atmospheric processes that it mediates.

Similarly, the actones of another person serve as signs of molar behavior. Just as we learn of changes in an electrical system through observation of mediating pointer excursions, so we may see what another person is doing in part through observation of his molecular behavior. Such actones as gestures and postural adjustments have actually been classified as "expressive movements."

The sign character of actones derives from their partial dependence upon actions. Our recognition of this dependency has been reinforced here by the principle that a molecular behavior manifold as a mediating process is in itself a more or less neutral composite whose form and organization depend in part upon forces in the context of molar behavior. Again, whether the steps of a child when he walks to a destination or his vocalizations when he says something are thus and so or otherwise depends significantly upon properties of the action in progress. The form of the action affects the form of the actone pattern in such a way that it represents in some degree the properties of the action.

The dimensions of actones per se are limited to such directly observable variables as amplitude and velocity as these appear, for example, in variations from large to small and quick to slow of locomotor, manual, laryngeal, and facial adjustments. Changes in these variables, however, are so correlated with changes in molar behavior that they provide essential information about the characteristics of actions. Here, in the sign function of actones as media, lies much of their pertinence to description of molar behavior, as we shall try to show more fully when the problem of recording molar behavior and it context is discussed.

ACTIONS AS UNIQUE EVENTS

When all has been said concerning the interdependence of actones and actions, their partial independence of one another remains. They are not univocally connected. A kind of transposability holds instead for the relationship between the units of the two orders.

First, an action is transposable from one to another manifold of actones. There *are* different ways to skin a cat. A child can memorize the rule for dividing fractions by writing it, reading it, or speaking it. Different letters and words might have been used for this paragraph.

Second, the same actones can be used for different actions. The same molecular manifold in walking or looking or speaking can mediate numberless different molar behavior units. Grasping with the hand can serve a thousand "purposes." So can saying *yes, no, why, I agree with you,* or almost any word or word combination. Different actions can be mediated even at one time by essentially the same actones. Walking, for example, can simultaneously mediate exercising, strolling for fun, and going to a particular place.

These observations imply that the most thoroughgoing scrutiny and reporting of actones by methods suited to the characteristics of behavior on the molecular level will not alone give an adequate description of actions. Insofar as the same action can be mediated by different actones and the same actones can mediate different actions, this must be true.

Reduction statements that specify actone correlates of actions have sometimes been made for the sake of simplicity and objectivity in descriptions of behavior on the molar level. One proponent of this tactic has stated, for example, that the ". . . response we call 'fear' . . . *is* a catching of the breath, a stiffening of the whole body, a turning away of the body from the source of stimulation, a running or crawling away" (Watson, 1924, p. 8; italics mine). "His body stiffened" is probably more credible as raw fact than "he drew back in fear." "John's fist swung upward through an arc of about 30 degrees and landed on Henry's chin" may be less assailable on the same basis than "John hit Henry hard with apparent intent to hurt him." But this kind of description is limited in discrimination power and sheer accuracy by the absence noted above of a one-to-one relationship between molar and molecular units of behavior. There must be many hundreds of ways in which the parts of a 10-year-old boy can behave while *he* is behaving avoidantly or aggressively, and these possible coordinations are complicated by the fact that the same parts can behave in many of the same ways while the boy is behaving nurturantly or submissively. Experimental indications (Sherman, 1927) that one kind of molar behavior cannot be distinguished reliably from another when its context is unknown cannot be surprising for this reason. The truth is that we now have little information as to what actone patterns go with such and such kinds of molar behavior. It is therefore impossible for an observer or behavior analyst to approach action by a person with a comprehensive set of coordinating definitions that give molecular indices of behavior on the molar level. Any reliable criteria of this kind have to be worked out while investigation proceeds.

One way to begin to describe the actions of persons is to record them as fully as possible in the idiom and by techniques which, in the light of our common social experience, now seem best adapted to the range of their own special characteristics. The idiom of common language and techniques that rely upon common observation appear to have the needed breadth and flexibility. One can include in what is recorded as data of interest in their own right and as material with sign significance for molar behavior all that can be observed of correlated molecular details. This liberal attack, upon which we have relied, has the advantage of encompassing at least partially and provisionally what there is to be reduced, where eventual reduction statements promise anything in credibility or simplification, and it has the advantage of leaving open the problem of relationships between the two orders of behavior units.

Actions differ greatly in kind and they have a multiplicity of dimensions. Different *modes* of action that correspond to commonly recognized "needs," "desires," "propensities," and the like occur in differing degrees. Examples are aggression, dominance, submission, nurturance, and avoidance. Actions vary in energy level, tempo, efficiency, persistence, manifest affectivity, in level of satisfaction or dissatisfaction, and emotional quality. Actions differ also in outcome. Some, for example, end in failure, and others in success.

Actually, psychology is by no means prepared to name systematically all of the properties, kinds, and dimensions of molar behavior. It has no adequate taxonomy of actions. As for the variables that we can now distinguish, our knowledge of their natural manifestations, of their relationships with one another, and of their situational correlates, even of the conditions under which particular sorts or characteristics of molar behavior units may be expected to appear, is greatly limited. We do not know enough about the natural history of actions to collect them for study by rigidly systematic techniques.

As for the later stages of the descriptive process, in which the recorded material is coded and quantified, development of criteria for analytical categories again requires reliance upon everyday knowledge and perception. Fortunately, ordinary social activity continually demands skill in identifying and describing the actions of our associates on the level of everyday behavior incidents; and it seems reasonable to rely upon the coupling of this skill with systematic application of descriptive categories.

PSYCHOLOGICAL HABITAT

HABITAT AND WHAT THE PERSON SEES

One might propose, for the sake of standardization and objectivity, to describe the surroundings of a person as they are perceived by people in general. This one can do efficiently with the help of a standard dictionary to establish what the surroundings mean. A Midwest child could see a motto and interact with it as only what the dictionary says it is, "an inscribed sentence, phrase, or word." But he might see it and interact with it at a given time as, say, a welcome birthday present or a stern reminder to be good or a familiar patch on a bedroom wall. The child could see his mother and interact with her as no more or less than a "female parent," although this seems improbable. It is not improbable that he will see her and interact with her at a given time as a person in a good mood or a bad mood who is presently helpful or hindering, bossy, protective, or generous.

Margaret Reid's mother urges some noodles upon Margaret in the setting, Home Meal, of Midwest. The mother smiles and is gentle but very insistent. It seems clear that Mrs. Reid is behaving nurturantly from her point of view, and it might be that she is behaving in a nurturant way from the dictionary's or Midwest's point of view, and from the observer's point of view. But more has to be added if we are to describe adequately Margaret's psychological habitat at the time. We have to tell how Mrs. Reid is behaving from Margaret's point of view. As Margaret sees it, is the behavior of the mother nurturant? Or, as the urging and insistence might suggest, is it not nurturant, but dominating? Or both? Or neither? The critically important parts of the psychological environment are in just such alternative characteristics of physical and social facts as they are perceived by the person. Then adequate description of psychological habitat has to heed these properties within a frame of reference that includes some form of the question: What does the person see and how does he see it?

One thing to be said for inquiry of this kind is that we practice it daily with confidence in the information it yields. We identify casually the thing others notice or do not notice, and see within limits how others look at, feel about, or "take" things, recognizing often that the viewpoint of another differs from our own. We see, within limits, what the actions of Y mean to X. Our belief in the correctness of such observation is strengthened by our finding that, very much more often than not, X sees our own behavior as we do. We often observe with confidence also the characteristics of "things in general" as they are for another person. Even when it appears to us that the "actual" circumstances of X are favorable, we may see that, "as far as he is concerned," his situation as a whole is confused or unhappy or threatening; and the reverse can occur. In these cases, too, we generally act in relation to X as much in terms of his situation as we think it to be for him as in terms of what we know about the "actual" state of affairs.

The ability to see what another sees in his habitat is a necessity of social intercourse. It alone enables us to deal with our associates on the basis of their goals, obstacles, paths, and values, and, thereby, to adapt ourselves appropriately to the actions of others. Errors in observation of circumstances as they are perceived by our associates do occur. Doubtless they are frequent on the level of conditions that go with very long behavior units and deeper motives. If only for reliability purposes, therefore, it becomes important that the research here is concerned with comparatively short behavior units that correspond to intentions of the person. We shall later try to define these targets with some precision. Meanwhile, a starting base in common perception for reliable observing of their environmental contexts is implied by the fact that, in the long run of minute-by-minute social interplay with others, we do generally adapt ourselves appropriately to their actions, which means that we must generally deal with them on the basis of their goals, obstacles, paths, and values, which is possible only in the degree that we do observe what they see in their situations.

How one observes the parts of another's habitat as he sees them is yet another problem for studies of social perception that cannot be discussed in any detail here. But we should like only to note as cues to such observation the present behavior of the person, the sequential context of the behavior, and the characteristics of present behavior settings and objects.

One may observe that a dog is a threatening or fearsome creature in the eyes of Joe Ward, of Midwest, in part because one now sees Joe run from the dog (the present behavior cue), in part because one saw the dog bite Joe an hour earlier (the sequential context cue), and in part because one notes that the dog is big and fierce by common Midwest standards (a behavior object cue). The present behavior probably is the most sensitive indicator. We observe that, as a child sees it, a thing is liked because he approaches it, disliked because he withdraws from it, funny because he laughs at it, or sad because it makes him cry. This lead alone obviously puts us in a circle. We get the characteristics of the environmental object from the behavior that we want to understand by relating it to the object. Fortunately, however, the present behavior cue generally does not stand alone; settings or behavior objects and sequence indicators provide stimulus information that is in some degree independent. One is moderately safe anywhere in asserting that a swarm of bees nearing a boy on his way to school is perceived by him to be menacing and dangerous even if, at the time, one can observe little or nothing of the boy's behavior. And, going by sequential context, one who momentarily loses sight of the same boy at home with his mother can have some confidence that, to him, her mood is unhappy if one knows that a minute before, he found her weeping over bad news. The behavior cue is needed to check other cues which, nonetheless, can be independently revealing.

Observation of another's situation in terms of what he perceives in it can be devoid of rational inference in the sense that one deliberately weighs criteria and deduces their consequences. It can be essentially direct. One may observe at once, without deliberation of any kind, that one or another aspect of a situation is now seen to be good, bad, indifferent, threatening, inviting, hot, cold, or whatever. As examples above suggest, however, such observation may always involve inference on some level. However this may be, it seems correct to generalize that the process of observing the facts with which we are now concerned does not differ in principle from observation of other complex phenomena.

A possible overinterpretation of the emphasis placed here upon the importance of getting at perceptually derived attributes of environmental parts is that adequate description of psychological habitat requires a mirroring of "private worlds." We have not meant to imply this. Whatever the potentialities in some phenomenological procedures, one who uses methods of observation and analysis from without cannot hope to break into the consciousness of a person and to come out with a description that duplicates its content through the shortest period of time. Only novelists who are free to improvise and to fill in another's experience with their own are in a good position to do this. Our aim has been only to represent the public side of private experience to the extent of exhibiting some properties that parts of a person's habitat have because they are objects of perception.

The relevant context of molar behavior includes by definition all of the conditions that make a difference to action by the person. Let alone the difficulties in apprehension of conscious experience from without, one cannot assume that these conditions are all represented in conscious experience. It would be superfluous to review here the common reasons for holding that many are not. Proof that an object or condition has entered the habitat of a person is established, in any event, by effectiveness rather than awareness; whatever has effects upon the molar behavior of the person exists in his psychological habitat. One can even doubt that the person is continually aware of habitat parts that derive from present behavior settings. It seems safe to say that Raymond Birch, whose mother works in the Midwest County

Courthouse, can traverse unerringly all of the corridors in this largest building of Midwest with his thoughts preempted by things that completely exclude the walls to his left and right. Yet the walls must continually make a difference to his behavior at the time. Otherwise, he would not continually avoid them. He must be less continually aware of them. Midwest children at school do not think to themselves all of the time, "I must not talk out loud without permission, I must not talk out loud without permission, I must . . ." Yet talking out loud without permission is a fairly rare exception to a rule of the Midwest school setting. The children "conform" to the rule, and thereby demonstrate its effectiveness, most of the time while the teacher who embodies it is present. But we outrightly doubt that they are aware of the rule through the whole of this time.

It is common practice in psychology to test the behavioral effectiveness of an observed condition in the situation of a person without any reference to private experience or to perception. One can do this in the case of the rule against talking out loud, for example, by observing the children both with and without the teacher in the room. On the same basis, one can compare the effects upon behavior of different conditions and use the observed differences in behavior to find by deduction the psychological properties of these conditions. This procedure, too, is common and probably offers the only available means of determining the particular characteristics of some facts in the context of behavior. It is no less true that the primary conditions in relation to which a person behaves at a given time are structured by and get their psychologically relevant properties from the processes of perception. Adequate effort to describe these conditions requires, therefore, a frame of reference and specific methods that enable one to identify these properties with the greatest possible clarity and directness.

There can be no getting around the fact that some "screening" and bias stemming from the standpoint of the observer can never be entirely escapable. All that a psychologist has to report on the parts of Midwest as they are seen by its children obviously will have to be accepted or rejected as *his* perceptions of what the children see. Psychology, where it undertakes representation of this kind, is enormously worse off as a descriptive discipline than many other sciences; but its position outside the facts is not unique in principle. An ideal view of a plant or a rock is biased and imperfect. This is true even of the view that reduces either to proton-electron aggregates as nearly ultimate realities; for these, to face the paradox of all searching investigation, are in fact only inventions by the observer. Ultimately, the only advantage on the side of being "scientific" that one investigation can have over another lies, not in any corner it has on reality, but in its better intersubjective tests. It follows that, however they stack up against the "true facts," descriptions of psychological habitat and of behavior should at least be as objective as reporting in this area will allow. This is to raise again the problem of reliability that will recur at several later points. No special measures to solve the greater validity problem will be offered. Our case here will have to rest upon the degree in which the findings on both habitat and behavior show internal consistency and otherwise make sense.

CONCEPTUALIZING HABITAT CONDITIONS

The greatest present need of research to describe psychological habitat is for adequate concepts by which to identify and relate different habitat conditions. In the absence of such concepts, one of two unsatisfactory alternatives must be chosen. The first is to link behavior directly with nonpsychological facts, i.e., with the physical and social conditions that only supply raw materials for the habitats of individual persons. This has been attempted in correlational studies of behavior and age or sex; behavior and climate; behavior and social class or caste; behavior and urban or rural life. It should not be surprising that the correlations obtained in these studies are generally low and often contradictory; for it is known that lawfulness and stability are to be found only in relationships between events and facts of the same order. Modern physics, for example, does not use in its derivations biological, economic, or psychological quantities. The best one can expect from linking behavior directly with nonpsychological conditions is indication of where some psychological truth may lie.

There remains the alternative of bridging the gap between behavior and nonpsychological habitat with the wisdom of common sense and art in the manner of the novelist or the biographer. One can go beyond a statistical correlation of behavior with birth order, for example, and describe the psychological habitat of, say, an only child in terms of his loneliness, the overindulgence of his parents, and the oppressiveness of an atmosphere that is overcharged with adult interests and standards. Representation of this kind has been condemned as subjective. The objective way out has often been seen as just that of relating behavior to nonpsychological facts. But it may be asked whether, for the purposes of understanding molar behavior, the facts of this order are rightly to be accepted as objective.

Objective conditions are generally held to be the ones that actually exist, unviolated by the biases or special viewpoint of the observer, in the context of the phenomena under investigation. It is by no means clear that, for example, social class or race or climate, as these are defined and measured by the sociologist, the anthropologist, and the meteorologist, do actually exist for a child in the relevant determining context of his behavior. On the other hand, it is clear that conditions vaguely identified by words like "loneliness" and "parental overindulgence" and the "oppressiveness of adult standards" do exist in the contexts of children's behavior as coercive facts. A primary task of ecological psychology where it is concerned with psychological habitat is the one of conceptualizing such facts with enough precision that they can be related to behavior in an orderly way. We have aimed to do this in applying the descriptive categories that are later to be presented. First, however, the recording of habitat and behavior has to be considered.

Chapter 3

RECORDING
BEHAVIOR
AND ITS CONTEXT

NATURALISTIC
PSYCHOLOGICAL DESCRIPTION

This chapter presents a rationale and the procedures of the *specimen record*, which is the basic psychological field device of the present method. We mean by a specimen record a detailed, sequential, narrative account of behavior and its immediate environmental context as seen by skilled observers. The account describes in concrete particulars the stream of an individual's behavior and habitat.

A *day record* and a *settings record* have been developed. The first extends through an entire day, from time of awakening to bedtime of the subject, and the second describes usually a complete visit to a behavior setting. Examples from our field work are in Chapters 4 and 7 and in previous publications (Barker and Wright, 1951; Barker, Wright, Barker, and Schoggen, 1961).

Records of the same general type also are in earlier contributions to child psychology that include writings of Dresslar (1901), Andrus (1924), Isaacs (1930, 1933), McFarland (1938), Fite (1940), Biber, Murphy, Woodcock, and Black (1942), Lafore (1945), and Hartley, Frank, and Goldenson (1952). Other ways of recording behavior without doing anything to change it have indeed been used, but space does not permit a review of these methods. Direct observational procedures have been given separate consideration in the literature of psychology (Heyns and Lippitt, 1954; Gellert, 1955; Wright, 1960; Weick, in press).

Specimen records give a multivariable picture of the molar and molecular aspects of behavior and situation. They preserve the continuity of behavior and save for study interrelations between simultaneous and successive conditions. They present undissected specimens of behavior and psychological situation.

Permanency and stability can be added to these advantages. Barring a revolution in written English and in the social conventions of western mankind, the specimen records of this research will have the same meaning in 2066 as they have now in 1966. This seems of no small importance. One cannot investigate adequately changes during the last century in the rearing and behavior of children because no scientific records of children's situations and behavior have been kept. Meanwhile, technological, economic, and political developments have been quite thoroughly recorded by social scientists. It seems safe to assume that comparison of change in these milieu phenomena with change in children's habitat and behavior would be rewarding. As matters stand, the best psychology can do to get data for such studies is to call upon lay writings and reconstruct from them in some degree the behavior and psychological situations of the past.

There remains as the distinctive characteristic of specimen records their theoretically neutral character. They are biased only by the predilections of common sense in the meaning of sense that most of us have in common. They are open to study for greatly differing interests, to placement in widely divergent theoretical frames of reference, and to analysis by a great variety of qualitative and quantitative procedures. They can be divided as one pleases and scrutinized part by part or reviewed and interpreted intact. Their word by word content demands no particular conceptual reformulation. Material in these records is often like behavior observed first-hand in the number and variety of the questions it raises and the answers it suggests.

Specimen records have many limitations. These include a lack of built-in provisions for quantification, dependence upon observation without instrumental aids, and sheer bulk. In making them, also, we have come up against a number of difficult problems that will now be discussed with attention to practicalities of the task and theoretical questions that surround it. This will require, at some points, review of problems raised in the preceding chapter.

MAKING SPECIMEN RECORDS

MOLAR AND MOLECULAR DESCRIPTION

It is possible to make a record that describes only molar behavior units like the following one.

George went berry picking for his mother.

Or one can make a record that includes subordinate molar units like those in italics below.

George *took a basket from the kitchen table* and *walked outdoors* where he *mounted his bicycle* and went to pick berries for his mother.

Finally, one can bring into a record molecular details like the actones italicized in the next version.

George, with his *lips quivering,* his *brows knit,* and the *corners of his mouth turned down,* took a basket from the kitchen table, and, with his *shoulders hunched,* his *chin sagging against his chest,* and his *feet dragging,* walked outdoors, where he mounted his bicycle and, with his *head still bent,* went to pick berries for his mother.

The first description identifies a *behavior episode.* This unit of the behavior stream will later be delimited as to size, examined in considerable detail, and used for a number of purposes. Meanwhile, for all of these purposes, it can be defined provisionally as an action of a person together with an immediate and coexisting situation in the life of the person.

An adequate sample of episodes, only identified, would be useful. It would tell us quite essentially what the chosen subject had been observed to do. Yet a specimen record that did no more than this would be deficient in description of *how* the subject had done what. Our main point here, though, is that the hows of actions are signified by actones, as anticipated in the preceding chapter. This is demonstrated best by the third present example, in which it clearly transpires from the quivering lips, the knit brows, and the dragging feet that George went to pick the berries unwillingly and unhappily.

Even the correct identification of an action, identification, that is, of *what* the person does, is facilitated by the recording of molecular detail. Consider another episode.

Henry, while sitting behind Susan in school, pulled Susan's pigtail.

Nothing is said in this description about the how of the action. But that is not all; questions may be raised as to what Henry was really doing. Was he hurting Susan? Was he only signalling her? Or was he teasing her? Information about the mediating actones would be pertinent. For example, recorded observations that Henry's jaws were firmly clenched and that his lips were drawn in a sharp line would support the first judgment.

Then information about actones and molecular components of situations is useful as a basis for diagnosing actions. Yet the necessity for including this information in specimen records might still be questioned, as it has been from time to time by some of our beginning observers. We can indeed gather from the several recorded molecular details that George undertook the chore for his mother unwillingly and unhappily. But the observer could have inferred and recorded the unwillingness and unhappiness from these same data on the spot. Similarly, an observer of the pigtail incident could report only that Henry intentionally hurt Susan by pulling her pigtail, and not that Henry's jaws were clenched or that his lips were drawn tight. It might be proposed, in short, that only generalizations about actions from molecular details, but not the details themselves, need to be put on record. Freedom of the observer to make and record such synoptic judgments seems desirable; there is often accessible on the scene of an action more or better data on which to base valid statements about events of any sort than can later be reproduced. We have nevertheless concluded that a record with molecular details from which characteristics of molar units are inferred is a better record than one containing only the inferences.

For one thing, generalizations from molecular to molar particulars can be wrong. Only records with adequate information about actones make it possible to check on these generalizations. Further, such records allow for conceptualization that may be difficult or is impossible for the observer while events are unfolding before him.

Language limitations also are important in this connection. Often it is impossible to find words for inferences about actions from actones. To do this one must ordinarily use adverbial expressions as direct qualifiers of verbs denoting molar units, as in George went unhappily. But such direct qualifiers often are unequal to subtleties that may nonetheless be expressed by actones. It is hazardous for a nonliterary person to stake much here on examples, but "William looked *with great wonder* at the gibbon" probably conveys less about molar behavior than "With his neck thrust out, his body rigid, his mouth wide open, and his eyes bulging, William looked wonderingly at the gibbon." Short of bringing in these actones, a gifted reporter might be able to improve upon our "with great wonder," but it seems doubtful that anyone could do much better without referring to molecular behavior units.

Novelists and poets have turned this idea to good advantage. Some Victorian novels represent actions in quite abstract terms. They lay molar units of behavior end to end and describe them frontally with generalizing qualifiers that strain with only moderate success to show what the characters are doing. Other novels, while no less essentially concerned with molar behavior, do not try to make actions stand without support from actones.

They weave in molecular details of behavior and situation that serve to describe actions concretely. The reader is at least given a fair chance to infer from actones qualitative aspects of molar behavior that cannot easily be generalized in words.

It remains true that the sharpest observer may not always perceive and be able to report actones upon which judgments about actions are based. The judgments may stem, not from "rational inference," for which the actone criteria are known, but from "perceptual inference," for which all such criteria are wholly implicit (cf. Heider, 1944). An observer may see only that John did thus and so wistfully or sheepishly or in a kind way or thoughtfully; and he may be unable to specify any of the molecular details behind the observation. The best observer cannot state all of the criteria by which he sees a stick and may not be able to state any of the criteria by which he sees the wistfulness of an action. Yet his perception may be entirely right in either case.

Consider again the pulling of the pigtail. It was easy to muster actone criteria for the judgment that Henry meant to hurt Susan. But it is hard to think of such criteria for the judgment that he was teasing her or signalling her, even though one might nonetheless have observed with confidence and correctly that Henry was in fact teasing or signalling. One cannot in any event bring into a narrow focus the person and only the most immediate parts of his situation and either infer from perceived actones or observe directly the meaning of his behavior, as we have aimed to show in Chapter 2. Perhaps the most reliable and valid observations of molar behavior are made upon the basis of gleanings from a partly inferential shuttling back and forth between molecular details and the larger contexts of actions. Our observers at any rate have made their reports under the premise that a good behavior record is one that reflects and aids such a process.

THE TASK OF THE OBSERVER

Observing for specimen records calls for no tricks, formulas, rules of thumb, or any special devices. If only for the sake of consistency, the observers have been called upon to side with the main intentions of this chapter. But this demands no more of them than that they go on doing what they have long been doing as a matter of course in their everyday lives, only with more vigilance and thoroughness than are common.

The observer is not asked to theorize; he is asked not to theorize. He is asked to suspend biases from formal psychological training, and to fall back upon the elementary, garden variety, spur-of-the-moment notions and hunches about behavior that are common to man as a socialized being, that could never be abolished or appreciably suppressed if this should seem desirable, and that cannot help but astonish anyone who stops to reflect upon them with their high ratio of accuracy to error.

A rough three-level classification of psychological descriptions may now be useful.

There are, first, running accounts of what a person is doing and of his situation on the level of direct perception or immediate inference. Here are some samples from one of our records. What we take to be immediate inferences are italicized.

Suddenly Raymond ran *eagerly* to another tree.
He started climbing the tree with great energy.
He remarked *in an offhand way*, but with slight emphasis on the second word, "I hope I can climb this tree." *He seemed to say this to himself as a form of encouragement.*
In a high-pitched, soft sing-song he said, "I hope, I hope, I hope."
Raymond continued climbing the tree, *cautiously* grasping one branch and then another, and fixing his feet firmly.
He called out to Stewart in a *playfully boastful manner*, "Stewart, this tree is harder to climb than the other one."
Stewart called back *very firmly and definitely*, "No, it isn't."
When Raymond was as high as it seemed safe to climb, he settled in a crotch of the tree with his hands gripped tightly around the branches.
Exuberantly he sang out, "Owww, owww, wheee. Do you see me?" (Barker and Wright, 1951, pp. 392–393.)

Second, there are minor interpretations in the form of statements *about* rather than descriptions *of* behavior or situation. Usually these are based upon observations covering a more or less extended sequence of behavior. Always they are couched in the idiom of everyday social experience, as below.

I had the feeling that, although the story wasn't especially interesting, he liked this restful part of the day when he could just sit (ibid., p. 220).

In handing his father the sugar bowl and salt shaker, Raymond was helping. Of course, he would have helped more if he had gotten up and put them in [the cupboard] himself. . . . I think Raymond wanted to be in on what was going on, that he wanted his father's continued attention more than to help. But the efforts were accepted as help (ibid., p. 27).

[In crossing the street] . . . he didn't seem to be worried or frightened but, rather, very cautious. It might be pertinent to mention that one of Raymond's closest playmates, Fred Wecker, had recently been in an accident on the square. Fred's bicycle had crashed with a truck (ibid., p. 52).

Minor interpretations like these often may be included advantageously in a record when the behavior and circumstances of the subject would otherwise remain obscure. They appear rather infrequently in our reports, however, and the observers are not pressed to offer them. When any such interpretation does occur in a record, it is set apart in an indented paragraph, where it can be studied for what it may be worth.

Finally, there are the technical or professional interpretations. We mean by these: generalizations based upon quite explicit theories about behavior.

The evidence suggests that in "accidentally" breaking the new briar pipe, after listening in on the argument between his parents, Tom was manifesting repressed aggression against his father.

The fact that Jim stopped working on his May basket as soon as the teacher left the room suggests that his earlier enthusiastic work upon this task was largely a product of induced forces stemming from the social power field of the teacher.

These statements exemplify the theorizing that the observers are asked not to do. The psychology of observing for a specimen record is not a depth psychology or a textbook psychology, but whatever psychology there is in common understanding of behavior. This leaves time enough for technical interpretation after a record has been made. It is then possible to study the recorded material in context and, by applying appropriate concepts, to get some quantified and conceptually disciplined understanding of what it means. To theorize in making the record would be like theorizing about the movements of the stars without at some time independently photographing their actual positions. The main difference here is that in psychological field studies the observer has to be the camera. We are not indifferent to the significant role that hypotheses and theories play in guiding scientific observation. But the fact remains that basic description of phenomena must occur at some stage in all empirical research.

Raising the question of objectivity, one might ask if all inferential description should not be left out of a specimen record, as it certainly would be if the observer were the astronomer's kind of camera. All one can say is that, in this case, the record could never make available for study what it is meant to preserve. Even if sound motion pictures were to be taken of the subject's activities, any attempt to theorize about the behavior still would have to be preceded by inferential description. A motion picture can show John throwing a ball toward Jim. But it cannot show whether John is trying to hurt Jim or to engage him in a game of catch in the same sure way that a photograph can show the position of a star. Only observation involving explicit or implicit inference can enable one to say what John is really doing. Trying to hurt Jim or to play catch with him and, to take other examples from our records, saying things "proudly and with definiteness," showing "evident surprise," being "motherly," speaking in an "authoritative tone," talking "with agitation," and "ominous quiet" go to make up the minimal phenomena of molar behavior; and any instrument that will not register them is no good for description of molar behavior.

The observer of human actions cannot be as precise as the observer of physical movements. It is doubtful, though, that he needs to be or that precision has the same meaning for both.

On the descriptive level, in any case, neither has to run theoretical risks. Essentially atheoretical recording of phenomena is possible in psychology as in other disciplines because the raw facts of behavior, rather than being accessible only through speculation or theory, are open to common observation, partly inferential though it has to be. If anyone still wants to challenge the objectivity of such description, he must give up hope that psychologists in their research or laymen in their daily affairs can ever study objectively what other whole persons do.

The line between partly inferential description of behavior and interpretation or theorizing about it probably can never be as sharp as the line between the former and perception devoid of inference. Where does the partly inferential description stop and outright interpretation or theorizing begin? There is hardly a dichotomy here, but we have not found this distinction difficult in practice. A working rule to aid it is that the observer should think of *intentions*, leaving the *dynamics* for later study. A record that does not permit approaches to dynamics must be of limited value. Again, however, such approaches can be made through systematic probing into the simultaneous and sequential facts of behavior and situation in the final narrative.

THE PROBLEM OF OBSERVER INFLUENCE

Making specimen records is vulnerable to interference by the observer with the phenomena to be recorded. When a geologist surveys and describes an area, he does not appreciably change the geology of the region, whereas an observer may well change the situation and behavior of the observed person. How can one keep the habitat of the person natural and so observe naturally occurring behavior when it is not natural for an observer to be present? It is probable that observer interference in psychological field studies can seldom be reduced to zero, which means that the problem is one of making it minimal, of defining it, and of keeping it as nearly constant as possible.

There is, of course, the possibility of concealed observation. But we have felt that people have a right to say whether their privacy is to be invaded, and that good public relations over the long run require a field policy of openness and candor. Following this policy, we have informed our subjects of each plan for observation in terms to suit their ages, with the exception that all children in public situations are observed without their consent.

Instead of resorting to concealment, the observer can do the opposite; he can get to know and be known by his subjects and their associates, and build for himself the role of a friendly, nonevaluating, nondirective, and nonparticipating person with interest in what people do. This tactic was adopted in Midwest, and our experience indicates that it goes far to ward off the guinea pig reaction. Observers of children in nursery schools and other settings have found the same to be true (one early example: Jersild and Meigs, 1939). Their experience is like ours in suggesting that most children "get used to" the presence of onlookers who, though friendly and not entirely anonymous or unresponsive, let what the child is doing take its course and rarely or never bother him. This holds especially if observations are long enough to permit adaptation to any new or uncertain elements of the situation that have at first been disturbing. A child cannot stop being himself for long, if at all, because someone is watching him, and outside forces must often be stronger than those induced by any onlooker.

It is clear that age is correlated with naturalness of behavior in the presence of an observer. Children of Midwest under 12 years do not generally show appreciable symptoms of sensitivity or self-consciousness under direct observation; and our records are restricted to subjects of this age range. We have not made specimen records on adolescents or adults.

The strategy of the field worker also is important for this problem. Activity and responsiveness certainly can make an observer stand out as a moving figure against a stationary ground, but inactivity and unresponsiveness may at other times make him stand out as a stationary figure against a moving ground. A good field observer varies his behavior as the situation varies so that he is not prominent and yet not elusive or secretive.

However the observer may complicate the situation of the subject, his influence need not be left unknown and unmeasured. Several checks upon how much and what kinds of difference he makes are possible. The behavior of the subject while the observer is likely to be most disturbing—as when he is alone with the subject—can be compared with his behavior while the observer is least disturbing, as when many others are present. Reports from parents, teachers, and others of deviations from characteristic behavior during periods of observation can be gathered. Also, the behavior of the subject with one observer and his behavior with others still can be compared.

When a record covering several hours is made, and efficiency requires the use of observers in turn, one probable result is a tendency for the different effects of different observers to cancel one another. At least, if several field workers take turns, as when our day records were made, the behavior of the subject is not bent in one direction by special interpersonal relationships between himself and a particular onlooker.

Finally, any interaction between a subject and an observer is real behavior with significance in its own right. It is behavior that shows as well as any other how a given person in a particular setting of a particular community reacts to a defined situation. Data on the social role and psychological effects of the observer will be presented in Chapter 8.

THE RELIABILITY OF SPECIMEN RECORDS

Are specimen records reliable? This may be like asking whether perception and language are reliable. No single answer to the question is possible; for the issue it raises is not a single problem, but a whole series of problems. Specimen records do not have only one reliability coefficient, as a mental test does; they have as many reliability coefficients as they have attributes that mirror the subject's behavior or situation. They have different reliabilities, for example, as sources of data on the games of children, on the amounts of time children spend outdoors, on the ways children are disciplined, on the number of overlapping episodes in which children engage, and on the occurrence of daydreaming in the behavior of children. We have identified many such variables in specimen records, and each presents a separate reliability question.

Owing to the great complexity of the issue and the prior necessity of developing analytical techniques, we are unable at this time to present data bearing directly on the reliability of specimen records. Yet we have felt justified in using the records without waiting for systematic studies of their reliability because of the following indirect and general evidence.

It has already been mentioned that the method of the specimen record is essentially the one by which behavior is observed and reported for the purposes of ordinary social intercourse. The whole experience of mankind indicates that the method is sufficiently reliable for many kinds of interpersonal understanding. Specimen records are not new creations; they represent the oldest means of collecting behavioral data. This indicates, at least, that the reliabilities of specimen records for assessing important characteristics of another's behavior are not zero.

One source of prima facie evidence is provided by records on the same subject made by different observers during consecutive observation periods. The reader can here experience reliability directly by reading a published day record (Barker and Wright, 1951). No one can doubt that the consecutive observers were seeing the same child and describing the same continuum of behavior.

The day records used below pool reports from different observers. No period of observation lasted more than 30 minutes, the order of the observers was randomized, the identity of the observers was not considered in analyzing the recorded materials, and all of the tabled data represent episodes from a number of observers. Any increment in reliability that arises from averaging measures drawn from a number of sources occurs in the final data.

The data from the present records give a generally consistent picture of the psychological habitats and behavior of the subject children. Various meaningful and congruent relationships between variables of descriptive categories that have been applied to the recorded specimen material are reported in later chapters. Such relationships could not appear frequently if the reliabilities of the records were low.

It seems probable that the reliabilities of specimen records are closely related to the reliabilities with which they can be analyzed for different behavioral properties. Characteristics of behavior that are observed and reported unreliably must almost certainly appear in the records with indefiniteness, ambiguity, and inconsistency, with consequent low reliabilities of the analyses. The reliabilities of the analyses are reported and considered in assessments of the findings.

It is reassuring to consider finally that, according to a reading of the history of science, the introduction of new methods usually moves through a practical sequence of two developments, namely, use of the methods in research, and, if the results are promising, detailed study later of their accuracy limits.

PROCEDURAL ROUTINES

In making specimen records, as in administering psychological tests, some standardization of routines is necessary. The following are suggested as practices that now appear to be advantageous.

1. OBSERVATIONAL PERIOD. The length of each period of observation should be limited. The observer must perceive and remember a multitude of simultaneous and sequential occurrences. This task is fatiguing, and no one can maintain for long the steady alertness it requires. Experience has shown that the maximum length of time for efficient observation is 30 minutes. This means that long records necessitate a corps of observers who take turns; at least six are needed for a day record.

2. NOTES. The observer should take notes on the scene of the observed behavior. Sufficiently detailed and accurate reporting of events and circumstances in their true order is otherwise

impossible. The Midwest observers have not recorded all verbalizations verbatim, but they have aimed to get down enough of the words spoken by the subject and his associates to permit near duplication of all verbal behavior.

3. TIMING.   Observations should be timed so that the duration of reported episodes may later be determined. Indications of the time at intervals of approximately one minute are sufficient for most purposes. For note taking and timing, observers use a 10-by-14-inch writing board with a metal clasp, to which a watch is attached. The use of a stopwatch was not found practicable.

4. DICTATION.   Observations should be recorded by dictation immediately after each observation period. It is probable that, when ratings and general summaries of behavior and situation are made, an interpolated interval allowing for perspective and insight is desirable. But when the emphasis is placed upon concrete details, as in making specimen records, immediate recording is essential. Following his notes, the observer narrates sequentially what he has observed. Not infrequently, an action or circumstance will remind him of something that occurred earlier. In this case, the observer should dictate a description of the earlier occurrence at the point of the recollection. Strictly sequential ordering of the material can come later.

5. INTERROGATION.   It has proved valuable to provide an interrogator who listens to the original dictation and, upon the conclusion of the report, questions the observer on unclear points and asks for elaboration where the account is lean. This allows both for spontaneity in the original narration and for subsequent corrections and additions. It usually requires at least an hour to record the observations of a 30-minute period, and often a longer time. With a team of observers, a schedule can be arranged whereby each observer serves also as an interrogator. Interrogation benefits both the observer's report and the interrogator's subsequent observations; it provides for a better record and for continuous training.

6. WRITTEN REVISION. After the dictated report has been transcribed, it should be revised by the original observer as soon as practicable. The revision should include deletion of duplications, correction of unclear or inaccurate statements, placement of all incidents in their proper order and, above all, filling in of newly recalled details that did not occur to the observer at the time of the dictated narration. This step is of the utmost importance. Often it makes the difference between a clear and rich report and one that is unclear and poor.

7. SUPPLEMENTARY INTERROGATION. Experience has shown that further interrogation is indispensable after the observer has revised his report. This seems to be even more profitable than interrogation when a report is first dictated. The interrogator raises questions about parts of the account that remain unclear or still appear to call for elaboration. When the report has been modified to meet these questions, it is ready for final typing. Even during the subsequent analysis of the record, however, the observer may be called upon to fill in gaps or to clarify unclear statements.

Probably these procedural routines can be improved. Meanwhile, they give a basis for making specimen records in an orderly way.

THE REPORTING PROCESS

Experience, especially in analyzing the records, has uncovered aspects of the task of reporting that need special emphasis. These have been generalized in the subjoined rules. In part, the rules only restate points that have been made earlier. But they bring together in one place a list of things to do and not to do which, in practice, have appeared often to make the difference between a good record and a poor one. Some of the rules are concerned mainly with the content of the report, others more with its form. All of them pertain in some degree not alone to reporting, but also to observing itself, for obviously the two processes are not entirely separate. The digest retains the style and imperative form of a field guide in the research files.

RULES OF REPORTING

1. *Focus upon the behavior and the situation of the subject.* This is one of the many points at which reporting certainly cannot be separated from observing.

The observer has a hard assignment in perception. What he must do is to see simultaneously the behavior and the situation that occurs with it. This means that his perceiving must be widely inclusive. At the same time it must be sharply exclusive; for no analysis of behavior and psychological habitat can use anything that falls outside the range of the subject, his behavior, and his situation. The situation of the subject includes only things that exist for him and make a difference to his behavior at the time. Our analyses sift out virtually everything else, as discussion in Chapter 2 anticipates.

The subject and his situation are invariably complicated enough to give the observer more than enough to deserve his undivided attention. It might seem otherwise at times. Observe a child at school while he only sits and reads a book for several minutes. Other children and the teacher are behaving, meanwhile, in more interesting ways. It is easy and tempting to turn and attend to these other children and the teacher, and later to add what they did to the report upon the behavior of the subject. But if the observer digresses in this way, the content of the record is almost sure to be weakened.

What one has to keep in mind is that, for analysis of a specimen behavior record, everything the subject does is interesting. The most common behaviors can be of as much consequence and have as many observable facets as the most unusual behaviors. A child can read a book, even a school book, in a great many different ways. If that is what he is doing, it is important to know whether he is reveling in the book, just tolerating it, bored by it, fascinated by it, hating it, amused by it, saddened by it, or sleepily indifferent to it; and the observer cannot see such things well and report them if he lets his attention wander to more intriguing actions of other persons.

There are two cases in which information about events or conditions outside the range of the subject—*his* behavior and *his* situation—are pertinent, and each needs consideration.

a. It is useful to report an action of someone other than the subject or a circumstance that apparently does not exist for him if the action or the circumstance is one that would ordinarily be expected to register upon and somehow make a difference to the subject. Suppose that, while Jimmy Vey, the subject, is drawing a picture, other children in the same room with him are filling it with noise. As far as can be observed, Jim is totally oblivious to everything but the picture; it appears that he might as well be all alone in the room. The observer should nonetheless report the noise, for one would ordinarily expect it to register upon and somehow make a difference to Jim. Clearly, in this instance, the information about the noise is useful. It tells something about the behavior of the subject; for it can be used as evidence that Jim was concentrating upon his picture. The need for exclusion of the extraneous remains. If something happens that evidently could not reach or arouse the subject, it should be excluded.

b. It is useful to report an action of someone other than the subject or a circumstance that apparently does not exist for him if the action or the circumstance is one that leads up to a change in the situation of the subject. A visitor walks into a schoolroom where Jim is seated and takes a seat. Jim is busy and evidently cannot see, touch, hear, or otherwise experience the newcomer. Later, though, he talks with her. Apparently she enters his situation only at this point. But she should not be left to appear from nowhere. A complete description must account for her presence in the behavior setting and place the conversation in a sequence of events that makes its occurrence intelligible. Otherwise, in all such cases, the record is short on continuity and context—as some of ours were before this qualification was urged.

The present rule remains as at least a practical necessity. One might wish for some purposes to describe everything that happens in a behavior setting, but one cannot do this and describe the situation of a person at the same time.

2. *Observe and report as fully as possible the situation of the subject.* The principle of exclusion in Rule 1 would be disastrous if it should be construed as requiring neglect of anything that does in fact enter the situation of the child under observation. If an associate of the subject talks with him, what the associate says is in every case fully as important as what the subject says. If an associate smiles, the record should tell that and how he smiles. If the subject looks at a picture or sings a song, the record should tell something about the picture or the song. And the aim should be to come as close as possible to an account of what the picture, the song, or whatever, is like for the child.

3. *Never make interpretations carry the burden of description.* There is a place for interpretations that go beyond perceptual inference (see pages 38–39) and generalize about the behavior or the situation of the subject. But interpretation cannot take the place of good description. One cannot conscientiously analyze an interpretation. All one can analyze is the behavior of the subject or some aspect of his situation. Interpretative comments are of value principally as means to the better understanding of what the observer describes. The least the observer can do is to push as far as possible away from interpretation as a substitute for concrete description. Any interpretations that he does offer should be expressed always in the idiom of everyday.

In the written revisions, all interpretative comments should be bracketed. The same should be done with statements about events or states of affairs that only lead up to a later change in the subject's situation. The bracketed material is indented in the final copy of the record, as mentioned earlier.

4. *Give the "how" of everything the subject does.* It is assumed that everything a child does is done some*how*. No child ever just walked, for example. The first time the subject walked he did so slowly, haltingly, awkwardly, unsteadily. Several years later, on his way to get a tooth pulled, he walked reluctantly.

Ben smiled. How? Common speech and literature confront us with countless differing ways in which persons walk, smile, stand, sit, say no or yes, ask for things, and so on endlessly; and we know that the differences from one way to the next are often behaviorially crucial. Roy raised his hand. How did he raise it? One observer said, "As if maybe he knew the answer and maybe he didn't." Roy walked to school. The how is given by this sentence from one report: "He swaggered as he used his entire body to hurry." Earlier, Roy had lingered in bed. The following effectively tells how. "He began kicking off the covers in a slow, leisurely fashion, raising one knee and slowly bringing it down, taking a long time as if savoring the lying in bed for a moment."

Often the answer to the one question, "how?" meets the requirements of the analytical procedures. In the "how" of the child's behavior, there is its constructiveness, its intensity, its social maturity level, its efficiency, the affect that accompanies it. Beyond this, one often can infer from the "how" of his behavior much about the situation of a child.

It may be that occasionally it is impossible for an observer to see at all or to interpret how a child does a thing. When such is the case, when the observer cannot give the "how" of an action, he should say so. It is true that children do not do everything dramatically, in some way that stands out—as tearfully, rapidly, gaily, gloomily, angrily. They do many things in an ordinary, average, routine way. But, again, when this holds, the observer should note the commonplaceness itself.

5. *Give the "how" of everything done by any person who interacts with the subject.* We have tried to state this rule carefully. The intention is to ask for the "how" of every action by a person who is in the psychological habitat of the child. This excludes the actions of all who are only in the child's physical situation. If, however, anyone talks to, smiles at, winks at, pushes, trips, hits, beckons, runs toward or away from, leads, follows, caresses, teases, joshes . . . the subject, the content of the behavior should be given as fully as the content of the subject's behavior. This rule develops Rule 2, which requires full description of the subject's situation.

6. *Report in order, in the final writing, all of the main steps through the course of every action by the subject.* The main point here is that continuous, unbroken records must be secured. All hands that go up must come down. A subject is said to be "on his way to the school basement." Up to this point, he has been sitting at his desk in the schoolroom. How did the behavior start? A child is at the front of the room talking to the teacher. The record says next that he is in his seat. How did he get there? In some analyses of the records, we have marked off every smallest molar phase in the child's behavior. This can be done completely only if the present rule is applied.

7. *Wherever possible, state descriptions of behavior positively.* It is possible to study only what the subject did do, not what he did not do. "Ben didn't say the words very loud." Then, did he say them "softly?" "He was not disturbed about being late." This tells something. But, should the following be correct, it would tell more: "Despite being late, Ben was calm and relaxed."

8. *Describe in some detail the scene as it is when each behavior setting is entered.* Even good novelists sometimes fail to keep their readers informed on the main parts of physical and social situations. One routine way to meet this problem calls upon the observer to sum up what he finds before him when he arrives on the scene of each new behavior setting. Nothing elaborate is needed here. The observer can do this much as a playwright does in setting up the scene of a play. Who are the main characters? What are their positions? What are the main features of the physical layout? Where, of course, is the subject, and where is the observer?

9. *Put no more than one unit of molar behavior in one sentence.* This rule should be kept in mind only through the work on the written revision. It doubtless would inhibit dictation.

Some of the methods of analysis separate from one another all distinguishable actions by the child; and it helps if the units come to the analyzer with no more than one of them in a single sentence. *In our record typescripts, every paragraph about a single molar behavior unit is blocked and single-spaced, and a double space precedes and follows every such paragraph. This format is strongly urged, for analysis purposes.* Molecular behavior units, of course, can be woven together within a sentence or paragraph, as in: "Head up and eyes widening, he . . ."

10. *Put in one sentence no more than one thing done by a person in the situation of the child.* This is Rule 9 applied to associates of the subject.

11. *Do not report observations in terms of time intervals.* The time is noted and reported at intervals of approximately one minute, but this does not mean that the reported actions are to be time bound. The observer should let the behavior set its own limits; he should not mark off a unit himself by referring to clock time. The following sentence illustrates time-bound delimiting. "He was concentrating on his work during this whole minute from 3:41 to 3:42." If, by coincidence, the child does begin concentrating on his work at 3:41 and goes on concentrating until 3:42, at which time he turns to something else, the observer should report:

3:41   He started concentrating. . . .
3:42   He turned away from his work. . . .

Often, when this rule is broken, we find lean, generalizing statements.

However correct and useful these rules may be, they are less important than the basic aim of the observer. The observer must approach the task of making a specimen record with the intention of seeing as nearly as possible everything the child does and everything in his situation, and of determing as truly and completely as possible the meaning to the child of his actions and the parts of his situation. He must aim to achieve a rich and full account of the concrete habitat conditions and the actual behavior of the subject. We have said that the best model for the observer is a good novelist when he faithfully devotes himself to reporting.

SETTINGS RECORDS AND DAY RECORDS

Specimen settings records have been taken in Midwest from continuously maintained behavior settings, such as the soda place of Clifford's Drug Store, and from relatively short, periodic, or occasional settings, such as the regularly scheduled meeting of an organization, an athletic event, a school program, or a children's party. To make a settings record the observer goes to the setting at a time when a child of a given age level and sex is known or expected to be present. The social group of the child is, in most instances, left to vary on a chance basis. Also, when the setting offers two or more children who are equally eligible in terms of the sampling schedule, a chance selection procedure is used to single out a particular child for observation. Where a setting is of limited duration and its standing behavior pattern has a clearly defined beginning, course, and end, as in the case, say, of an organizational meeting, the behavior of the observed child through the entire time span of the setting may be recorded. This has not always been practicable. In every case, however, the intention is to secure a record that does not violate either the integrity of the setting or the continuity of the child's behavior.

Naturalistic descriptions in psychology have so often violated the continuity of behavior. Our settings records have done this in some degree by recording limited sequences of episodes. So have earlier anecdotal records, by reporting single incidents, and so have time-sample records, by reporting only fractional aspects of behavior or situation. Case studies and biographies usually retain the rough temporal order of the reported events, but they leave many gaps. All of these methods have selected material of value from the continuity of behavior and habitat. But they have generally left out the vitally important factor of the continuity itself. This aspect of behavior is preserved by the day record. A related consideration is that the possibility of a biased selection of episodes is reduced as the length of a recorded sequence is increased. A record covering a complete waking day of a Midwest child contains from 600 to 1300 episodes. A day record, therefore, as compared with a shorter record, is equivalent to a larger rather than a smaller population sample.

Despite its several advantages, the specimen day record is not an ideal tool for a thorough and efficient survey of the behavior-habitat units in a community. The process of making it is demanding. It requires the concerted efforts of a staff of 8 to 12 trained persons, including secretaries, over a period of no less than two weeks. The cooperation of several individuals of the community, including the subject, his parents, and his teachers, must be secured; and all of these persons must be carefully prepared for the procedure by interviews and visits before the observations begin. It is quite impracticable to get a sample of behavior-habitat units that is balanced as to the age, sex, and other stable characteristics of the subjects and that represents adequately all of the behavior settings of a community by this one method alone. The day record, however, does appear to be of unique value for work upon a number of problems.

One way to use specimen records scientifically would be to deposit them in museums. They qualify as science end products insofar as they are true records of what they aim to record. Another way to use them scientifically is to subject them to conceptual and quantitative analysis. This has been done. In the Midwest project we have experimented with different kinds of such analysis among many other kinds that are possible. The following chapters, in which the procedures and results of this experimental work are reported, may show at least that the recorded material has significance for certain varieties and levels of psychological problems.

Chapter 4

DIVIDING THE BEHAVIOR STREAM

EPISODES AS MOLAR UNITS

A specimen record collects behavior episodes; here it is made for this purpose. Yet, because it makes no systematic reference to parts of the behavior stream, each record leaves undone the delimiting of these descriptive targets. This task is treated in the present chapter, which contains also some preliminary discussion of what we have done with episodes to describe children's habitat and behavior.

Margaret Reid of Midwest was wakened by her mother at 8:10 on a June morning. The first thing she did was to mutter sleepily from her bed something about going to Bible School that day. Then, while continuing to talk with her mother about Bible School, she stretched, groaning and extending her arms. Next, she proceeded to dress and, meanwhile, (a) said sleepily, "I want to lie down," did so, and (b) stretched again, this time "raising up and wiggling," (c) playfully pulled several bobby

56

pins out of her hair, (d) conversed about her curls with her mother, entering upon this action while still working with the bobby pins, and continuing it after pulling out the last pin, (e) hugged her mother when the latter said that she, Margaret, walked "like an old lady," (f) went to the bathroom, and, on the way (g) took note for the first time of a nearby spectator with a writing board.

These are things that Margaret was observed to do by a trained observer. They are actions that might have been seen by Margaret's mother, who was present most of the time, or by any present and normally perceptive adult. We may assume that each of them was perceived by Margaret herself as something she was doing. They have all been recorded in detail in a specimen record, and each, together with the situation in which it occurred, is an episode.

These episodes are presented below as they were marked off on the record, each delimited by a marginal bracket and identified by a number and title. As indicated already, Margaret's behavior here was not, throughout, entirely one thing after the other, but also, at points, two or more things at the same time; during parts of the sequence, two episodes and, later, three, occurred at once. Such concurrence of episodes is called *overlapping*, to be considered later in detail. Overlapping is graphed on the records by parallel placement of episode brackets which shows here, for example, that the whole of *Lying Down* (5) overlaps with an early part of *Getting Dressed* (4). Note also that the forepart of *Discussing Curls with Mother* (8) overlaps with the concluding part of *Taking Out Bobby Pins* (7) and with an intermediate part of *Getting Dressed*.

Mrs. Reid has just entered Margaret's bedroom.

1

Coming Awake

The mother went into the bedroom and said, "Margaret, Margaret, it's time to get up; you have to go to Bible School," coaxingly calling Margaret out of her sleep.
Margaret muttered very, very sleepily, "I hope they don't start," as if she didn't want Bible School to be.

Coming Awake

I took this to mean that if Bible School didn't start she wouldn't have to get up.

The mother said very pleasantly, "Yes, dear, it does start."

Margaret rolled over.

Mrs. Reid walked out of the room.

Margaret was again seemingly sound asleep.

2

8:11   Returning, the mother said more firmly, "Margaret, get up so you can get to Bible School on time."

Then she turned to me and said, "She's sleeping so soundly I hate to wake her."

Turning to Margaret, she said coaxingly and in a loving tone of voice, "Come on, honey, get up; you have to get ready for Bible School."

3

Stretching

Margaret groaned and stretched way out.

The mother pulled down the covers.

Margaret put her arms clear above her head and raised herself by using her heels and her head as supports, wiggling as she did so.

Exchanging Remarks with Mother

The mother then asked, "Well, how do you feel?" in a very pleasant tone of voice, as she sat on the edge of Margaret's bed.

Margaret said very, very sleepily, "O.K.," and the mother absently murmured, "Huh?"

Margaret said, "O.K., I don't have a cold."

This was said a little less sleepily in the tone of one who is telling something of great interest.

The mother asked, "You don't have a cold?"

Margaret muttered, "Huh," still rather sleepily, lapsing back to her former sleepy state.

The mother asked pleasantly, "Do you want to go to Bible School?"

Margaret murmured, so sleepily as hardly to say a word at all, "Yes."

4

8:12   The mother urged, "Well, let's get dressed."
As Margaret started to slide off the bed, her mother said quickly, "Wait." Then she explained, "Get your shoes and socks so you won't have to get your feet dirty."
Margaret sat on the edge of the bed where she was before her mother's voice arrested her slide to the floor.

5

As the mother reached for her foot, Margaret said sleepily, "I want to lie down."
The mother laughed and said, "So you want to lie down and go to sleep again."
She let Margaret lie down.
Margaret lay with her head at the foot of the bed this time.

6

Margaret then stretched as far as she could with her arms back, raising up and wiggling.
It was almost as if she were shedding her sleep like a snake sheds its skin.
Her mother laughed at her pleasantly.

7

Margaret said cautiously, "A hairpin came out."
   Her hair was done up in bobby pins for curling purposes.
Then she asked with a great deal more interest, much more animated than she had been, "Do you see a curl?"
Margaret wiggled some more.
The mother didn't say anything.
"I took a hairpin out," said Margaret with firmness, almost with a note of defiance.
The mother said, "So you took a hairpin out," as if "so what."
   I gathered that Margaret was pestering her mother.
   After saying the hairpin came out had brought no

Getting Dressed

Lying Down

Stretching

Taking Bobby Pins Out

reprimand, she seemed to be trying to get one by saying she took it out.

Margaret took out several more hairpins, reaching rather lazily up to remove them.

She looked cautiously at her mother.

Getting no response, she didn't bother to look at her mother any more.

Margaret watched her mother's hand as if to make sure she was keeping the hairpins safely.

8

8:13   She took several more hairpins from her hair and said, "Do you see a curl?" rather eagerly.

The mother said, "I see a lot of them that are going to be curls."

Margaret took a few more bobby pins out and said again, "Do you see a curl now?" a bit more eagerly.

The mother answered, "Yes, I see a curl," as if she knew she had to say so before she would have any peace.

The mother finished putting on the shoes and socks for Margaret and told her to take off her pyjamas and put on her panties.

Without saying anything, Margaret put her feet off the bed rather lazily.

She slid slowly to her feet.

9

Margaret kind of wobbled and took several steps toward her mother.

Mrs. Reid laughed and said, "Think you can walk this morning, honey?" in a very loving tone of voice.

She added, "You walk like an old lady."

Margaret giggled and laughed.

She put her arms affectionately around her mother's neck.

As her laugh subsided, the mother said, "Take off your pyjamas and I'll put your panties on you," in a pleasantly firm tone of voice.

The mother unclasped Margaret's arms from her neck and let them slide down.

The mother pulled Margaret's panties on rather snugly but in a loving way.

She gave Margaret a little pat on her rear.

10

Margaret came out of the bedroom and into the dining room, prepared to go to the bathroom.

11

She finally noticed me.

The observer was sitting in the dining room near the door to Margaret's room.

She opened her mouth in surprise.

She really seemed surprised to find me there.

She almost stopped, but didn't, and walked on to the bathroom.

8:14 The mother followed her and asked, "About through, honey?"

I thought I had better not go into the bathroom at this point.

There were sounds of splashing water as the mother helped.

8:16 Margaret came out of the bathroom, through the kitchen, and into the dining room.

As she stood there, she pulled on her housecoat that her mother had left on a chair for her.

(left margin labels, top to bottom:) Getting Dressed | Going to Bathroom | Noting Observer

An action and a situation stand out as parts of every episode.

The action is in some instances single and undivided, as in *Noting Observer*. It is in other instances divided into subordinate parts or *phases,* as in *Getting Dressed*. Yet it is always unitary. The situation is the person's psychological habitat when the action occurs. It includes the needs and working abilities of the person and coexisting objects of the environment. Where the action is divided, the situation also is divided; habitat objects, working abilities, and needs change as the person goes from one phase of an action to another. Yet the total situation also has unity; its parts form on the environmental side one set of outer conditions to be dealt with in some way at one time for one purpose.

The title, *Lying Down*, for example, identifies an action. The situation includes the need state, signified by Margaret's sleepiness. It includes also the friendly mother and all parts of the behavior setting that made a difference to Margaret Reid while she was lying down, as these are represented in the record.

One cannot hope to find in a specimen record a complete description of either the action or the situation of an episode. The state of the person and the content of the environment cannot be completely determined by presently available methods; nor is it possible to describe fully by any available means the content and properties of an action. We nonetheless hope to show that some dimensions of the molar behavior unit and its context in an episode can be reconstructed usefully on the basis of material in a specimen record.

Naturally occurring episodes are the events that people write personal letters about if they write daily. They are, as a rule with exceptions, too small, vestigial, and numerous for annual letters and they are comparatively rare for the same reasons in biographies, novels, and histories, but they generally form the plot units of short stories and plays. They are the molar behavior phenomena that parents, teachers, neighbors, storekeepers, and others note as a matter of course in the lives of children, and that adults in general often praise or blame, abet or hinder, delight in or deplore. Behavior units that fall short of or exceed the size range of episodes do not always go entirely unobserved. At times, for example, a mother will notice a subepisodic unit, as when she commands her child to stop absent drumming with his fingers. Frequently, also, she will take note of superepisodic units, especially to encourage very long ones, as when she urges upon a backward violinist the advantages in musical skill. More often, however, adults attend to and get concerned about the intermediate behavior parts, episodes, that are perceived while they occur by children themselves in their own behavior. As behavior-situation units, in short, episodes are of intermediate size. They are denotable first of all as neither the very small, nor the very large, but the moderately extended units of the behavior stream that external observers and the behaving person normally perceive. Occurrence within the evident view by the person of his own behavior will indeed be proposed in due course as a fundamental criterion of an episode. Before identifying episodes further, however, we should like to consider briefly their place in the study of behavior.

RESEARCH USES OF EPISODES

Basic laws of molar behavior can appear in the observable action-to-situation relationships within episodes. Belief in this is implicit in the fact that, to test hypotheses about interdependencies between situation and action, laboratory psychologists commonly create episodes, often called "trials." Experimental conditions are manipulated so that the experimenter contrives trial by trial a situation that elicits one or another action. These manipulated conditions bring about, in short, a particular episode in which, say, a cat escapes from a puzzle box, an ape rakes a banana into his cage, a child strives to reach a playhouse on the other side of a screen, or a man makes a hatrack out of two poles and a table clamp.

These and many other laboratory episodes give leads to laws of molar behavior. But their analogues are abundant in naturally occurring units of the same order whose variables of action and situation are no less uniform. For example, the paradigm of a child, something the child wants, and an interposed obstacle occurs many times over in our records on Midwest children. It is possible to collect from such records an adequate sample of episodes in which individuals of any chosen age, sex, social group, or other nonpsychological classification behave in situations that present in one or another degree a particular type of frustration, failure, success, social pressure, conflict, or the like. It also is possible to hold other situational variables essentially constant through selection, with the end result that one can determine relationships between the independent, situational variables and such dependent variables of behavior as, say, energy level, efficiency, or constructiveness.

What this comes to is that a planned collection of naturally occurring episodes in specimen records can supply experimental trials in nature. These, moreover, have some advantages over comparable events of the laboratory.

Foremost here is the advantage that one can find in life episodes environmental conditions that cannot be contrived easily, if at all. Consider the properties of other persons. Warm affection, an observable, reliably measurable, and frequently occurring property of a parent in a home or of a playmate, cannot readily be managed in a laboratory associate of a laboratory subject. The same holds for intense aggression, which occurred, for example, in one recorded episode as a property of a Midwest four-year-old girl when she hit her brother over the head with a bucket.

Another special advantage in episodes of specimen records is that they give a unique chance for study of sequential interdependencies. The situations and actions of consecutive episodes can be rated on selected variables, and profiles can be drawn of change from unit to unit in the continuing behavior and its context. Using a collection of episodes records, one can do experiments of a kind on interunit relations. It is possible to set up almost any constellation of situational variables or behavior variables, or both, to find the constellation in particular episodes, and then to determine the situation, the behavior, or both, in flanking antecedent and subsequent episodes.

The experiments in nature of naturally occurring episodes have apparent limitations for research on general psychological laws. They do not permit the efficient accommodation of conditions to hypotheses, the positive separation of independent variables, and the elimination of extraneous factors that are characteristic of good laboratory procedures. Yet they offer possible corroboration of laboratory findings and they stand to turn up new hypotheses.

Recorded episodes clearly have greatest significance for behavior problems on the level of particular actions and their more immediate contexts. Personality problems clearly require identification and study of long biographic units whose determining contexts include lasting and characteristically stable needs and goals of the person. Yet action-and-situation units on the episode level are used in clinical practice and research. The diagnostic interview, for example, often discloses particular "incidents" that are thought to be revealing parts of a life history, and so do associated testing procedures.

The foregoing leaves as the first research value of the episodes in specimen records their store of information about the distribution of different kinds, properties, and conditions of molar behavior outside the laboratory and clinic. One can take these descriptive units, much as a medical student takes histological slides, and study them one by one from the standpoint of their action and situation content. But they also have significance for our natural history problem from an entirely different point of view.

To episode a record is to find boundaries between the parts of a whole behavior sequence. One can then inquire into the relations of part to whole and part to part within the sequence without any reference to what the parts contain. This is to ask about the structure or anatomy of the behavior continuum. The problem is analogous to the one presented by part and whole relations of a skeleton, a plant, or a rock formation, except that the whole is extended in time as well as space in the case of behavior with its context.

Given a behavior sequence through a known period of time, to what extent, in the first place, is it differentiated into parts? How many episodes does it include? How many "things," for example, does a normal Midwest 2-year-old do in a day? A Midwest 11-year-old? How are the episodes of a behavior sequence related interpositionally, whatever the degree in which the total sequence is divided? How often do they occur one by one in single file? How often, on the other hand, do they overlap, and with what variations in the form and complexity of the overlapping? Also to be considered here are dynamical factors closely associated with the anatomy of behavior. What conditions act at the beginning of an episode to get it underway or at its end point to break it off? Under what conditions do episodes interact? One can ask also about cross-effects between different units of a sequence. When episodes overlap, for example, in what degree may they interfere with, complement, or reenforce one another? Such questions identify the problem of *behavior structure*.

We have analyzed both the action and situation content of individual episodes in records on Midwest children and also the structural properties of episodes. Results of these different kinds of analysis are presented in succeeding chapters. The problem of structure, meanwhile, points back to the task of discriminating episodes in specimen records.

To meet this practical problem, we had to develop a pilot theory of behavior unit formation. The theory, which owes most to Lewin (1938), may have pertinence for general questions of behavior perception. Also, some developments of it in the following discussion may say something of behavior structure on the side of results, because the formulations stem partly from discoveries made in work with specimen records.

PLOTTING BEHAVIOR STRUCTURE

IMPLICIT AND EXPLICIT CRITERIA

Some circumstantial observations on our experience with episoding may be helpful.

We have found that, on the average, it takes a trained episoder 12 minutes to divide one page of a specimen record. On this basis, 54 minutes were used in episoding the excerpt above from the day record on Margaret Reid. A part of the time was spent only in reading through the material and in inscribing episode brackets and titles. Most of it, however, was spent in applying criteria for telling episodes apart. This may seem out of line with our statement that each of the episodes in the sequence might easily have been discriminated at the time of its occurrence by any present and normally perceptive adult. We have indeed said that such action and situation units are characteristically open to ordinary perception by others. What is the need, then, for the special criteria?

As a matter of fact, we had no explicitly formulated guides to episoding at the time of setting out to divide the records. We began instead with little more than the word "episode" as a name for a commonly recognized or recognizable unit of action with its context. Yet, lacking substantially more than this to go upon, we were nonetheless able to find in the records units that stood out clearly to us and that seemed likely to have been open to easy discrimination by others when the recorded behavior occurred. Also, we agreed among ourselves more often than not in marking off these units. Some of them were spotted without hesitation or any dissent. For example, we can now say with confidence that no one of the pilot episoders would have missed *Getting Dressed* of the Margaret Reid record if it had occurred on the first page of our first episoded record.

Despite agreeing more often than not in this earliest dividing of the records, we did not agree often enough to meet adequate standards of reliability. One episoder would see a particular part of a sequence as a discrete and entire unit, while another would see it as only a part of a larger unit, and a third might see the same part as two or more episodes. Certain nodal points, each denoting the end of one episode and the start of another, were marked in extended sequences with firm unanimity among as many as three independent episoders. Between these nodal points, however, discrepancies occurred rather often. And there were frequent instances in which units seen as concurrent or overlapping by one analyst would be seen by another as only subordinate parts of a single episode.

These disagreements led us to consider that, although there are easily and often recognized intervals of action and situation within a certain behavioral range, this range includes different and more or less equally perceptible units. Consistency in episoding required, therefore, some positive specifications that could be used to judge whether a given unit was or was not to be marked off as an episode. The need for the subsequently developed criteria is, first, a need for such consistency. An episoder has to go by what he sees, no less than anyone else, which means that these criteria cannot take the place of common perception. They probably do not even make common perception more than ordinarily correct. Perhaps the best they can do is to increase its stability within the range of ordinarily recognized behavior units. In any case, evidence will be presented to show that the episoding of a specimen record with the help of these criteria is a reliable and repeatable process.

A second advantage of the criteria at last developed has been clarification of episode properties as objects of study. This would seem desirable apart from the objective of consistency or reliability in episoding.

PROXIMAL EPISODE CUES

Study of episoded records suggests that the following cues have influenced our marking of the beginning and end points of episodes.

1. Change in the "sphere" of the behavior from verbal to physical to social to intellectual, or from any of these to another.
2. Change in the part of the body predominantly involved in a physical action, as from hands to mouth to feet.
3. Change in the physical direction of the behavior. Now, a child is walking north to a sandpile; next, he is going up a tree; later, he climbs down the tree.
4. Change in behavior object "commerced with," as from a knife to a watch to a dog to a person.
5. Change in the present behavior setting. When his teacher says, "Pass," Henry leaves the classroom setting and, at the same time, starts a new action.
6. Change in the tempo of activity, as when a child shifts from walking leisurely to running toward a friend.

These and other like indicators, many of them doubtless subliminal, necessarily affect discrimination of episodes. Yet such empirical marks are by no means bound in a univocal way to behavior units on this level. The changes noted under 1, 2, and 3 actually are very often only changes in the actone manifolds that mediate continuing units of molar behavior (see pp. 17–22).

The situation is like that in perception where the recognition of a geometrical form, such as a circle, is possible under a great variety of stimulus conditions. In the case of the form, the necessary conditions do not have to be defined for the person who sees it. Three-year-olds who know nothing about the laws of object constancy can identify a circle, for example, whether you lay it on a table or pin it to a wall. Similarly, persons in real life or episoders can recognize episodes under enormously varied, molecular, phenotypic, or proximal conditions, which no one has defined for them, and which, moreover, we are in no way prepared to define for the present purpose. Our problem, then, is to find indicators that remain essentially invariant while these conditions change; it is to find criteria that sustain to all such signs something of the relationship that the distal form properties of the circle sustain to its changing proximal characteristics.

PRIMARY CRITERIA OF EPISODES

CONSTANCY IN DIRECTION

The behavior of an episode is constant in direction. Thus, in main principle, a change in episode occurs for every change in the direction of behavior. Muenzinger (1942) has made direction constancy the key feature of a *start-end unit*, which has other features in common with an episode.

Another episoded sequence will now be useful; we shall refer back to it repeatedly. It is taken from a day record on Dutton (Chuck) Thurston. The sequence begins at 7:32 on a November evening in the back yard of the Thurston home, where Chuck is setting on the hood of a truck while his father stands nearby.

Going Inside

7:32 The father called good-naturedly, "Come on, Chuck. Come along, boy."

Chuck jumped down easily and quickly.

He trotted a few steps ahead of his father.

Mr. Thurston caught up at the back door of the house. There he said briskly, as he opened the door, "Come on; let's get inside."

Chuck bounded into the house.

He walked quickly through the kitchen and dining room into the living room, where his mother sat resting on a couch.

Taking Off Wraps

He started to peel off his jacket.

Commenting on Cold

At the same time, he remarked companionably to his mother, "It's cold outside. It's really cold out there." He said this in a very adult way.

Only smiling pleasantly, his mother seemed to take it that way.

7:33 Chuck pulled his jacket down from his shoulders; but it stayed on because the sleeves jammed against the bulky gloves he was wearing.

Getting Mittens Off

Chuck demanded of no one in particular, "Mittens off!"

His mother said nothing and made no move to help.

Chuck resolutely walked over to his mother.

Standing before her with his coat sagging, he soberly held out his hands.

The mother reached over toward him.

Then, while he helped by pulling back a little, she tugged off his gloves.

Chuck wriggled on out of his coat, letting it drop where he stood.

Putting Wraps Away

His mother said firmly, "Chuck, put your hat and coat away."

He just stood there.

His mother repeated her command very firmly.

Chuck asked, looking impish, "Shall I get the ruler, Mommie?"

> Earlier in the day Chuck had refused to put away his wraps, whereupon his mother had said threateningly, "Now, where is my ruler?" So, in asking now if he should get the ruler, Chuck evidently was just beating his mother to the draw.

Chuck did not press the question about the ruler. Before his mother could answer it, he picked up his hat and coat. Then he carried the wraps into the bedroom. He was smiling.

He returned to the living room at once.

The direction test is exemplified by the judgment that, so long as he behaved in the episode, *Going Inside*, Chuck was engaging without a break in the action that took him from a starting position—outdoors, on truck, near father—to a new position, inside the house, which he had intended to reach from the starting position. It is exemplified also by the judgment that, when Chuck began to take off his wraps, his behavior took a new directional tack in a new episode; and so on through the remaining units, except for *Getting Mittens Off*, as later explained.

Several marks of directedness as a property of behavior are in the psychological literature, and some of them can be used as aids to recognition of change or continuance of direction in the behavior stream. Representative clues of this kind are listed below, each with a psychologist who has advocated it and also with an example, adapted in most instances from our records.

1. Action persists in the absence of instigating conditions (McDougall, 1923).

Mrs. Logan, the second grade teacher in Midwest, says, "Turn, stand, pass," and Ben Hutchings proceeds to walk out of the classroom, to go on out of the building, and to walk a distance of three blocks to his home.

The instigating conditions act more like a goad than a continuing push from behind. They set the action off. Then it seems to maintain itself, not in a situational vacuum, but without continuance of the initial stimuli.

2. Change in position toward a part of the environment is renewed after forced digression or delay[1] (McDougall, 1923).

Raymond Birch uses his wagon to haul a large and wobbly old crate across a lot. The crate falls from the wagon repeatedly, and, each time it does, Raymond stops pulling the wagon, hurries to one side of it, works the crate back onto the wagon, and goes on his way.

3. "Preparatory adjustments" appropriate to imminent situational change, to which the observed action contributes, accompany the action (McDougall, 1923).

A Midwest 11-year-old "primps" often and turns repeatedly to look at her reflection in store windows while she half runs to a birthday party.

Here, there is a getting ready for the change in situation that the action itself is to bring about. This getting ready in the behavior confirms the observation that the child is indeed going in the direction of the party.

McDougall gives as a classical example the postural and pointing adjustments of a predatory animal, stalking its prey.

4. Sustained movement is abruptly discontinued after an end, provisionally identified by the observer, has been reached (McDougall, 1923).

Jimmy Hebb, observed across a street, is wandering somewhat lackadaisically in his front yard. His head is bent. Every now and then he gets down on his hands and knees and runs his fingers through the grass. What *is* he doing? It begins to look as if he might be looking for a four-leaf clover. Confirmation is finally given to the best guess that all of the behavior is toward this end when Jimmy

[1] One version of what McDougall says about "variation in the direction of persistent movements."

looks at something in his left hand, audibly counts "1–2–3–4," and then flops down, stretches out on the grass and lies very still for a few seconds.

It is as if the sought end had been the reason for being of the action, so that the action loses its dynamics when the end is reached. Actually, however, one need not suppose, as we do not, that the end causes the action.

5. Action between observable beginning and end points shows continuity (Köhler, 1925).

This holds for each of the foregoing examples. Throughout the length of all such behavior segments there are no gaps. Differing individual, subordinate, molar units of behavior occur. But these are scarcely seen singly, as a matter of course; one often has to search for them. The whole action, however, appears as a good figure. The distinguishable lesser actions show a connectedness that arises from their implementing progress toward the stopping point.

6. Action between beginning and end points follows the shortest available path (Adams, 1931–1932; Wheeler and Perkins, 1932).

Ben Hutchings on his way home from school cuts across a vacant lot.

Ben might have gone "the longest way around," say with a friend. In this case, however, we doubtless would have marked two overlapping episodes, the one: *Going Home from School*, and the other: *Walking with Friend*. Ben's continuously maintaining the closest possible connection with *home* by taking the shortest available route implies directedness as a feature of the behavior and, beyond that, helps to establish the true action in progress.

There is considerable experimental evidence to show that this sign of directed action is a basic characteristic of molar behavior. Such evidence has been generalized by Adams (1931–1932) as "parsimony," by Gengerelli (1930) in the principle of "maxima and minima," by Bingham (1929) in the rule of the "easiest means," and by Wheeler and Perkins (1932) in the "law of least action."

7. Variance in behavior is concordant with variance in the position of an environmental object (Baldwin, 1955).

Stella Town is rushing pell-mell back and forth across the school playground. What is *she* doing? Her behavior looks quite random and aimless—until the observer discovers Sammy Sherwin on the other side of a grouping of children, and finds that every time Sammy runs north or south, so does Stella. Now, the behavior looks thoroughly directed. And the particular directed action in progress is now evident. Stella is chasing Sammy, or, at least, as some other noted facts suggested, putting on a good show of doing this.

All of these indicators are available to observers and analysts of molar behavior and its conditions. We cannot profess to their intentioned, systematic use in episoding. Yet we do assume that these and probably other equally important signs of behavioral direction are used almost inevitably, both as evidence that an action by a person is in progress and as a means of telling one action from another, in common social intercourse—and in dividing a specimen record. Our main point in any case is that direction as an attribute of molar behavior has clear empirical marks.

Guides to detection of constancy and change in direction are *present position, change in position,* and *terminal intended position.* Synonyms of terminal intended position are *goal* and *end.* The episoder continually looks ahead to diagnose the position intended from the present position of the person. Once a particular end has been fixed, all behavior seen to bring the person nearer to it is considered to lie in the same direction. The observed progress can be great or small or, in the limiting case, zero. Also, a change in position can occur when there is no observable movement in physical space. The person can move in a social sphere of action, as when the child speaks a piece, or in an intellectual sphere, as when a child solves a mathematical problem.

The behavior theory behind the episode is that an action changes the position of the person on a path in the space of a situation; the person locomotes on this path toward a new, intended position. The test, then, of whether a particular action occurs in the same direction as a preceding, simultaneous, or subsequent one reduces to a single question. Does the action carry the person nearer to his goal in any of the compared actions? If it does not, its direction is different and the uniqueness of the action is established.

Two processes in episoding are implied here. The first is diagnosing the end toward which the person is moving, and the second is judging whether the "movement" brings the person nearer to that end. The total process is circular. The new position is determined from the behavior of the person and the direction of the behavior is determined from its relation to the new position. In reality, however, the judgments usually are not analytical. The direction of the behavior in relation to the new position and vice versa generally are immediately apprehended; the unity of the action in an episode generally is perceived almost as immediately as the unity of a visual form or an auditory pattern.

Continual rediagnosis of the terminal intended position is nevertheless essential in episoding. A change in the position of a person can bring about a realignment of psychological forces such that, at any point, a new goal or end can arise. Wesley Mead, in a darkened room, turns on a light. Then he goes at once to a wall and stands before it, looking at a picture. Is *Turning on Light* a separate episode or is it only the first phase of a larger episode, *Looking at Picture*? This question can be answered only by finding whether or not, in turning on the light, Wesley intended to view the picture. If so, there is only the one larger episode; if not, there are the two smaller ones. We have found generally in such cases that the facts needed for a reasonably confident decision are available.

A further complication is that the goal of an episode is not necessarily reached. It can be relinquished, as in failure. Theoretically, however, if not always demonstrably, an episode never ends so long as the goal sought when it began persists: the action in every episode extends through its issue, where issue means outcome, whether the outcome be failure, success, satiation, or some other terminal development in the behavior. Issue is defined more fully in Chapter 5. When the person does fail or is forced to quit an action by pressure or blocking from without, and the goal is not relinquished, an interruption occurs, in which case the episode may or may not be subsequently resumed. Examples will be reviewed when special consideration is given later to the problems of episode interruption.

The episoder has to recognize that direction is a genotypic factor in behavior that can be clothed in diverse phenotypes; there are no behavioral specifics for either constancy or change in it. One must recognize also that direction refers to an attribute of behavior as it is for the behaving person. This means that the observation of its constancy or change must always be tentative. One continually tests such observation in daily life by questioning the other person or by trying out responses to him that he "takes" in such a way as to clarify what he is aiming to get done. A similarly experimental approach must be followed in the episoding of a record. The same tests cannot be literally applied, and yet somewhat equivalent hypothetical tests are possible. Would the child feel interrupted if the observer broke the behavior here? Would the loss to the child be the same if the observer broke it here or there? Such probing has been found useful. But the major requirement of episoding from the standpoint of the direction guide is mastery of the genotype and wide familiarity with its differing manifestations.

OCCURRENCE WITHIN THE NORMAL BEHAVIOR PERSPECTIVE

Our second primary criterion of an episode concerns its size. We have seen that molar behavior units can differ in size, as they can indeed, from minimal ones, like *Stepping Down from Curb*, to short ones, like *Crossing Street*, to rather extended ones, like *Walking to School*, to long ones, like *Working to Pass from the Third Grade*, through still longer ones, like *Getting an Education*, to very long ones, like *Climbing to the Top in Life* or, if some psychologists are right, *Earning Approval from Mother*. All of these could make up for a child at one time a hierarchy of molar behavior units corresponding to a hierarchy of goals.

The importance of this variable for episoding derives in part from the fact that size of behavior unit and direction of behavior are related. A Midwest six-year-old who has been ordered sternly by his mother to stay at home first runs off to the school playground and then goes to the house of a friend. We probably would mark *Running to School Playground* and *Going to House of Friend* as separate episodes on the grounds that the two actions differ in direction. But, within the compass of such a behavior cycle as *Breaking Away from Parental Domination*, for example, both could have the same direction and consequently belong to the same unit. This does not mean that the one judgment would contradict the other. Both could be true. The direction of flow of the Missouri River is 14 degrees south of east between Kansas City and St. Louis; it is 37 degrees east of south between the more inclusive points of Rapid City and New Orleans. Both statements are correct.

Some designation of limiting points on the continuum of behavior analogous to zone restrictions on a geographical map is needed to fix the size range of episodes. How long is an episode? We have answered by defining episodes as molar behavior units that the person himself perceives to be in progress. This designates by a perceptual coordinate the points on the behavior continuum within which episodes fall. It eliminates, as subepisodic, molecular and short molar units that run off with no or only vague awareness by the person; and it eliminates also, as superepisodic, long units that are maintained outside the limits of clear perception. The span of attention or clear perception by the person of his own behavior-in-progress we have called the *normal behavior perspective*, and our second criterion places episodes within this span.

The idea of behavior perspective brings to bear upon the perception by a person of his own behavior three characteristics of perception in general.

1. SELECTIVE AWARENESS. The part of the action continuum within the behavior perspective stands out as a figure against an undifferentiated behavioral background. Other parts are in the peripheral zone of faint perception, while still others lie entirely outside the perceptual field.

2. LIMEN OF SENSITIVITY. Just as the resolving power of sensory surfaces for visual, auditory, and other stimuli are finite, so that limens exist below which discrimination is impossible, there are corresponding limits of perception by the person of his own behavior. Some molecular units or actones cannot be perceived at all, as earlier suggested, and some extended molar units are equally imperceptible.

3. RANGE OF SENSITIVITY. The range of stimuli for any sensory modality within which a person can discriminate is wider than the range within which he does discriminate. This also appears to hold for the behavior continuum, in that the range in size of the behavior segments a person *can* perceive, from the largest episode in progress to the smallest perceptible actone, is greater than the size range of the segments he normally *does* perceive. The maximum behavior perspective within the total range of sensitivity is achieved only by special techniques, as in cases of "insight" under clinical direction. This does not mean that the normal perspective is rigidly fixed; it varies instead from moment to moment, although its limits appear to be quite sharply defined. The behavior units outside this range are real and legitimate. They are left out of direct account in episoding, however, for the reason that, by definition, a unit outside the perspective by the person on his own behavior is not an episode. The behavior perspective is an aperture past which the continuum of action by a person must pass and through which one can see episodes of behavior. This perceptual coordinate, in other words, is a range finder. One can use it to say how big episodes are, to identify units of the prescribed size, and to exclude those either larger or smaller. On the other hand, it says nothing about the essential nature of episodes, certainly not that they have only heuristic, perceptual significance. An episode is a natural unit of action and situation with an integrity that depends first upon dynamical and structural properties.

As the most generally perceived behavior units, episodes have basic evolutionary significance. Just as there probably is survival value for man in the normal range of his visual acuity for size and distance, there also may be adaptive value in the normal behavior perspective. We might be grateful to see neither more nor less that it discloses of our own behavior. Self understanding and guidance would be inadequate if we saw much less, while confusion would increase if we saw much more. Insight into the longer parts of the behavior stream and into the ordinarily "hidden" motives that underlie them can occur and is now generally thought to be hygienic. But such insight comes only in flashes, with the fortunate result that we do not have to live continually with its revelations.

How, in the dividing of a behavior sequence, are the limits of the behavior perspective to be set?

The nub of the problem is that the behavior perspective of a person, like the direction of his behavior, is defined by what exists for the person, which means that, like direction, it cannot be observed directly. No observer can pretend to get into private worlds in using this or other tests for an episode. Yet certain marks of action limits are perceived no better by the person than by an observer. The observer sees from the outside what the person sees from the inside. The result is that we all are able to detect in the continuing behavior of our associates, units that evidently match well their behavior perspectives. Even small children are remarkably sensitive to the intended boundary lines between the actions of their mothers, fathers, and teachers; children of five and six years know rather well, many exceptions to the contrary nothwithstanding, when to break in or hold back on occasions when adults are intermittently busy.

Persons could not hope to "get on" with others without ability to discriminate their intended actions. We have to know with some precision when the things our associates do and mean to do, begin and end. Otherwise we would be continually interrupting one another. But others do not generally cut in on our actions as we see them or generally complain of the reverse. On the other hand, persons do not commonly see in the daily lives of their associates long trains of behavior that encompass different actions in dissimilar directions. By and large, it is only when one deliberately adopts the characteristic orientation of the psychiatrist, the counselor, or the biographer that this happens. The upshot is that, in applying the criterion of occurrence within the normal behavior perspective, the episoder has available another one of the common skills that must be used in naturalistic psychological studies.

The idea of behavior perspective is related in some respects to the concept of time perspective (cf. Frank, 1939). Both refer to perception by the person of processes within the continuum of behavior. Time perspective, however, is broader in scope. It embraces all of the psychological present, past, and future as these are seen by the person. Behavior perspective extends through only a part of the person's behavior-in-progress, namely, the part within the span of clear perception.

What is the child now doing at the most as he sees it? This question, later formulated in terms of behavior perspective, gave our first explicit guide to episoding. We applied it at the outset to specimen day records, and our case for it was that a day of episodes, defined from this standpoint, would represent the parts of a child's day as they were for him. Such representation provides a defined base of one kind for work on a variety of psychological problems.

SUPERIOR WHOLE POTENCY

Episodes are sometimes undivided, single molar units, as when a child answers only "Yes" or "No" to a question. *Commenting on Cold* of the Chuck Thurston sequence, above (see p. 70), is another example of an undivided episode. More often than not, however, an episode is divided into consecutive parts. The reader can easily find in *Going Inside* of Chuck's behavior, for example, such episode divisions as *jumping down from truck, trotting ahead of father*, and *bounding into house*. The person is "involved in" one or another of the parts of a divided episode at every moment while he is involved in the whole. The whole and the part coexist as units with some degree of independence, with each part an action and a minor, dependent, included situation.

As a subordinate complex, every part unit of an episode makes a greater or lesser contribution to the whole of the ongoing behavior; each, compared with the whole, has a greater or lesser degree of importance for the total behavior of the person. To say this with better conceptual language from Lewin (see 1938, especially), every part, relative to the whole, has a greater or lesser degree of potency or weight. The potencies of the whole unit and any part unit are by definition relative to one another, so that when the weight of either goes up, that of the other goes down. But the relative weights of part and whole can differ from one segment of an episode to another. For example, we would judge that, as a part of *Going Inside, bounding into house* had a greater potency when it took place than just *trotting ahead of father* at the earlier time of its occurrence.

Our third primary criterion of an episode refers to the potency relationship of part to whole within the total episode unit by affirming that an episode as a whole has greater potency than any of its parts. A group of persons presents an analogue. Social group unity depends in part upon group action in some one direction. But it depends also on potency relationships in the sense that the unity of a group can be destroyed if one of its members "outweighs" the rest. The unity and integrity of an episode depend similarly, not only upon constancy in direction of the included action, but also upon superior whole potency. A corollary of this is that, if any part unit of a behavior sequence with a constant direction either exceeds or equals the whole in potency, that unit becomes a separate episode. The part in this case outweighs the whole, in the behavior perspective of the person and in the dynamics of the behavior.

In the Chuck Thurston sequence, *Getting Mittens Off* was seen to have the same direction as *Taking Off Wraps*. But the episoder judged that, while Chuck was involved with the troublesome mittens, this lesser, included unit had at least as much weight as the whole of the larger, containing segment of behavior. *Getting Mittens Off* was therefore singled out as a separate episode. Units individuated in this way are said to be *contained*. Every contained episode overlaps with the containing *parent* unit, for it necessarily occurs while the latter is in progress. Yet coexisting contained and containing episodes differ from other overlapping episodes in that they have the same direction, with the result that they leave the behavior continuum the less widely split.

Although superior whole potency and behavior perspective are conceptually independent of one another, their behavioral signs are correlated. In general, a unit tends to move toward the periphery of the behavior perspective as its potency goes down; and units with zero potency are thought to be not perceived at all by the person. Yet we have assumed that action units with relatively high potency can occur outside the behavior perspective, as in fugue or trance behavior.

In episoding, we have used as indicators of high potency wide involvement of motor, verbal, and other behavior mechanisms, "indifference" to potentially distracting conditions, and high energy level of the behavior. Factors in the situation of the person, such as high resistance and strong interpersonal stimulation, also are associated with high potency.

SPECIAL COMPLICATIONS OF
BEHAVIOR STRUCTURE

Episoding consists mainly in using the ideas of constancy in direction, behavior perspective, and relative potency as guides to episodes in a specimen record. But the method takes into account also the following special features of behavior structure which, at some points, require qualification of the primary criteria.

EPISODE PARTS

There are, again, both undivided and divided episodes. We have found in divided episodes three classes of parts. Although these are not marked off in episoding, they have significance for the process of dividing a record and for the larger problem of behavior structure.

1. *Phases.* Consider again *stepping down from curb, crossing street,* and the circumjacent episode, *Going to School,* all drawn earlier from the Raymond Birch record. The first of these is a *phase,* defined as any molar unit among sequential, least inclusive units in an action hierarchy. A succeeding phase here was *darting back to curb.* A phase is a minimal action in that dividing it would break it into actones.

We see as a phase Chuck Thurston's jumping down from truck. It is a part of *Going Inside.* It presents something Chuck did in relation to molar parts of his environment. *Bounding into the house* is taken to be another phase. But we find no recorded evidence of actions by this child within these phases. Divide the jumping unit and you get movements of the arms, trunk, and legs, for example; not actions, but actones.

The phase, like an episode, contains an action and also its own minor context. Dynamically, it differs from an episode chiefly in that the action in a phase is directed toward a subgoal, whereas the action in an episode is directed toward a goal which, within the limits of the behavior perspective, is terminal. As a minimal molar unit of behavior toward a subgoal, a phase action contributes one step in the direction of the terminal goal of an episode.

A practical complication in episoding concerns what we have called *precursory* and *sequent* phases. A precursory phase amounts to a step that takes the person up to the point at which the prevailing action of an episode begins; it is linked functionally with the prevailing action as a necessary antecedent. A sequent phase, on the other hand, amounts to a step out of an episode; it is linked functionally with the prevailing action as a necessary or at least "natural" sequel. Likely examples of precursory and sequent phases, respectively, are the entrance before and the exit after a speech. We have found that one must be vigilantly on guard against marking either precursory or sequent phases as episodes in themselves.

2. *Stages.* Once begun, the action of an episode continues until a new action begins. This follows from constancy in direction as a trait of an episode. We have left implicit another consequence of the direction principle, namely, that an episode includes, not only the behavior in getting to a goal, but also the behavior in going

through the goal region. Each of these two behavior segments, with its context, we have called a *stage*. The behavior and situation in "getting there" extend through a *transitive stage*, the behavior and situation in "being there" through a *consummatory stage*. A transitive stage is illustrated by getting an ice cream cone, through the point of handing the clerk a nickel; and eating the cone illustrates a consummatory stage.

Strictly, the shift from a transitive to a consummatory stage brings change in direction of the continuing behavior. The behavior in a transitive stage is directed from one part to another more or less distant part of a situation. The behavior in a consummatory stage is directed toward the present region. This difference, however, is not as great as it might at first seem; because, in every observable case of consummatory action, the present region, i.e., the goal area, is differentiated into parts from one to the next of which action is continuously in progress, which means that, in a consummatory stage, the present position and the intended terminal position of the person are not identical. Yet the person is at each moment in a "plus" area; and, characteristically, as in a game played purely for fun (so that "the running is as good as the winning"), all parts of this area are homogeneously *plus*. One is not "spurred on" or "attracted," and meanwhile made more or less miserable, by something better at a distance. Also, resistances and distances to things seen ahead are virtually zero in a consummatory stage whereas, in a transitive stage, they can be maximally high.

In theory, both of these consecutive stages occur always in a complete episode. But both do not always appear in behavior. Often, as far as one can see, the goal is only a point reached rather than an area enjoyed. A consummatory stage cannot be observed when this is true. Raymond walks briskly onto the schoolgrounds and so reaches the goal in *Going to School*. But there is nothing in the record to show that the region of this goal is differentiated. As far as one can observe, a new goal arises instantly when two stray dogs snarl at him. For the observer, at least, the terminal position in *Going to School* was a *point region* that Raymond reached and passed through at one and the same time.

Conversely, it is sometimes impossible to observe a transitive stage. Shortly before crossing the busy street, Raymond digressed from his path to school to the extent of behaving through the following episode.

Rocking Bench

Raymond sat down on one of the benches [on the Courthouse yard] with a pleasant, relaxed expression.

He rocked the bench back and forth for a few seconds, sitting with his hands stretched out and holding the edges of the bench to brace himself. His feet were out in front of him, flat on the ground.

He hummed a little to himself, very softly, contentedly.

He jumped up and began rocking the bench as he stood on the ground at one end of it. He held onto the seat and the back and pushed the bench back and forth.

He gave me the feeling of his having lots of energy ready to spill over, although he was going about all this rather quietly.

We can find here only a consummatory stage, with the possible exception of the first phase, in which Raymond sits down on the bench.

In line with the foregoing, we have distinguished transitive episodes, consummatory episodes, and episodes that are both transitive and consummatory. Here are titles of some transitive episodes from a day record on Mary Ennis.

Looking for Socks
Getting Milk from Refrigerator
Making Own Bed
Working Problem on Blackboard

The following are titles of consummatory episodes from a day record on Jimmy Sexton.

Bouncing on Bed
Drinking Milk
Singing to Self

Below are representative titles of episodes with both a transitive and a consummatory stage, each of which was detectable.

Hanging and Admiring Picture
Retrieving and Bouncing Ball

3. *Sections.* We have seen that a phase is directed toward a subgoal on the way to the terminal goal in an episode. A transitive stage can include also any number of superordinate subgoals to which the lesser goals in a series of phases are subordinate. The behavior

directed toward such a superordinate subgoal, together with the context of this behavior, we have called a *section*. Such a unit always is made up of more than one, but fewer than all, of the phases in a divided transitive stage. Structuring of this kind does not occur in a consummatory stage, where all phases, as steps in a terminal goal region, are on the same valence level, so that a superordinate subgoal cannot occur. But for its high potency, which makes it a contained episode, Chuck's *Getting Mittens Off*, on page 70, would be a section.

These intermediately large parts of an episode have theoretical importance for study of the hierarchical structuring of behavior. Also, they have a practical application in episoding for the reason that episodes individuated by potency are almost invariably units which, were it not for their relatively high weight, would be sections, the only exceptions being contained episodes which, but for the same reason, would be phases. What this comes to follows. *Given a behavior sequence with a constant direction toward a terminal goal, no part of that sequence is ever segregated as a contained episode unless it has integrity based upon constant direction toward the superordinate subgoal of a section* or, in some rare cases, the minor subgoal of a phase. It turns out, then, that a contained episode, like any other, has its own beginning and end, from which it follows that, *within the frame of the parent unit*, it is unique in direction. A contained episode may therefore be said to conform in principle to uniqueness in direction as the pivotal test of an episode. This qualification of the potency criterion is an important episoding guide.

Episode parts are themselves real integral units of a behavior sequence. Because of their limited content, little could be gained and, because of their dependence upon the including episode, probably much would be lost, by singling them out for separate analysis. Yet it may now be evident that it is necessary to consider these subordinate units with care in any attempt to divide a behavior sequence validly or to understand its structure.

OVERLAPPING

As anticipated earlier, overlapping takes place when eposides occur, wholly or in part, at one time. As this implies, each of any two or more overlapping episodes has a potency greater than zero.

We have distinguished three major types of overlap: the *coinciding*, *enclosing-enclosed*, and *interlinking*, each graphed by episode brackets in Figure 4.1. Enclosing-enclosed examples are frequent in earlier parts of the chapter. Interlinking occurs in the Margaret Reid sample, on page 60. A common example of coinciding, rare in our records, is that of the man who eats his breakfast and reads his morning paper simultaneously from start to finish. These three types of overlap generate four types of overlapping episodes, explicated in Figure 4.1 and below.

A *coinciding episode* (CND) is one such that the whole of it intersects with the whole of another.

An *enclosing episode* (ENG) is one such that a part of it overlaps with the whole of another.

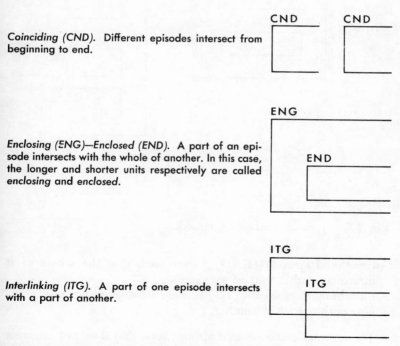

Coinciding (CND). Different episodes intersect from beginning to end.

Enclosing (ENG)—Enclosed (END). A part of an episode intersects with the whole of another. In this case, the longer and shorter units respectively are called *enclosing* and *enclosed*.

Interlinking (ITG). A part of one episode intersects with a part of another.

Fig. 4.1. Different types of episode overlap.

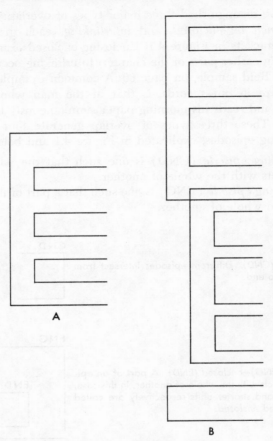

Fig. 4.2. Types of overlapping episodes.

An *enclosed episode* (END) is one such that the whole of it
   intersects with a part of another.
An *interlinking episode* (ITG) is one such that a part of it overlaps with a part of another.

There remains the *isolated episode*, one that does not intersect
with another at any time.

As many as four, though rarely more than three, episodes have been found to overlap at one time in our records. A result of overlap involving more than two units is that any one of them can be of mixed type. At one time, for example, an episode can be enclosed in relation to a second, enclosing in relation to a third, and interlinking in relation to a fourth.

These statements have dealt entirely with simultaneous overlap. As some of the sequences here have shown, different episodes can overlap sequentially with a given episode in progress, as shown in Figure 4.2A.

Also, various complications are possible in a sequence of simultaneous overlaps. More or less extended *linkages* of overlapping episodes can occur, as in Figure 4.2B, which includes also an isolated episode, from a record on two-year-old Mary Chaco.

The gap between a linkage and either another linkage or an isolated episode we have called a *break*. In this relation it is convenient to identify an isolated episode as a *link*.

More on these specifications is in Chapter 5.

RELATIVE WEIGHT OR POTENCY

An important feature of the dynamical relationship between episodes that overlap is their relative weight or potency.

Although it is convenient to attribute potency to an episode as such (or one of its parts), potency is more strictly a characteristic of the situation in an episode. This concept refers specifically to the degree in which the total behavior of a person is determined by the forces of a situation the person has entered and in which he is presently behaving. To say that a person is in a situation is to say that its forces are now operative in some degree, so that it has some importance for the total ongoing behavior. Thus, each situation of any two or more that overlap has a potency greater than zero.

The weights of overlapping situations are always relative, so that, if the weight of one goes up, that of the other must go down equally. If a person is in only one situation, it has by definition a potency of 1, which implies that at the given time the potency of all other situations is 0. Stating that a person is in only one situation or saying that a situation the person is in has a potency of 1 are ways of saying the same thing. When more than one present situation exists, as in the case of overlapping episodes, the potency of each must vary between .9 and .1.

Criteria of potency are on page 82, and a scale of potency values is left for Chapter 5, pages 104–105.

INTERRUPTION

Interruption has figured significantly in experimental research, as in studies, by Rickers-Ovsiankina (1928) and Zeigarnik (1927), of unfinished tasks. If only for this reason, we have dealt with it carefully in episoding.

Interruption is defined by a drop in potency of an episode to zero before the person has reached his goal in the given action. This criterion implies that need tension persists after the interrupting break. Such persisting tension can either be diffused or act to bring the person back to the interrupted behavior, which means that an interrupted episode may or may not be resumed. We have marked interruption, however, only when resumption does occur, because of inability to detect, short of resumption, the persistence of tension after an interrupting break.

Wally, a disabled four-year-old, is coasting in his wagon when two older boys, Jim and Ben appear. Read the account on page 91.

We judged that the potency of the coasting situation was lowered to zero by Jim's interference. As the analyst saw it, *Coping with Jim* took over and supplanted entirely the coasting in Wally's perspective on his own behavior in progress, so that, for a while, Wally was only in the situation imposed by Jim's meanness, and out of the one that engaged him while he tried, not to resist another boy, but to make the wagon go. We judged, in short, that the potency of *Coping with Jim* went up to 1, with the necessary result that the potency of *Coasting* went down to 0. When Jim first rode up on his bike, Wally had not reached the coasting goal, and tension corresponding to this goal must have persisted through the coping period. Otherwise, why did Wally

Coasting

Wally raised himself on his arms and feet in the wagon. Shifting his position abruptly, he managed to move the wagon several inches.

Coping with Jim

3:14 Jim rode up on his bike and asked Ben with mock solicitousness (to judge from his playful facial expression and tone of voice), "Do you want me to bump into him?" Wally called, "No," as if he were afraid Jim might.
Wally's position looked precarious.
Jim bumped the bike against the wagon with a rather mean gleam in his eye.
Wally fell with the bump to a less precarious position in the wagon; he was half lying, half kneeling.
Jim rode up the walk.
3:15 Wally said vociferously, with real anger, almost raging, "Goddam it, Jim; goddam it, Jim."
Jim came back and bumped him again.
Wally fell out of the wagon with the force of the impact. He fell gracefully and adeptly, and apparently wasn't hurt.

Coasting

Immediately he grabbed onto the wagon and raised himself to his feet, reaching down to maneuver his leg into a better position.
He went on shifting his leg until it was in the wagon.
With his left knee in, pushing with his right foot and steering with his hands, he moved the wagon a little.
He maneuvered the wagon slowly up into the front yard.

so promptly clamber back onto the wagon and go on his way?

We have found it useful to think here of three levels on a continuum.

1. ONE-UNIT CONTINUANCE. An isolated episode E_1 proceeds continuously. Its situation, as the only one existing for the person, has a potency of 1. The person behaves toward one terminal intended position.

2. OVERLAPPING. At this level, episodes E_1 and E_2 occur simul taneously. The situation in each has a potency greater than 0 but less than 1. The person behaves toward different termina intended positions, each in a different direction.

3. INTERRUPTION. An interrupting episode E_2 proceeds con tinuously between the fore part and the latter part of an inter rupted episode E_1. The situation in E_1 has a potency of 0, while the situation in E_2 has a potency of 1. The person behaves again toward one terminal intended position.

Owing to the close dynamical and structural connectednes between interrupting and interrupted episodes, for certain pur poses, to be developed in Chapter 5, we have considered the relationship between them to be one of *secondary overlap*. Thus for these purposes, *Coasting* and *Coping with Jim*, by Wally Wolfson, become cases in point. This leaves interruption open for study as a special psychological phenomenon, without loss for study of overlapping.

An important line of inquiry about interruption concerns the factors that bring it about. Interrupting factors that we have found in our records include *new positive valences*, as when a child is pulled away from a sandbox by a flight of planes, *intrusion of negative valences*, as when a child stops making a mud pie after being nipped by a stray dog, *environmental cessation*, as when the projector at the Midwest movie breaks down, and social pressure. These changes come in upon the child from the outside. There are also interrupting factors, such as failure, that are partly intrinsic to the ongoing behavior.

All interrupted units that are later resumed present segments separated by one or more episodes. These separate segments can be analyzed independently or treated together as a single unit. We have done the latter because our standard target is a whole episode with limits defined by the beginning and end points of an entire action toward a goal.

RESTLESS BEHAVIOR

Restless movements are often found between the start and the finish of an episode. For example, the subject may fidget in various ways while he reads a book. When recorded in separate sentences, these behavior elements are set apart by marginal brackets, each labeled *R*. We have at times found somewhat extended blocks of restless behavior that occur between the end of one episode and the beginning of the next. The marking for these is the same as for a regular episode, except that the bracket line is again labeled *R*. R segments, which usually are actones, often illuminate including or flanking episodes.

ADDENDUM: PRACTICAL ROUTINES

Some procedural requirements and conveniences in episoding need consideration.

READING THE RECORD. Our experience shows that, to episode either a day or a settings record, one should first read all of it; finding the parts evidently requires knowing the whole.

READING AHEAD. The episoder will save a great deal of erasing by making sure that he knows clearly and definitely what is coming next in the record. Reading a whole record is not enough, alone, to guarantee this. Our practice has been to episode in blocks of 30 to 40 pages. The material of every such block should be studied intensively before any marks are drawn. Mental notes can be made on the main units while the reading continues. Usually, we have set down rough episode lines between such notes and the final bracketings.

RULE OF MAXIMUM INCLUSIVENESS. One is in doubt most often in trying to decide whether a minor segment is an integral part of an episode or in itself a shorter, overlapping one. When these alternatives have seemed about equally correct, we have included the segment in the more extended unit. Violating continuities has seemed the less desirable risk.

EPISODE TITLES. A participial phrase is used to describe as concisely as possible what the child is doing in the episode. The title has little significance later, but we have found that a clearly fitting one usually gives partial proof of a correctly discriminated episode.

NUMBERING. We have numbered the episodes of a record by the order in which they start, placing the numbers over the episode brackets. Wherever overlapping episodes start together, they are numbered by the order in which they end. An arbitrary choice is made in the rare instances of coinciding overlap. Episode numbers are indispensable for machine coding.

WEIGHT DESIGNATION. The potency of every overlapping episode is designated by putting over the episode bracket a number on a scale for relative weight, presented in the following chapter.

CONTAINED OVERLAP. We have given every contained episode a special notation, the letters *CTD*, placed to the left of the episode bracket. Otherwise, the markings themselves are left to show type of overlapping.

APPLICATIONS AND RELIABILITY

The method has been applied to day records, partial day records, and settings records of the Midwest collection as shown in the breakdown of Table 4.1. The table shows that this work has made available for study 19,654 episodes, 14,417 of them in records of Midwest children, and the remaining 5,237 in records on nearby disabled children.

Most of the episoding was done during one year by a team of five analysts that included a supervisor who reviewed the work by the other four. The supervisor made some changes in the original episoding, usually after consultation with the analyst concerned, so that continuous training was provided.

Periodical tests of interanalyst agreement will be represented by procedures with parts of 14 day records.

Sequences varying in length from 30 minutes to 90 minutes and covering approximately one-fourth of the subject's waking time

TABLE 4.1.   Midwest Collection of Episoded Records

Subjects	Type of Record	Number of Records	Pages	Episodes
Midwest Children	Day	12	4627	11567
	Partial Day	1	192	480
	Settings	130	948	2370
	All	143	5767	14417
Disabled Children	Day	4	1393	3482
	Partial Day	4	322	805
	Settings	52	380	950
	All	60	2095	5237
All	All	203	7862	19654

during the recorded day were marked off in each record. There were 50 sequences, chosen from different parts of the records to give variety in kinds of behavior and situation.

Eight episoders, who had received similar training in the method, were paired in complete rotation for the test procedures, and the 50 sequences were distributed as evenly as possible among the different pairs. A copy of every sequence was divided into episodes by each member of the team to which it had been assigned, after which the two episoders jointly compared the marked transcripts. The pair members recorded the title of every episode either had discriminated, and checked all instances of agreement and disagreement. Agreement was credited whenever an episode marked by one analyst was essentially the same in span, content, and identifying participial phrase as an episode marked by the other. Differences in the marking of units as isolated or overlapping were not scored as disagreements. Commonly, however, where there was agreement on identity, there also was agreement on position. Other characteristics of episodes were not considered in the comparisons.

In every case, the paired analysts reconciled their differences and, leaving the independently marked transcripts intact, jointly episoded a third copy of the material on the basis of their pooled best judgments. Finally, the leader of the episoding team reviewed the joint product and made some, though never extensive, changes in the markings. Because it represents a best effort to apply the method correctly, we shall refer below to the final outcome of these several steps as the criterion version.

For each of the episoded sections of the sample an estimate of accuracy was secured by applying the following formula.

$$\text{Estimate of Accuracy} = \frac{\text{Episodes Marked by } X \text{ Marked Also by } Y}{\dfrac{\text{Episodes Marked by } X + \text{Episodes Marked by } Y}{2}}$$

where X and Y are any two independent analysts.

The numerator is the number of episodes on which the two independent analysts agreed. But it is not necessarily the true number. On the contrary, it is open to two errors. First, it may include units incorrectly identified as episodes by both analysts. Second, it may include units correctly identified as episodes by one analyst, but not by the other. The denominator is the best available estimate of the true number of episodes. It is the mean number discriminated by both analysts. Its rationale assumes that any analyst trained in the method will approximate the correct total number of episodes. Actually, of course, every analyst will

TABLE 4.2. Estimate of Accuracy Obtained by Comparing the Episoding by Independent Analysts of 50 Sequences in 14 Day Records

Estimate of Accuracy	f
72–74	3
75–77	4
78–80	16
81–83	11
84–86	10
87–89	5
90–92	1
Total Number of Sequences	50

make errors of two kinds. He will identify two or more episodes where there should be one (overestimate the true number) and he will combine into a single unit two or more episodes where there should be more than one (underestimate the true number). If these are chance errors, averaging of the judgments by more than one judge should come closer to the true number of episodes than the judgments of a single person. In any case, the quotient gives that proportion of the "true" number "correctly" discriminated independently by each analyst.

Application of this formula to the 50 sequences of the sample yields estimates of accuracy ranging from 72 to 92. Table 4.2 presents a frequency distribution of these measures. An overall estimate was computed by summing for all 50 sequences and then substituting in the formula. This gives a value of 81.1, which represents the central tendency shown in the table.

One can classify as major all episodes rated primary in relative weight and as minor all rated secondary and tertiary in weight. See the scale for judgment of relative weight on page 104. An estimate of accuracy was computed independently for the major episodes, the minor episodes, and all of the episodes in each of 10 sequences, 4 from one day record and 6 from another. For this purpose, the weight ratings of the episodes in the criterion version were used. Episodes of lower than primary weight are

TABLE 4.3. Estimates of Accuracy of Episoders on Major Episodes, Minor Episodes, and All Episodes in 10 Sequences of 2 Day Records

Section	Episoders	Estimate of Accuracy			Number of Episodes		
		Major	Minor	All	Major	Minor	All
1	A, B	87	41	76	72	35	107
2	C, D	91	72	84	50	34	84
3	B, A	92	50	84	68	24	92
4	D, C	93	70	86	79	37	116
5	B, C	91	35	73	38	19	57
6	A, B	92	67	80	36	28	64
7	B, D	94	62	80	29	20	49
8	C, D	95	64	87	32	19	51
9	D, A	96	47	73	35	21	56
10	C, A	98	42	72	23	23	46

characteristically overlapping, enclosed, short, and often undivided units, usually eliminated from later analysis because
there is not enough in them for special study. The data from
these groupings are in Table 4.3, which shows that, for all of the
different episodes discriminated in the various sections of the two
records, the accuracy estimates range from 72 to 87, and that, for
major episodes, they range from 87 to 98.

These data are taken to imply sufficient reliability of the
method as it is applied in the discrimination of whole episodes.

Chapter 5

ASPECTS OF

BEHAVIOR

STRUCTURE

PROBLEM AND MATERIAL

This chapter[1] reports an exploration into the structure of molar behavior. The data are from 16 episoded day records from the Midwest and nearby disabled children who are introduced in Chapter 1 (pp. 9–10) and the Appendix.

All of the episodes in the 16 records were used for certain purposes. For other purposes, we have sampled the total episode population. Earlier analyses had shown for every entrance into a behavior setting the number and name of the setting, the identifying numbers of all included episodes, the total number of these episodes, and the time of occurrence and duration of behavior in the setting. There was available, then, a minute by minute and setting by setting breakdown of each recorded day.

[1] The chapter is based on the doctoral thesis by Phil H. Schoggen (1954).

With presently negligible exceptions, we included in the sample from every record all of the episodes that occurred during alternate visits to each setting.

An advantage in the selection method is that it gives nearly proportionate representation to behavior settings of widely differing importance, as measured by time spent in them. Thus, nearly 40 percent of the behavior in the 16 records occurred in Home Indoors. The sampling plan gives a similar proportion of episodes from this setting. Another advantage is that it preserves the natural continuity of extended behavior sequences.

The total sample consists of 7749 episodes from nearly all of the different settings entered by the 16 children. This is 52 percent of the entire episode population. The chosen target units range from 45 to 56 percent of the episodes in each record.

DESCRIPTIVE CODE

Most of the data were obtained by applying categories to all episodes in the sample. Some of the categories deal with structural characteristics of episodes, others with related dynamical factors. Each category will now be itemized and defined.

STRUCTURAL CHARACTERISTICS OF EPISODES

1. Episode Length

1.	15 sec.	7.	5 min.
2.	30 sec.	8.	6–7 min.
3.	1 min.	9.	8–10 min.
4.	2 min.	10.	11–14 min.
5.	3 min.	11.	15 or more min.
6.	4 min.		

Category 1 provides a measure of episode length in clock time. The analyst was guided by the time notations of the observer.

2. Total Number of Overlapping Episodes

1. 1
2. 2
3. 3
4. 4
5. 5

6. 6–8
7. 9–11
8. 12–14
9. 15 or more
10. DNA (Isolated Episode)

Category 2 is used to record for the target unit the total number of episodes that overlap with it throughout its course. In Figure 5.1, for example, episode 1 has five others overlapping

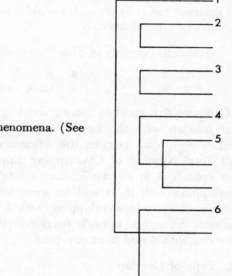

Fig. 5.1. Overlapping phenomena. (See text, categories 2 and 3.)

with it; episodes 4 and 5, two, and every remaining episode, one. Episodes with no overlapping at any time are tabulated under 10, DNA, meaning does not apply.

For this category, as for categories 3 through 6, below, the evidence of reliability in application is indirect. Each of these categories deals with an aspect of behavior structure identified in the episoding process. Thus, the question of reliability goes back in each case to the episoding itself, the reliability of which was tested by procedures described in Chapter 4.

Our tests of episoding reliability, as may be recalled, measure only agreement between independent analysts on presence or absence of episodes. Such determinations as the position of units in relation to others were not considered in the agreement computations. We have considered, however, that agreement on episode interrelations is likely to have been tolerable where the reported agreement levels were high. It is doubtful that two episoders could agree satisfactorily in identifying episodes and yet disagree radically on such variables as number of overlapping episodes or type of overlap.

3. Maximum Number of Simultaneously Overlapping Episodes

| 1. | 1 | 3. | 3 |
| 2. | 2 | 4. | DNA (Isolated Episode) |

Category 3 is used to record the largest number of episodes that overlap with the target unit at any one time during its course. Figure 5.1 clarifies the difference between this variable and Total Number of Overlapping Episodes. We noted above that episode 1 in Figure 5.1 has a total of five other episodes overlapping with it. It will be seen, however, that the largest number of episodes overlapping with 1 at one time is two. On the same basis, one episode overlaps with 2, 3, and 6, and two episodes with 4 and 5, at one time.

4. Type of Overlap

1.	Coinciding	4.	Interlinking
2.	Enclosing	5.	Interpolated
3.	Enclosed	6.	DNA (Isolated Episode)

Category 4 describes the structural form of relationships between overlapping episodes.

Except for item 5, Interpolated, the several types of overlap have been defined and illustrated on pages 86–89. Item 5 applies wherever the target episode occurs between the arrows to indicate interruption of a previously begun and subsequently resumed episode. An example is in Figure 5.2 on page 111, where each bracket represents one episode. Item 5 applies to episodes 11c and d, 12c, d, and e, and 13c, d, e, and f. This item makes possible the segregation of episodes in occurrences of secondary overlap.

Wherever a target episode sustains more than one type of overlap relation to others, each type is checked. Thus, in Figure 5.2, episode 6a is interlinking in relation to 6b, but enclosing in relation to 6c. Therefore, both items, Enclosing and Interlinking, apply to 6a.

5. Form of Transition

1. Abrupt   2. Merging

Category 5 is concerned with the structural relationship between the target unit and other episodes at its terminal point, i.e., at the point of transition to the immediately subsequent behavior segment, which can be a new unit or the remaining part of a more extended overlapping episode. The category measures smoothness of behavior flow. Where an abrupt transition occurs, the target unit is immediately succeeded by a break in the behavior sequence. Where, on the other hand, a merging transition occurs, the target unit ends while an overlapping episode is still in progress. Among others of Figure 5.2, episodes 1, 2a, 6b, and 12c illustrate abrupt transitions. Examples from this figure of merging transitions are in episodes 2b, 6a, and 12b.

6. Continuity

1. Continuous   2. Discontinuous

Category 6 is used to measure the frequency with which episodes are broken into more than one segment.

Item 1 applies where the target unit proceeds continuously from its beginning to the point of final termination, whether or not the goal in the episode is reached. An episode is considered

continuous only if it is judged to maintain potency greater than
0 throughout its course.

Item 2 applies where a unit is interrupted and resumed one
or more times. As many as 20 separate interruptions of an
episode have been marked in the records. Note that the category
is not concerned with ultimate completeness of an episode; a
judgment is not made as to whether the child ever reaches his
intended terminal position. The question of completion or
incompletion is raised by a later category.

Every episode of Figure 5.2 is continuous, except for 11a, 12a,
and 13a, which the arrows identify as discontinuous.

CONDITIONS RELATED TO STRUCTURE

Dynamical factors associated with behavior anatomy follow.

7. Basis of Episode Discrimination

    1. Direction   2. Potency (Contained Episode)

Category 7 distinguishes between contained episodes, discriminated solely on the basis of their relatively high potency,
and episodes discriminated on the basis of unique direction.

The analyst only notes whether the target unit has been
marked a contained episode during the episoding process. Thus,
the question of reliability again goes back to agreement on
episoding. In this case, however, no evidence of interanalyst
agreement is available; differences between independent episoders as to whether a given episode was contained were not
considered in the episoding agreement tests.

8. Relative Weight

1.	Primary	6.	Primary, Tertiary
2.	Primary, Tied	7.	Secondary, Tertiary
3.	Secondary	8.	Primary, Secondary, Tertiary
4.	Tertiary	9.	Does Not Apply (Isolated
5.	Primary, Secondary		Episode)

Category 8 treats the relative importance of different simultaneously overlapping episodes. The weight of every episode among two or more involved in an overlap at one time is ranked in order from primary through tertiary. Occurrence of more than three simultaneously overlapping episodes has been negligible in the present records.

Item 1 applies when the target episode clearly outranks the other overlapping units in potency throughout its entire course. Item 2 applies when the first rank in potency is shared by the target unit and another episode at some point during the course of the former, i.e., when neither appears to have greater potency than the other. An episode of secondary weight could be equaled in potency, but instances of this have proved to be negligible. Whenever three episodes were found to overlap simultaneously, one of them was always clearly tertiary.

Items 5 through 8 represent combinations of items 1, 3, and 4. These apply when an episode of some length is judged to have different weights at different intervals during its course.

The relative weight of a long, enclosing episode may vary from time to time, depending upon characteristics of the episodes it encloses. Thus, for example, item 5 applies when the target unit is primary in potency through a part of its course, but secondary at one or more points.

As anticipated in Chapter 4, the episoding process included application of the category, and interanalyst agreement on this phase of the process was not tested. The upcoming data on relative episode weight must be evaluated accordingly.

9. Episode Initiation

| 1. | Spontaneous | 3. | Pressured |
| 2. | Instigated | 4. | Can Not Judge |

Category 9 is concerned with self regulation versus external regulation of behavior structure.

Item 1, Spontaneous, applies whenever the action of an episode begins in the apparent absence of external instigation, defined as any observed and reported change in the child's situation. In these cases, the child is seen to behave as if he "just happened to think of something to do"; action is initiated without evident dependence upon active behavior objects. When, in the case of social behavior objects, the child is seen to react to the presence, as opposed to the activity, of an individual, the initiation is spontaneous, as when Lewis Hope was observed to interrupt his father, who was reading, long enough to get some information about a camera. The essential element of spontaneous initiation is an apparently voluntary "selection" of action by the subject. One can not assume complete detachment from environmental conditions. Yet we have found that behavior with the *appearance* of spontaneity stands out in the records, and believe that sense made by findings concerning it has justified special consideration of this behavior.

Item 2, Instigated, applies when the child is seen to respond to some observable event or change in his situation, provided only that the event does not exert pressure, as this is defined below. An event here means any observed and reported occurrence referable to some source other than the subject. Someone enters the subject's presence; a tractor drives past on the street; someone speaks; a paper flutters; a whistle blows; a clock chimes; a book falls.

Item 3, Pressured, applies when an episode appears to start in response to pressure upon the child. Pressure means here external influence of any kind that is in any way inconsistent with the child's own momentary needs and goals. Although social pressure accounts for a majority of these cases, other kinds of pressure are included, as when Raymond Birch was "forced" by rain to leave his play and go indoors. *Practicing Piano Lesson,* which began when Raymond's mother called him in from his play for it, exemplifies socially pressured initiation.

This is one of the four categories upon which specific agreement tests were made. An assistant applied each of these categories to a number of episodes that had been marked off by the principal analyst. In all, there were eight blocks of 50 episodes each in the agreement sample. These blocks were taken from eight different records and selected, from different behavior settings, to provide a variety of target material.

The category tests show exact agreement between independent analysts in 91 percent of 400 episodes. Taken separately, the agreement percents for each of the eight blocks of episodes range from 80 to 98.

10. Episode Issue

This category is used to describe aspects of the target episode for the child at the point of episode termination.

A decision is made first as to whether the episode is complete or incomplete. In the case of transitive or goal-seeking behavior, this amounts to deciding whether or not the child reaches his goal. In the case of consummatory behavior, i.e., behavior within a goal region, the analyst judged only whether or not satiation occurred. When confident judgment as to the completeness of an episode could not be made, the analyst marked the unit Can Not Judge. The items follow.

Complete Episodes		Incomplete Episodes	
1.	Acquittance	7.	Nonattainment
2.	Attainment	8.	Frustration
3.	Gratification	9.	Failure
4.	Success	10.	Consummation: not satiated
5.	Consummation: satiated	11.	Other
6.	Other	12.	Can Not Judge

A set of criteria was adopted for each item, which applies only when all of the criteria are met.

1. Acquaintance
   a. The action is a single minimal molar unit.
   b. The action is characteristically brief.
   c. Resistance is virtually zero.
   d. The episode is "unimportant." If involved in an overlap, its relative weight is secondary or less.

2. Attainment
   a. The goal in the episode is reached only after the child has overcome appreciable resistance.
   b. The child does not attribute credit to himself or to anyone else for reaching the goal; there is satisfaction, but neither pride nor gratitude.

3. *Gratification*
   a. The goal is such that the child could not reach it by his own efforts without overcoming resistance.
   b. The child attributes credit for reaching the goal to someone besides himself or to external circumstances.

4. *Success*
   a. The goal in the episode is reached only after the child has overcome resistance.
   b. The child attributes credit to himself; there is satisfaction and pride in accomplishment; the child feels that he has "done something."

5. *Consummation: satiated*
   a. Resistance against locomotion is virtually zero; the child is free to move about with little or no difficulty.
   b. All activity regions are homogeneously positive; there is virtually no valance differential between any present position and any next step.
   c. Distance to ends sought is virtually zero.
   d. The episode terminates because the child becomes satiated with the goal activity; the activity becomes neutral in valence.

6. *Other: complete*
   This item is used when a judgment of "complete" seems correct, but when the criteria for no one of the above issues are met.

7. *Nonattainment*
   a. The child gives up only after overcoming appreciable resistance.
   b. The child does not place any blame for not reaching his goal; he does not blame others or himself.

8. *Frustration*
   a. The child gives up only after overcoming appreciable resistance.
   b. The child places blame for not reaching the goal upon someone besides himself or upon external circumstances.

9. *Failure*
   a. The child gives up only after overcoming appreciable resistance.
   b. The child places blame for the outcome upon himself; he feels not only dissatisfaction, but also some shame.

10. *Consummation: not satiated*
    a, b, c. Each is the same as for item 5, above.

    d. The episode terminates because of a factor other than satiation, e.g., a new positive valence or social pressure.

11. *Other: incomplete*

This item is used when a judgment of Incomplete is made, but when the criteria for no one of the above issues are met.

Tests show exact agreement between independent analysts in 56 percent of 400 episodes. The percents for each of the eight test blocks range from 26 to 74, with a median of 59. These data for the individual items of this category are not reassuring. But we are dealing with large numbers of cases. If the errors of judgment are random, some confidence can be placed in the frequency data on the different kinds of episode issue. Separate agreements were computed for judgments on episode completeness. They show that the analysts agreed on 81 percent of the 400 episodes. The percents on each block of 50 range from 64 to 98, with a median of 83. This means that judgments as to whether episodes terminated, in general, either satisfactorily (complete) or unsatisfactorily (incomplete) were made with considerable agreement.

11. Episode Termination

    1. Spontaneous   4. Pressured
    2. Instigated   5. Can Not Judge
    3. Environmental Cessation

The category complements and is patterned after category 9, above, on episode initiation. Item 1, Spontaneous, applies where the action of the episode appears to terminate from within. If the child apparently just quits upon reaching his objective or upon tiring of the action, termination is judged to be spontaneous.

Item 2, Instigated, applies where termination appears to occur in response to an external change, provided that the change (a) does not consist in reaching the goal of the episode, and (b) does not conform to items 3 and 4 which, as will be seen, are only special cases of instigated termination. This item is directly analogous to the one of the same name under category 9; the definitions and examples cited there are applicable here as well.

Item 3, Environmental Cessation, applies to termination caused by withdrawal of necessary behavior supports, as when riding a bike stops because a tire goes flat. The behavior of the episode is sustained by external forces and then brought to an end by disappearance of these forces.

For Item 4, Pressured, the definitions and examples given for the item of the same name in category 9 apply.

The accuracy tests show exact agreement of independent analysts in 82 percent of 400 judgments. The percents for each block of 50 episodes range from 70 to 94.

SPECIAL PATTERN FACTORS

The marking conventions used in episoding a specimen record bear information about the patterning and differentiation of behavior sequences that can be obtained readily by simple inspection and counting procedures. We have used such procedures to obtain data on both episodes and linkages as behavior parts. These data are based upon study of all episodes and linkages in each of the 16 episoded day records. They are derived partially from distinctions as to kinds of linkages, which we shall identify briefly before turning to results.

A linkage is a sequence of episodes connected with each other by overlapping. The minimal sequence is an isolated episode, otherwise identified as a link. Linkages range upward in complexity to those including even as many as 60 episode links. Figure 5.2 illustrates some of the more common patterns formed by these linkages. The columns show different complexity levels of simultaneously overlapping episodes, ranging from the isolated episode or single link to the pattern of four simultaneously overlapping episodes. The examples in each row are intended to show that the number of sequentially overlapping episodes varies for each pattern of simultaneous overlap. Thus, in the case of linkages at the level of triple overlapping, exemplified in the third column, the total number of episodes may vary from a minimum of 3, as in the first row, through 6, as in the last row, on up to the

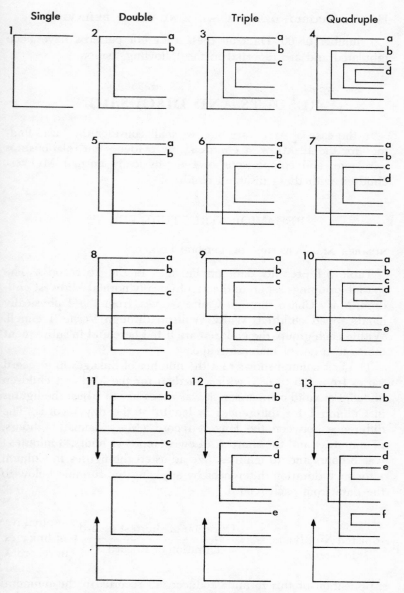

Fig. 5.2. Common linkages. (See text.)

top number of 60. Data on these different patterns have been tabulated and are reported in the following section.

RESULTS AND DISCUSSION

In the case of each variable, we shall consider the basic findings for the 12 Midwest children, any evidence on relationships with age, and comparisons of the physically normal Midwest children with the 4 disabled children.

BEHAVIOR STRUCTURE PER SE

NUMBER AND DURATION OF EPISODE LINKAGES

Table 5.1 presents data on linkages in the 16 records. The spatial groupings separate the 12 physically normal Midwest children, Mary Chaco through Claire Graves, from the 4 physically handicapped children, Wally Wolfson through Verne Trennell. Within each group, the children are listed here and in subsequent tables in order of increasing age.

The first column shows that the number of linkages in a record varies from 135 to 683, with a median for the Midwest children of 428. For valid comparison, it was necessary to adjust the figures in Column 1 for differences in length of the day records. The difference between the longest record (Mary Ennis; 14 hours, 27 minutes) and the shortest (Lewis Hope; 11 hours, 8 minutes) was 3 hours and 19 minutes. We adjusted the figures in Column 1 for such duration differences by applying the formula below to the data from each record.

$$\text{Adjusted } N \text{ of linkages in record } X = \frac{\text{Duration of shortest record}}{\text{Duration of Record } X} \left(\begin{array}{l} \text{Actual } N \\ \text{of linkages} \\ \text{in record } X \end{array} \right)$$

Application of this formula reduced all records to the temporal base of the shortest day: 11 hours, 8 minutes.

The adjusted numbers of linkages are in Column 2, which shows a range from 105 to 683. The differences between children are not distributed randomly. There is a relationship with age, as shown by a rank order correlation between the adjusted number of linkages and age of —.67, significant beyond .01.[2]

TABLE 5.1.   Number, Partition, and Duration of Episode Linkages

Child	Age to Nearest Month (Yrs.–Mos.)	Actual Number of Linkages (1)	Adjusted Number of Linkages[a] (2)	Average Number of Episodes per Linkage (3)	Average Duration (Minutes) (4)
Mary Chaco (MC)	1-10	667	626	1.65	1.06
Jimmy Sexton (JS)	1-11	656	653	1.56	1.02
Lewis Hope (LH)	2-11	683	683	1.95	0.98
Dutton Thurston (DT)	3-10	544	471	2.13	1.42
Margaret Reid (MR)	4-6	427	357	2.48	1.87
Maud Pintner (MP)	5-0	499	491	2.39	1.36
Roy Eddy (RE)	6-2	249	206	2.80	3.24
Ben Hutchings (BH)	7-4	296	264	2.28	2.53
Raymond Birch (RB)	7-4	430	353	2.32	1.89
Mary Ennis (ME)	8-7	370	285	2.62	2.34
Douglas Crawford (DC)	9-2	307	240	3.06	2.78
Claire Graves (CG)	10-9	135	105	3.66	6.37
Range		135-683	105-683	1.56-3.66	0.98-6.37
Median		428	355	2.35	1.88
Wally Wolfson (WW)	4-3	390	381	2.32	1.75
Sue Dewall (SD)	7-1	138	113	5.59	5.66
Bobby Bryant (BB)	7-4	225	193	3.03	3.45
Verne Trennell (VT)	7-5	307	238	3.18	2.80

[a] Adjusted for differences between children in length of day.

In Column 3 of Table 5.1, the average number of episodes per linkage is given for each child. Two-year-old Jimmy had the smallest average, 1.56, and 11-year-old Claire the largest, 3.66. The median for the Midwest children is 2.35. Relationship with age is apparent from inspection of the table; and this is demonstrated by a rank order correlation of .73, significant beyond .01.

Finally, the data on average duration of linkages are shown

[2] All p tests of the study are two-tailed.

in Column 4. For these values, the range is 0.98 minutes to 6.37 minutes, the median duration 1.88 minutes, and the correlation with age .67, again well beyond chance expectation. The data in Columns 3 and 4 are not, of course, independent of those in Column 2; for, with length of record held constant, where the total number of linkages in a record is smaller, each linkage must include more episodes and last longer.

These data indicate that for the older children there is consistently a higher degree of connectedness among episodes. The older children tend to keep more activities going at a given time; they more frequently begin a new action while still finishing an earlier one. It is true that the specific changes with age here are not fully represented by the quantitative data. But they become amply evident if one inspects the episoded records.

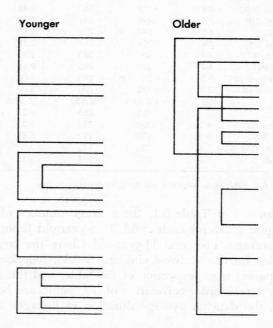

Fig. 5.3. Typical sequences of episodes for younger and older children.

Typical sequences for younger and older children are shown in Figure 5.3. Five linkages are shown for the younger child and one for the older. The data in Column 2 of Table 5.1 demonstrate that in some cases, as in that of Lewis (2–11) versus Claire (10–9), this ratio is more than 6 to 1.

There is no suggestion of a difference in linkage patterns between disabled and normal children, which suggests that peripheral disablement does not necessarily interfere with behavior complications of the kind occurring in extended chains of behavior episodes.

NUMBER AND DURATION OF EPISODES

Table 5.2 presents, for episodes, data comparable to those in Table 5.1 for linkages. The actual number of episodes in each

TABLE 5.2. Number and Average Duration of Episodes

Child	Age	Actual Number of Episodes (1)	Adjusted Number of Episodes[a] (2)	Average Duration (Minutes) (3)
Mary C.	1-10	1103	1036	0.64
Jimmy	1-11	1027	1022	0.65
Lewis	2-11	1335	1335	0.50
Dutton	3-10	1159	1004	0.66
Margaret	4-6	1059	885	0.75
Maud	5-0	1196	1178	0.57
Roy	6-2	699	579	1.15
Ben	7-4	675	603	1.11
Ray	7-4	1000	821	0.81
Mary E.	8-7	969	746	0.89
Douglas	9-2	940	735	0.91
Claire	10-9	494	383	1.74
Range		494-1335	383-1335	0.50-1.74
Median		1014	853	0.78
Wally	4-3	907	887	0.75
Sue	7-1	771	629	1.01
Bobby	7-4	683	587	1.14
Verne	7-5	977	759	0.88

[a] Adjusted for differences between children in length of day.

record is in Column 1. As with linkages, the original number of episodes is not directly comparable from record to record, owing to differences in length of day. Hence, these figures were adjusted by a formula like that used for the number of linkages. The adjusted figures are in Column 2.

The actual number of episodes for the Midwest children ranges from a low of 494, for Claire, to 1335, for Lewis, with a median of 1014. When length of day is reduced to the shortest day (11 hours, 8 minutes), the range is from 383 to 1335. The figures for Claire, the oldest child, and Lewis, one of the youngest, show a striking difference in the behavioral partitioning of the two days. Claire's day was made up of a relatively small number of large parts; several of her episodes lasted as long as 50 minutes, one of them 2 hours. Lewis, on the other hand, engaged in few long episodes; his day consisted of many small parts. Comparisons of other older and younger children reveal similar differences.

The age relationship suggested by these data is borne out by a rank correlation coefficient of —.61, significant beyond .01. Column 3 of Table 5.2 presents the same results in different terms: the total number of minutes in the day over the actual number of episodes, for each child. The age relationship for Column 3 is, of course, identical with that of Column 2, with the sign reversed. A finding of fewer episodes of longer duration as age increases is clearly established for these children.

It is apparent from Table 5.2 that the four disabled children do not differ significantly from the Midwest children in differentiation of their days into episodes. On a plot to show relationship with age, the curves for the two groups are scarcely distinguishable.

LENGTH OF EPISODES: INTERVAL ANALYSIS

Beginning with Table 5.3, all results are based, not upon the entire record on each subject, but upon the sample (see pp. 99–100) of about one-half of the episodes per record.

Looking first, in Table 5.3, at the distribution of the percents

TABLE 5.3. Percent of Episodes with Stated Length

Child	Age	N	¼ m	½ m	1 m	2 m	3 m	4–5 m	6–10 m	11 m or more
Mary C.	1-10	615	50	20	21	4	2	1	1	+
Jimmy	1-11	490	54	22	18	4	1	1	1	+
Lewis	2-11	653	53	20	17	6	1	1	1	+
Dutton	3-10	633	58	19	12	4	2	2	2	+
Margaret	4-6	582	39	33	18	4	2	2	1	2
Maud	5-0	607	51	21	18	5	2	1	1	1
Roy	6-2	326	29	22	31	8	3	2	2	3
Ben	7-4	358	32	23	25	9	4	1	3	2
Ray	7-4	511	42	18	24	9	2	2	2	1
Mary E.	8-7	545	41	18	27	5	2	3	2	2
Douglas	9-2	422	42	20	22	7	2	2	1	3
Claire	10-9	233	27	20	28	11	4	4	3	4
Tau with age:										
COEFFICIENT			−.45	−.21	.48	.54	.44	.62	.59	.74
p VALUE			.05	.37	.04	.02	.06	.01	.01	.001
Wally	4-3	499	45	18	25	5	3	2	2	1
Sue	7-1	423	40	21	26	4	2	2	2	3
Bobby	7-4	337	30	20	30	9	3	3	3	2
Verne	7-5	513	36	24	27	5	2	2	2	2

of episodes with different temporal durations, one finds that, for every child, more than 70 percent of the episodes lasted less than two minutes. The number lasting two or more minutes totals no more than 26 percent in any case. The findings are consistent with those on average duration of the episodes in each record, as presented in Table 5.2, where it may be seen that the mean episode duration ranged from half a minute to a minute and three-quarters. Supplementary analysis reveals that, on the average, the children entered upon a new episode, which is to say that they set out toward a new goal, once every 45 seconds. Table 5.3 shows that this average is heavily weighted by many very short episodes.

The two rows just below the data for the Midwest children record correlations with age. The coefficients show that correlation between age and length of episode is negative for the shortest episodes, and gradually shifts to positive for longer ones until it reaches a high and significant positive value for the longest episodes. Change from negative to positive correlation occurs between the time intervals of 30 seconds and 1 minute. The reversal was implied earlier by figures on average episode duration for each record. But the point at which the shift occurs is shown here, and so also are comparatively high correlations with age for both the short episodes at one extreme, and the longest at the other. Again there is no evidence that the disabled children differed from the Midwest children.

These data on number and duration of episodes are basic data on the partitioning of behavior in naturally occurring situations. They show that the Midwest children did from about 500 to about 1300 things in a day, that the average duration of these commonly discriminated actions was short of half a minute, that the number of episodes was negatively correlated with age, and that the duration of episodes was positively correlated with age. There is no evidence that the disabled children differed from the normal children in these respects.

FREQUENCY AND COMPLEXITY OF OVERLAPPING

Data on episode overlapping are presented in Tables 5.4 through 5.6. They supplement and refine some of the information from analysis of linkages.

To what extent did overlapping of episodes occur in the recorded days? Table 5.4 answers in percent of all episodes found to overlap with one or more others. Of the Midwest children,

TABLE 5.4.   Percent of Episodes Found to be Overlapping

Child	Percent of Episodes	Child	Percent of Episodes
Mary C.	53	Roy	77
Jimmy	51	Ben	75
Lewis	67	Ray	63
Dutton	64	Mary E.	76
Margaret	75	Douglas	83
Maud	71	Claire	78
Wally	66	Bobby	80
Sue	89	Verne	74

Jimmy behaved in the smallest and Douglas in the largest proportion of overlapping units, as indicated by percents of 51 and 83, respectively. The median percent is 73. A relationship between amount of overlapping and age appears in a rank correlation of .61, significant beyond .01. Only about one-fourth, over all, and never more than one-half, of the episodes occurred in isolation. For the greater part, the children did not do one thing at a time; they were involved preponderantly in multiple-track action. This, further, was true more frequently of the older children.

Although Sue, disabled, has the highest percent of overlapping episodes, the four disabled children as a group do not appear to differ greatly from the Midwest children on this variable. The relatively high weighting for Sue may stem from the high concentration of social behavior objects in her life situation. It will be recalled that Sue spent her entire day at the Lawton School where solitude was not often possible.

We have determined for each overlapping episode, first, the total number of others that overlap with it throughout its course and, second, the largest number that overlap with it at any one time (see categories 2 and 3, above). The measurements indicate that most of the overlapping units intersect with only one other. For any single child of the sample, the target overlapping episodes that were overlapped while in progress by two or more episodes in sequence did not exceed 27 percent. A positive relationship with Tau .50 and p .03, was found between age and the percent of overlapping episodes having more than five others overlapping sequentially with them.

Simultaneous overlapping (category 3) of two or more episodes with the target unit accounted for percents of overlapping episodes ranging from a low of 1, in the Jimmy Sexton record, to a high of 20, in the Ben Hutchings record, with a median of 9. These percents are somewhat higher for the older than for the younger children. A rank correlation of .38 suggests relationship in the expected direction, but the significance of the coefficient is doubtful, with p at .10.

There is no evidence to suggest that the disabled children differ from the nondisabled in frequency of overlapping.

TYPE OF OVERLAP

Overlapping episodes differ with respect to their interpositional relations, as treated by category 4, Type of Overlap. Results here for the children of Midwest are summarized in Table 5.5. The table shows that, for every child, most of the overlapping episodes were of the enclosed type. These and enclosing episodes account for about 90 percent of the overlapping in the 16 day records. Interlinking episodes are rare.

TABLE 5.5. Range and Median Percents of Overlapping Episodes of Stated Types: Midwest Children

	Coinciding	Enclosing	Enclosed	Interlinking	Combinations
Range	0–+	13–28	65–78	0–4	2–11
Median	0	18	72	2	5

The data show additionally that for the Midwest children the frequency of both enclosing and enclosed episodes is correlated with age. Rank order coefficients for these two types of overlapping respectively are −.45 and .52, with significance levels of .05 and .03. These findings show that the behavior of the older children occurred in fewer but longer encompassing segments, which means that the older child managed to maintain goal-directed actions with greater persistence in the face of potentially interrupting action units. The findings are consistent with those reported above on number and duration of episodes and linkages. No evidence was found that the disabled children differed here from the nondisabled.

FORM OF INTEREPISODE TRANSITION

Results from category 5, Form of Transition, are summarized in Table 5.6. The percents in this table are based upon the total number of episodes in the respective samples, not only the overlapping units, as in preceding tables. These data are not entirely independent of other results presented above, but they represent a somewhat different approach to the problem of describing the structural interrelationships of episodes.

As Table 5.6 suggests, the different transition forms occur with varying frequencies in the behavior of different children. In Jimmy Sexton's record, 67 percent of the episodes show abrupt termination, only 33 percent merging transitions. In general, these percents are reversed for the older children. They are 37 and 63 respectively for Claire. The median percent of merging transitions for the Midwest children is 55. A correlation of .64 ($p = .01$) was obtained between age and percent of episodes

TABLE 5.6. Range and Median Percents of Episodes with Stated Form of Transition at Point of Termination: Midwest Children

	Abrupt	Merging
Range	34–67	33–66
Median	45	55

with merging transition. These data substantiate earlier evidence that the behavior of the older children was less broken or saltatory than that of the younger children. The younger children tended to do things sequentially, one at a time, whereas the actions of the older children were more interlaced. There is no consistent difference between the disabled and the nondisabled subjects.

CONTINUITY AND INTERPOLATION

The concluding structure data are on behavior continuity and the incidence of interpolated episodes.

Discontinuous episodes are quite infrequent, up only to 3 percent for one record, Bobby Bryant's. There is no correlation between age and the proportion of these interrupted units.

The percents of interpolated episodes range from 1 to 9, with a median of 4.5. A correlation of .42, with a p of .07, indicates a weak relationship between age and percent of interpolated episodes. Thus, although the frequency of discontinuous units varies little from record to record, units between beginning and ending segments tend to increase among the older children. This would suggest increase with age in ability to sustain need tension corresponding to an incomplete action.

The findings on these two variables for the disabled children differ little from those for the Midwest children. A tendency was found toward more interpolated episodes for the disabled than for their nondisabled age-mates. Bobby Bryant had more interpolated episodes than even the oldest nondisabled child. Conceivably an increased ability to maintain tension toward the goal of an incomplete action through a number of interpolated episodes is a compensating factor in peripheral motor disability.

CORRELATIVES OF BEHAVIOR STRUCTURE

Factors associated with structural characteristics of behavior will now be considered.

INCIDENCE OF CONTAINED EPISODES

The percent of contained units among all overlapping episodes was determined for each record. For the Midwest children the percents range from a low of 4 for Margaret to 14 for Claire, with a median of 8. No correlation with age was found. Among the four disabled, the range is as great as for the Midwest children, i.e., 2 to 12. Each episode contributing to these percents is a part of a larger, unidirectional unit from which the part is segregated solely on the basis of its high relative potency. The data indicate that the frequency with which parts of episodes become so segregated varies from child to child, and it may be that equal or even greater variation occurs for the same child in different situations. An adequate accounting for these variations could be made only by a special investigation.

RELATIVE WEIGHT

Data behind Table 5.7 show that 65 to 85 percent of the overlapping Midwest episodes were of primary weight for at least a part of their duration. Episodes never less than *primary tied* (1' in the table) account for 55 to 72 percent of the overlapping units. There are no significant relationships here with age and no evident differences betweeen the disabled and non-disabled children.

TABLE 5.7. Range and Median Percents of Overlapping Episodes with Stated Relative Weight: Midwest Children

				Relative Weight				
	1	1'	2	3	1, 2	1, 3	2, 3	1, 2, 3
Range	22–51	12–42	14–35	0–2	7–18	0–1	0–+	+–3
Median	38	25	22	1	12	+	0	2

EPISODE INITIATION

Table 5.8 gives data on episode initiation. For all but two of the Midwest children, the percent of spontaneous starts is greater than the percent of instigated starts which, in every case far exceeds the percent of pressured starts. The consistency

TABLE 5.8. Percent of Episodes with Stated Types of Initiation

Child	Spontaneous	Instigated	Pressured	Can Not Judge
Mary C.	59	35	5	+
Jimmy	58	40	2	+
Lewis	62	35	2	1
Dutton	62	34	4	+
Margaret	49	43	8	+
Maud	56	42	2	+
Roy	49	45	+	6
Ben	40	50	7	3
Ray	56	40	3	1
Mary E.	53	42	3	2
Douglas	60	34	3	1
Claire	42	54	0	5
Range	42–62	34–54	0–8	
Median	49	41	3	
Wally	50	47	2	2
Sue	45	54	1	+
Bobby	36	63	1	1
Verne	44	53	2	1

of this frequency order is demonstrated by a Kendall (1948) W of .86, significant beyond .01.

A correlation with age of $-.33$, even though it has a p of but .16, raises the possibility that spontaneous episode starts decline as age increases. A possible explanation is that many settings entered by the older children, particularly at school, prescribe quite uniformly required actions more than the settings, such as Home Outdoors, in which the younger children spent much of their time.

For three of the four disabled children, the percent of instigated starts exceeds the percent of spontaneous starts. The coefficient of concordance, W, for this pattern is .81, significant at .05. Thus the disabled childern tended to have consistently higher percents of instigated starts. Differences in behavior settings again seem important for interpretation. Sue Dewall spent her entire day, and Verne Trennell a large part of his, in the Lawton School, where individual freedom was considerably limited by group routines; and Bobby Bryant, who has the highest percent of instigated starts, was similarly surrounded by associates, according to data from the study reported in Chapter 8.

EPISODE ISSUE

Table 5.9 gives the Midwest data on Issue of Episode. As in the original itemization of the category, the issues are grouped according to whether the episode was complete or incomplete.

Complete units make up 72 to 83 percent of all episodes for the Midwest children, with a median of 76 percent. A negative relationship between age and percent of incomplete episodes is shown by a correlation of $-.74$, significant beyond .01. Thus the younger children stopped short of the goal more frequently than the older. In a clear majority of their episodes, however, all of the children finished what they started.

Summed, the percents for success, frustration, and failure range from less than 1 percent to 7 percent, with a median of 2. Life for the children was in larger part on an even keel than one

TABLE 5.9.   Range and Median Percents of Episodes with Stated Issues: Midwest Children

Issue of Complete Episodes

	Acquit-tance	Attain-ment	Gratifi-cation	Success	Consum. Sat'd.	Other	Total Completed Episodes	Can Not Judge
Range	8–18	3–15	+–4	+–4	+–8	32–63	72–83	9–16
Median	11.5	7.5	2	1.5	2.5	50.5	76	11

Issue of Incomplete Episodes

	Nonattain.	Frustration	Failure	Consum. Not Sat'd.	Other	Total Incomplete
Range	+–8	0–3	0–+	2–6	1–7	4–17
Median	1	1	0	4	3	11

might be led to expect from the amount of attention given to these outcomes of action in research and writings on child behavior.

For every child, the percent of good outcomes (attainment, gratification, and success) is higher than the percent of bad outcomes (nonattainment, frustration, and failure), with the median percents 11 and 2 respectively. Correlations of age with percent of good and bad outcomes are $-.36$, with a p of .11, and $-.42$, with a p of .07.

A correlation of $-.45$, significant at .05, between age and percent of consummatory episodes suggests that activity valued as an end in itself declined as age of the children increased.

Again there is no indication of difference between the disabled and the nondisabled children. The data carry no evidence that motor disability inflicts characteristically bad episode endings.

EPISODE TERMINATION

Table 5.10 presents the findings on episode termination. The frequency pattern is even more consistent than for initiation. For every child the rank order is the same, viz., *spontaneous, environmental cessation, instigated,* and *pressured,* in order of mention. Viewed together, these data and those reported above on episode initiation indicate high independence of the children in starting and stopping their action units.

TABLE 5.10.   Percent of Episodes with Stated Episode Termination

Child	Spontaneous	Instigated	Environmental Cessation	Pressured	Can Not Judge
Mary C.	62	11	18	6	4
Jimmy	62	11	22	2	2
Lewis	65	8	19	4	4
Dutton	65	10	16	3	6
Margaret	57	11	21	6	5
Maud	62	11	18	4	6
Roy	51	11	26	2	10
Ben	59	10	21	4	7
Raymond	67	8	19	1	5
Mary E.	66	5	22	2	6
Douglas	63	9	17	5	6
Claire	59	6	23	0	12
Range	51–67	5–11	16–26	0–6	
Median	62	10	20	3.5	
Wally	54	14	24	2	6
Sue	55	8	26	1	10
Bobby	56	9	29	1	6
Verne	52	13	27	2	6

The frequency ranking is the same here for the disabled children as for the Midwest children. But the disabled stand generally lower in percent of spontaneous terminations. This trend is like that for episode initiation. The two sets of data suggest that behavior structure was determined more by external forces among the disabled children.

REVIEW

Evidently the stream of behavior has characteristics that can be described reliably in the language and dimensions of behavior structure. The evidence for this is of four kinds: (1) agreement between independent analysts in episoding, (2) agreement between independent analysts in application of structure categories to episodes, (3) internal consistency of the structure data, and (4) agreement of the findings with theories of behavior that have wider confirmation.

The particular categories of the present study have not all been subjected to direct tests of interanalyst agreement. The balance of the evidence obtained where such tests were made, however, and converging lines of indirect evidence indicate that episodes themselves, some of their structural features, and certain of their properties that relate to behavior structure can be identified dependably.

The internal consistency of the structure findings appears especially in age relationships. Different indices of behavior complexity show the same trend toward greater complexity in behavior of the older children, with none of the findings at odds with this trend. Thus, the younger children did more things in a day and their action units generally were shorter than those of the older children. In other words, the number of units, both episodes and linkages, was negatively correlated with age, and the average duration of units was positively correlated with age. Further, the older children as compared with the younger showed:

more episodes in each linkage;
more overlapping episodes;
more instances of three or more simultaneously overlapping episodes;
more instances of five or more sequentially overlapping episodes;
more episodes that ended by merging into the subsequent behavior units;
more episodes between the segments of discontinuous episodes;
more completed episodes.

These findings are mutually supporting. They indicate marked differences between the younger and older children in structural characteristics of behavior. The younger tended to do things sequentially, one at a time, to shift frequently from one action to another, and to persevere in a given activity a relatively short time, whereas the older tended to engage in actions of longer duration, to pursue more than one action at a given time, and to carry to completion a higher proportion of their episodes.

The data on relationships between behavior structure and age have points of affinity with developmental theories of Lewin (1935, 1936), Kounin (1943), and Baldwin (1955).

Lewin and Kounin assert that the psychological person is structured into parts corresponding to different behavior possibilities. These regions or action systems of the person necessarily have boundaries, one property of which is their rigidity, defined as the inverse of communication between neighboring systems. The more rigid the boundary between two regions, the less a change in one affects the other. Further, rigidity increases with chronological age. With increase in age, then, the parts of the person become increasingly independent. Because it brings increasing independence of action systems, increasing age also should effect decreasing susceptibility to diversions, with consequent gain in the frequency of completion and the duration of episodes. Thus the findings that the older children engaged in characteristically longer episodes and that they completed a higher proportion of the things they started are consistent with the theory. Also, the greater ability of the older children to maintain simultaneously different courses of behavior, as shown by the increase with age in frequency of overlapping episodes, can be derived from the comparatively high inviolacy of the boundaries between their action systems.

In his description of the maturity continuum, Baldwin (1955) holds that expansion of the psychological world is a central feature of the developmental process. This expansion is marked by an increase with development in the temporal and spatial remoteness of things that engage the child. It is understandable in these terms that the older child should pursue remoter goals and so have longer episodes. The Baldwin conception leads also to the expectation that, because they are bound less tightly to immediacies, the older children should become involved more in multiple-track action. Our data and these derivations agree.

We have seen in the anatomy of behavior an essentially new problem with inviting ramifications, and the foregoing results encourage us to believe that the basic method of this volume or similar methods can be used to pursue it in a productive way.

Chapter 6

AN INSTRUMENT FOR

PSYCHOSOCIAL

DESCRIPTION

TARGETS AND CATEGORIES

Some of our data suggest that Midwest children transact behavior in 60 to 80 percent of their daily episodes with mothers, fathers, teachers, neighbors, peer friends, and other associates. What properties do these social carriers of psychological effects have for the children? How do others behave in relation to the children, how do the children behave in relation to others, and with what frequency and potency do the actions on both sides give rise to conflict, cooperation, and social interaction of other types?

Toward answers to these questions, we have a set of categories to describe some elemental aspects of habitat and behavior in social action and interaction.[1] Most of these categories are

[1] Jack Nall participated in the development of these categories in connection with an independent research project. Also, he contributed as an analyst of specimen records and as a supervisor of analytical work with the records to the study of Chapter 8. John Lubach contributed similarly in the later stages of this part of the Midwest research.

thought and talked in one idiom or another in the everyday management of human affairs. Parents and teachers use them to state and solve problems in their everyday dealings with children; and so do child, social, and clinical psychologists in their practice and in their experimenting and theorizing about human social behavior on all developmental levels. These analysis guides are commensurable and therefore give a basis for systematic study of interdependencies in the context of social behavior.

This chapter contains definitions of the categories, a summary of data on their reliability, and discussion of problems met in applying them to recorded episodes. Chapter 7 presents an episode exhibit that exemplifies most of them and displays concrete social behavior and situations of individual children. Finally, Chapter 8 describes in quantitative data from application of the categories some aspects of social habitat and behavior in both Midwest children and comparable disabled children.

The categories are named and classified below.

Outline of Categories

General Factors
  Associate Complexity
  Sociality of Episode
  Action Circuit
  Social-Field Potency
  Action Sequence
  Relative Power
  Strength of Motivation
  Centrality of Motivation
  Episode Weight
  Behavior Setting

Action Modes
  Dominance
  Aggression
  Resistance
  Submission
  Nurturance
  Appeal
  Avoidance

Action Attributes
  Pressure
  Affection
  Mood
  Evaluation

Interplay Variables
  Interplay Type
  Accord

Subject Constants
  Age
  Sex
  Social Group

Associate Constants
  Age and Sex
  Social Group
  Role Classification

General Factors include such basic variables as behavior setting and motivation strength. They include also relative power and other central aspects of the relationship between S and A, the subject and associate in an episode. Action Modes, as common words under this heading in the outline suggest, are qualitatively different kinds of action by S in relation to A, and by A in relation to S; each mode of action by subject and associate is identified and rated as to strength. Action Attributes are primary aspects of social behavior, like affection, that enter into every kind of interpersonal action. Here, also, ratings are made on both action by the subject and action by the associate. Interplay Variables enter into interaction as a process supraordinate to the actions of A and S. Included, for example, are such kinds of social interplay as cooperation and conflict. Subject Constants are stable characteristics of the subject, and Associate Constants are stable characteristics of the associate as a social behavior object. Role Classification refers to such *associate classes* as parent and teacher.

Each category will now be presented. An item of every category, though one rarely used with most, is *can not judge*. We shall append to several of the definitions references to illustrative episodes in Chapter 7.

GENERAL FACTORS

ASSOCIATE COMPLEXITY

1. Simple: one alone
2. Simple: one of two or more
3. Compound

An associate is defined as any social behavior object that gets into the psychological habitat of S. One can demonstrate this event only if the subject acts in relation to the object. An associate is defined, therefore, as a physically present social behavior object O in relation to which the subject acts. Any kind of directly observable action that involves or requires O in any way or degree, such as striking O, pushing, pulling, talking to, smiling at, or only listening to or looking at O, satisfies this criterion. The behavior object can be a single individual, called a *simple associate*, or a complex social unit, formed by any number of individuals, called a *compound associate*, as the items of the category provide.

Where the subject acts consecutively with two or more individuals or groups during an episode, the one of these judged to have the greatest influence is made the associate. Independent analysts (see pp. 161–162) have agreed well upon associates.

If judged to be in the background throughout an episode, like an unused piece of furniture, the observer is not classed as an associate. This rule is difficult. We have assumed in applying it that the observer is lost in the background so long as there is no positive evidence to the contrary. In effect, here, a judgment is made as to whether or not the subject "pays any attention" to the observer.

We have segregated as *observer episodes* all in which the observer is either a simple associate or a member part of a compound associate. This leaves as *standard episodes* all in which the observer is in no way a social behavior object.

SOCIALITY OF EPISODE

> 1. Social
> 2. Potentially Social
> 3. Nonsocial

A social episode is one in which the subject has an associate. A potentially social episode is one in which, although the subject does not have an associate, at least one other person is present. A nonsocial episode is one in which the subject is alone. Only social episodes are analyzed by other categories of the instrument.

ACTION CIRCUIT

> 1. Open
> 2. Closed

Again, an associate is by definition an individual in relation to whom the subject acts. But the associate may or may not act in relation to the subject. If action by A in relation to S does not occur, the action circuit of the relationship is left open. If, however, A does act in relation to S, the circuit is closed.

An open action circuit limits greatly the range of psychological effects that can be carried by an associate. It eliminates all variables of social *inter*action, and all variables in the instrument on the associate's behavior with the exception of *mood*. Accordingly, our analyses have dealt mainly with closed social episodes.

SOCIAL-FIELD POTENCY

1. Low
2. Medium
3. High
4. Unity

Mary Ennis, in *Telling Mother Goodbye* on leaving for school, transacts behavior only with her mother. This episode is all social; nonsocial behavior objects are in no way required for the action unit or used in it. Later, in *Playing with Paints,* at home, Mary gets "absorbed" in a behavior transaction with a box of water colors, a brush, water in a glass, and a bathroom washbowl. The most she does in relation to a social behavior object during the episode is to mumble indifferently to the observer about her activity in progress. This episode is almost entirely nonsocial.

Social-Field Potency refers to the degree in which the behavior of an episode is transacted in relation to social behavior objects. *Unity* holds when the required and used objects are exclusively social, or virtually so, as in *Telling Mother Goodbye. Low* applies when, as in *Playing with Paints,* the required and used objects are predominantly nonsocial, *High* when the reverse is true, and *Medium* when nonsocial and social objects are required and used about equally. Two fields of situational content, the social and the nonsocial, are distinguished by the category, which rates the relative weight of the social field.

ACTION SEQUENCE

1. S-A
2. S cycle
3. A-S
4. A cycle
5. Does Not Apply

Action Sequence has two dimensions, one concerned with order, and the other with complexity, of interaction. The category applies only where S and A are involved in a bilateral action relationship.

Interaction initiated by S (items 1 and 2) and interaction initiated by A (items 3 and 4) account for the order possibilities. Two complexity levels are differentiated. There occurs on one an initiating action folowed by a concluding reaction (items 1 and 3) while on the other and more complex level there is an initiating action, a reaction, and at least a subsequent action by the initiating participant (items 2 and 4).

RELATIVE POWER

1.	$A <<<<< S$	
2.	$A <<<< S$	
3.	$A <<< S$	1–5: A has less power
4.	$A << S$	
5.	$A < S$	
6.	$A = S$	6: A and S have equal power
7.	$A > S$	
8.	$A >> S$	
9.	$A >>> S$	7–11: A has more power
10.	$A >>>> S$	
11.	$A >>>>> S$	

Relative Power is in application the most difficult category, conceptually and empirically, of all in the instrument. Power, here, means ability of A as perceived by S to change the behavior of S. As perceived potential to change behavior, power may be used in any degree or not used at all in social pressure (see pp. 145–146). Each item of the category expresses a ratio. The analyst compares the degree in which A is able to change the behavior of S with the degree in which S is able to change the behavior of A. This comparison is made on the basis of what S is judged to see of the total interpersonal relationship.

To try to rate, not the overt behavior of S, but the way in which S sees, not the behavior A, but only the ability of A to change the behavior of S as compared with the ability of S to change the behavior of A, suggests the height of temerity. The effort is tested in some degree, however, by checks on the reliability of the ratings and the sense made by findings on relative power in Chapter 8. This is indeed the better part of our case, not only for the present category, but also for others that follow.

Power is defined in part by correlations with relatively stable traits of A and S that signify ability or inability of each to affect action by the other. Often these are marks of "influential position," which is to say that power is made to include status. Characteristics and appurtenances of high power include large physical size, known skill or wisdom, adulthood, parenthood, grownupness, any kind of leadership role, repute for difficult or heroic accomplishment, belongingness to or "connections" with the elite, with officialdom, with the "varsity," with "the gang," or the like, uniforms of rank, and various titles, degrees, badges, and medals. Owing to its derivation from such relatively stable properties of individuals, the power ratio between A and S in a particular episode depends, first of all, upon who A and S happen to be.

An analyst must nevertheless look for signs of relative power, episode by episode. He must continually ask: as far as S is concerned, to what extent is A now able, under all of the circumstances, to change the behavior of S? Because these circumstances do include characteristics of A that exist and may be known to S outside the limits of any one episode, sequential context is decisively important for correct judgment.

"Situational factors" leave relative power more stable for a given associate than other variables of the instrument. Our ratings generally place mothers, fathers, and teachers in the $A > S$ part of the scale, peer friends or siblings near the $A = S$ part, and pets, younger children, and infants somewhere in the $A < S$ part. Generally, for a particular associate, the situational factors only bring about fluctuations within a certain range. It has seemed important, however, to try to measure these fluctuations and their cumulative outcomes; and this can be done only if ratings are made an episode at a time.

Illustrative episodes: 3 and 4.

MOTIVATIONAL CONDITIONS

Strength of Motivation and Centrality of Motivation are not represented in the data of the study in Chapter 8, for which reason neither will be elaborated here.

These categories have been applied along with others of the instrument to all records that we have processed. The resulting data have pertinence for description of social action chiefly as means to reclassification of findings from other categories. For example, they enable one to distinguish social conflict under weak and peripheral motivation from social conflict under strong and central motivation. Such refinement has raised difficult problems of analysis and interpretation for additional study.

Illustrative episodes: 1 and 2.

EPISODE WEIGHT

1. Primary
2. Below Primary

Episode Weight refers to the relative potency of the target episode. This variable has been defined more fully in Chapter 4.

Item 1 applies under either of two conditions: (a) the target episode is isolated, so that its potency from beginning to end is primary in the meaning stated in Chapter 4, and (b) the target episode overlaps with another, but is of primary weight during all or any part of its course. Item 2 applies to every episode which, throughout its course, is of less than primary weight.

BEHAVIOR SETTING

Behavior Setting, contingently itemized, provides for identification of the setting in which each target episode occurs. We shall not report data from this category for two reasons. First, the number of episodes in different settings common to all of the subjects proved to be rather small. Second, where common settings did occur, these were found to be tied closely to common social habitat objects, which are here of central concern. For example, for the records we have used, to describe social interaction with a mother, a father, or a sibling usually is to describe social interaction in the home setting.

ACTION MODES

These variables have their analogues in needs distinguished by Murray (1938). Here we are concerned, however, not with needs or any other determinants of action, but with qualitatively different ways of behaving. Murray's exegeses on needs have nonetheless contributed the bulk of the material in our definitions. We have used a modification of his scheme for need analysis and also have taken the liberty of paraphrasing passages and adopting terms in his descriptions of related needs. Yet the aim throughout has been to develop criteria with special pertinence for actions as against enduring needs or wants. Murray himself has recognized the possibility of deconceptualizing his needs to just kinds of actions. The names used here for modes are the same as Murray's for needs in the instances of *dominance, aggression,* and *nurturance*; and modes that are called submission, resistance, appeal, and avoidance, respectively, are like his needs of *deference, defendance, succorance,* and *rejection*.

We do not have here an exhaustive list of significantly differing kinds of social action, but do have seven ways of behaving by a person, X, in relation to another, O, that are fundamental. The rationale for selection of these and no more reduces to this and the fact that dominance, aggression, resistance, submission, nurturance, appeal, and avoidance have met, better than other kinds of social action, the more or less formal tests of reliable and fruitful description.

Every definition begins with a general identifying statement. A presumed end sought by the person, X, as an *effect* (cf. Murray, 1938) of the behavior is then noted. There follow specifications about the occurrence of the mode in relation to action by the other person, O. Two possibilities are open here. First, the behavior can be *spontaneous* in that it is not activated necessarily by a particular kind of action by O, as in nurturance; and, second, the behavior can be *reactive* in that it does presuppose a particular kind of action by O, as in submission, which implies instigating dominance or aggression (cf. the concept of *press* in Murray, 1938, pp. 115–123). Where the behavior is reactive, commonly observed kinds of activating or instigating O behavior are noted. Also, whether the behavior is classified as spontaneous or reactive, or both, kinds of behavior that it commonly activates are mentioned. Common variants of each mode are then indicated. Descriptive terms often used in referring to the characteristic behavior conclude each analysis. Following Murray's example and freely borrowing his items, we have assembled diverse clues to correct identification. These clues often rest upon untested theory about the concomitants and correlates of the behavior concerned, but better leads to follow are not now available.

Where a mode is found in the target behavior, its strength is rated on a scale of three points which, added to zero, give the following items.

0. Zero: absent
1. Lower range
2. Middle range
3. Upper range

It is mentioned again that every mode is applied to both the subject S and his associate A. A rating on A refers always to the behavior of A as S sees it. With this understood, the definitions will refer to any individual, X, with any other, O, so that each statement can be adapted to the subject or the associate.

In this study, the policy at first was to stay clear of elaborate definition, in the belief that judgments could be made least equivocally on the basis of essentials only. But experience with the records led to a change of mind. The great complexity of behavior, with its never ending variations on the same themes, made fairly complex specifications necessary.

DOMINANCE

X rules or seeks to rule O by exerting social pressure in an arbitrary way. Dominance is power used in authoritarian pressure.

END SOUGHT. To influence, direct, or control O by gaining ascendance over O; to gain such ascendance as an end in itself.

OCCURRENCE RELATIVE TO ACTION BY O. Spontaneous or reactive. When reactive, instigating O behavior includes dominative action itself. Instigated O behavior includes submissive action, resistance, counter dominance, aggression, and avoidance.

COMMON VARIANTS. To sway, lead, boss, direct, regulate, govern. To organize or supervise. To pass judgments, set standards, lay down principles, give decisions, settle things. To prohibit, restrain, confine. To demand an audience, command attention. To impose conditions or requirements.

COMMON DESCRIPTIVE TERMS. Masterful, forceful, assertive, authoritative, disciplinary.

The verbal model for dominance is the order, "You do that" or "Do not do that," especially when a "because I say so" is expressed or implied. By invoking the rule, X personifies power which, although it is otherwise impersonal and one step removed from him, is still essentially arbitrary. Any "explanation" of an order or a rule reduces the degree of dominance.

Illustrative episodes: 5 and 6.

AGGRESSION

X attacks and harms or tries to harm O or any object forming a unit with O, such as a thing or person owned by, liked or made by, or "in league with" O.

END SOUGHT. To make O suffer. Subsidiary ends include revenge, punishment, defense. The suffering X aims to inflict may be any such bad state as pain, discomfort, loss, embarrassment, or frustration.

OCCURRENCE RELATIVE TO ACTION BY O. Spontaneous or reactive. When reactive, instigating O behavior includes aggressive action, dominative action, or resistance. Instigated O behavior includes submission, avoidance, resistance, counter aggression, and dominance.

COMMON VARIANTS.   To be assertive in any hostile or threatening manner. To willfully exasperate or annoy; to tantalize. To "pick a fight." To frighten. To criticize, deprecate, slander; to censure; to reprimand, blame, scold. To be "mean."

COMMON DESCRIPTIVE TERMS.   Aggressive, combative, belligerent, pugnacious, quarrelsome; destructive, cruel, vindictive; accusatory, abusive.

Illustrative episodes: 9 through 12.

RESISTANCE

X "holds out against" dominance, aggression, appeal, or action of any kind in which O exerts social pressure.

END SOUGHT.   To withstand coercive social influence or to ward off harm and consequent suffering.

OCCURRENCE RELATIVE TO ACTION BY O.   Reactive only. Instigating O behavior includes aggressive action, dominance, and appeal. Instigated O behavior includes dominance, aggression, or a resurgence of pressure.

COMMON VARIANTS.   With aggression as instigating O behavior: X defends himself physically, or verbally, as in protesting criticism. With dominance or social pressure as instigating O behavior: X withholds compliance; he "gets his back up"; he actively ignores demands or requests; he "takes a stand" and "sticks to it" in the face of appeals or arguments.

COMMON DESCRIPTIVE TERMS.   Unyielding, disobedient, refractory, stubborn, recalcitrant.

Illustrative episodes: 7 and 8.

SUBMISSION

X "gives in" to dominance, aggression, entreaty, or action of any kind in which O exerts social pressure.

X sees that O is trying to get him to do something or to refrain from doing something and he lets O have his way. He "takes" action by O upon him. He is nonresisting. The behavior of X in submission always means for him: "I am being coerced; O is pushing or pulling me."

END SOUGHT.   To eliminate or meliorate stressful interaction between X and O. In submitting, X does not aim to benefit O, as in nurturance, but only to ease the pressure on himself.

OCCURRENCE RELATIVE TO ACTION BY O.   Reactive only. Instigating O behavior can include dominance, aggression, appeal. Instigated O behavior varies greatly. Submission can invite dominance or attack. Another possibility is instigation of nurturance "out of sympathy" when submission has occurred as a reaction to dominance or aggression.

TYPICAL BEHAVIOR.   To "take" injuries, blame, criticism, punishment, or bossing without defense, resistance, or retaliation. To resign oneself to imposed conditions. To adopt a passive, meek, humble, or servile attitude. To let others push and get the better. To allow oneself to be "talked down," bullied, or dispossessed. To give things up or relinquish own aims in favor of another's.

COMMON DESCRIPTIVE TERMS.   *Submissive,* acquiescent, pliant, meek, humble, servile, abasive, resigned, patient, passive.

Submission and avoidance differ. Both can occur within the same episode. In submission, however, X does not move away or hang back from O with fear or dislike. Instead he stays and "takes it."

X can react compliantly to pressure so low that the meaning of being coerced is not realized in his behavior, for him or for an observer. This appears most often in passive and immediate reactions to mild appeal. All instances of such ordinary *compliance* are separated from submission. Accordingly, in Chapter 8, data on compliance are given independently of data on submission.

Illustrative episodes: 13 and 14.

NURTURANCE

X extends himself to benefit O.

X sees that O has a need and he tries to meet it. He actively gives or tries to give O something, to help O, or to protect O.

Nurturance of an associate A is rated if it is judged that, as the subject S sees it, A is doing or trying to do something for S.

END SOUGHT.   To gratify the needs of O.

OCCURRENCE RELATIVE TO ACTION BY O.   Spontaneous or reactive. Instigating O behavior includes appeal. In the absence of appeal, any sign of need may instigate nurturance.

Nurturance entails positive action to benefit O, no less when it is reactive than when it is spontaneous. Thus, there is no nurturance in only passive giving in to appeal or pressure. This holds even when the effect of the giving in is beneficial to O. Whereas nurturance is action by X for the sake of O, the passive behavior of giving in is generally action by X for the sake of X, to free X of pressure from O. Whether the behavior of X is spontaneous or reactive, it is nurturant only if X in some way extends himself to benefit O.

Instigated O behavior can include resistance.

TYPICAL VARIANTS.   To administer sympathetically to a weak, disabled, tired, inexperienced, humiliated, lonely, ill, or helpless O. To be "moved" by distress. To support, console, comfort, nurse, heal. To extend lenience or indulgence, to give freedom, to condone. To be protective when O is maltreated. To encourage, pity, console, sympathize, assuage, calm, appease. Only to be nice to O.

COMMON DESCRIPTIVE TERMS. Nurturant, sympathetic, compassionate, maternal, paternal, benevolent, altruistic; indulgent, merciful, charitable, lenient, forbearing, forgiving, tolerant; generous; helpful, supporting; protective.

Illustrative episodes: 15 and 16.

APPEAL

Reliable judgments proved to be more difficult with this mode than with any other. The present formulation was adopted only after many unsuccessful attempts to define appeal so that it meant nearly enough the same thing to different analysts.

X solicits benefit from O; he asks O to meet or to help him meet a need.

Satisfaction of the need expressed by X in appeal is in some degree "put up to" O. Thus, in appeal, X places himself in or exploits a dependent position.

The essence of appeal is a direct bid for need satisfaction. To be scored on appeal, an action must have this significance for X and it must be such that X evidently expects it to have this significance for O. The action must mean to X and he must expect it to mean to O: "I am behaving as I do now to express a need to you. This is my purpose. I want you to meet or to help me meet the need. I acknowledge some dependence, at least for the time being, upon you. You can turn me down or not. I have to depend on you. It's up to you."

The conditions can be realized in a high degree, as in begging; or in a very low degree, as in many mild requests. But routine, casual, matter-of-fact inquiries made in the ordinary course of conversation quite generally do not meet these conditions.

END SOUGHT.   To have own needs gratified by the sympathetic action of O. To be supported, sustained, helped, protected, nursed, advised, guided, indulged, forgiven, consoled; to be benefited in any way by another.

OCCURRENCE RELATIVE TO ACTION BY O.   Spontaneous or reactive. The situation giving rise to appeal can be simply one in which O is not at the moment meeting a need on the part of X. Thus, instigating O behavior can include abandonment, "pointed" unconcern, aggression, dominance, or any kind of pressure; in such cases, X asks O to refrain from what he is doing.

For the reason that appeal involves pressure, it is a kind of action to which O can react with any of the reciprocals to pressure. These include resistance and submission. O can hold out against appeal, or, without doing anything for the sake of X—i.e., without being nurturant—simply give in to it. A remaining possibility is that, in response to appeal, O can actively extend himself in behalf of X; O can react to appeal with nurturance.

COMMON VARIANTS.   To seek out a nurturant O, one in a position to give help, gratuities, or protection. To ask, with dependence, for information or understanding. To bid for tenderness and affection, as in claiming an ache. To invite sympathetic attention by telling of misfortunes, hardships, accidents, or failures; by exaggerating difficulties or injuries, by complaining of discomfort, anxiety, sadness, or depression. To call upon the good nature, generosity, understanding, tolerance, mercy, or forbearance of an O.

COMMON DESCRIPTIVE TERMS.   Succorant, dependent; helpless, suppliant, petitioning, begging, pleading, entreating.

Illustrative episodes: 17 and 18.

AVOIDANCE

X increases or keeps his distance from O in the face of aggression or any negatively valent feature or effect of O's behavior or of O; X hangs back or draws back or withdraws from O.

END SOUGHT.   To avoid any dissatisfying effects of O's company, of O's behavior, or of any part or aspect of the situation that forms a unit with O.

OCCURRENCE RELATIVE TO ACTION BY O. Generally reactive. Avoidance can by spontaneous, in effect, when X is shy or apprehensive in a situation such that no danger or threat can be detected. When reactive, instigating O behavior includes aggression, dominance. But any dangerous, threatening, unpredictable, or unpleasant action or characteristic of O can instigate avoidance. Instigated O behavior can include nurturance, "out of pity."

TYPICAL BEHAVIOR. To stand still and make no noise so as to be unobserved; to "freeze up" in the company of an O. To hide. To keep clear of unpleasant or threatening Os or of Os who create unpleasant or menacing conditions. To flee from attack. To just shy away.

COMMON DESCRIPTIVE TERMS. Timorous; afraid; hesitant, wary, careful.

Illustrative episode: 19.

ACTION ATTRIBUTES

Let the behavior of X with O be of any mode at all. In this case, X can exert strong or weak *pressure* and plus or minus *affection*, good or bad *mood*, and positive or negative *evaluation*. Each of these is an attribute of social behavior. Action attributes are like attributes of sensation, modes of action like sensory modalities.

PRESSURE

		X is now acting to change O's behavior
0.	Zero	in no degree
1.	$> O$	very little
2.	$>> O$	little
3.	$>>> O$	moderately
4.	$>>>> O$	much
5.	$>>>>> O$	very much

Pressure is applied power; it is used ability to change the behavior of another individual.

Pressure can occur in different forms, depending on the mode of action by X, its agent. Authoritarian pressure occurs with dominance, hostile pressure with aggression. Equally strong pressure goes with appeal, as when X begs O to do something. Also, pressure can occur with nurturance, as when a host urges more pie upon a guest.

Although pressure presupposes power, we have assumed that an individual whose power is low, as he and his associate see it, can exert high pressure. For example, in begging for food or a toy, a baby can act effectively to change the behavior of a parent, who is withholding the object. One might say that in these cases pressure is high in proportion to a necessity of compensating for low power. On the other hand, with power high, pressure can be low, as indulgent parents often show.

It may be incorrect to use a dichotomy of absence (O) and presence (>O). Perhaps, so long as two individuals interact, each acts in some degree to change the behavior of the other. Practically, however, the records present cases in which the degree of pressure is at least virtually zero. Pressure loses its meaning if, for example, it is ascribed to a father who only answers a child's question in a nice way.

Illustrative episodes: 20 and 21.

AFFECTION

1.	− − − − −	
2.	− − − −	
3.	− − −	1–5: The feeling is negative
4.	− −	
5.	−	
6.	N	6: The feeling is neutral
7.	+	
8.	+ +	
9.	+ + +	7–11: The feeling is positive
10.	+ + + +	
11.	+ + + + +	

Affection means momentary feeling on the part of X toward O as a social habitat object. This variable forms a U-shaped continuum with a negative segment, a neutral break, and a positive segment.

Positive affection refers to momentarily favorable feeling toward O, commonly denoted by such words as *affectionate, friendly, tender, fond, loving, sympathetic*. Negative affection means momentarily unfavorable feeling toward O, denoted by words like *hostile, cross, irritated, spiteful, antagonistic*. Minus affection is bad feeling in the sense that it always carries an element of hostility. Thus, even "coldness," so long as it is not in some degree mean or hostile, is not negative on the scale. In minus affection there is always some "feeling against." In plus affection there is always some "feeling for."

Neutral affection refers to absence of either plus or minus feeling. It is denoted by words like "indifferent" and "unconcerned," and includes "coldness," so long as it is not active in the meaning of hostility or "feeling against."

There are episodes in which both minus and plus affection toward O appear. Extended experience with the records has shown that, when this holds, confident judgment of equality as between plus and minus elements is rarely possible, whereas judgment of preponderance on one side or the other can generally be made. In all such instances, therefore, either plus or minus affection has been marked, usually without appreciable forcing.

At the time of a particular interaction, X may have plus affection for a person whom he generally dislikes or minus affection for a person whom he generally likes. Baldwin (1955) has suggested that the frequency of such imbalance rises with increasing maturity. Affection in any case should not be confused with like or dislike as a stable attitude. A child may like his mother and know it in a basic way through the time of a quarrel, while at the same time his momentary feeling for her is negative. It may be necessary to go to adults of high sophistication for cases in which X dislikes O as a person, knows it at the time, and yet momentarily has positive feeling toward O. Still, in rating affection, one does not try to measure like or dislike as a general attitude. The rating is shifted up and down with any evident change in momentary feeling.

Illustrative episodes: 22 through 25.

MOOD

1.	$- - - - -$	
2.	$- - - -$	
3.	$- - -$	1–5: X is unhappy
4.	$- -$	
5.	$-$	
6.	N	6: X is neither $-$ nor $+$
7.	$+$	
8.	$+ +$	
9.	$+ + +$	7–11: X is happy
10.	$+ + + +$	
11.	$+ + + + +$	

Mood means a momentary state of X that exists without reference to O is an object. Unhappy and happy moods are distinguished on a continuum that includes a neutral zone.

Mood can change suddenly, although a "bad" or a "good" mood often hangs on through an extended time. It is generally necessary anyhow to study a somewhat extended sequence of episodes to judge the mood of S or A in any unit of the sequence.

Terms denoting qualitative variations in both unhappy and happy mood are given below. In some instances, the distinctions refer at least in part to differences in degree. The clues to mood in a record include words like these and also explicit references to common actone signs of the named affective states.

Unhappy mood: anxious, troubled, worried, fretful, distressed, disturbed, discontented; irritable, riled, angry; annoyed, vexed, cross; despondent, miserable, bitter, despairing; dejected, sad, depressed, gloomy, melancholy.

Happy mood: gay, merry, glad, gleeful, elated, joyous, blissful, delighted; cheerful, comfortable, gratified, contented.

It is clear that the words in each of these groupings refer to feeling states by no means all the same. For some purposes, too, it would be desirable to measure the different variants of happy and unhappy moods; and probably the material in specimen records would permit reliable judgments upon some of these. But more refined distinctions have not seemed profitable in the present context.

Neutral mood means absence of either plus or minus affect, denoted by words like impassive, wooden, and apathetic.

Mood and affection are positively related, yet vary independently, as our ratings show. Minus mood with plus affection is not uncommon. For example, a Midwest mother, in tears because a hail storm is destroying her husband's wheat, can clasp her child warmly while the hail falls.

This category obviously only touches a class of very complex phenomena that include such feeling states as excitement and calm and many differing emotional qualities.

Illustrative episodes: 26 and 27.

EVALUATION

1.	− − − − −	
2.	− − − −	
3.	− − −	1–5: X is disapproving
4.	− −	
5.	−	
6.	N	6: X is not judging
7.	+	
8.	+ +	
9.	+ + +	7–11: X is approving
10.	+ + + +	
11.	+ + + + +	

Evaluation means critical assessment by X of O's behavior. A U-shaped continuum is formed by negative evaluation, absence of evaluation, and positive evaluation. Approval of behavior and disapproval of behavior, respectively, are the plus and minus segments.

Evaluation is a property of X as judge or critic. The target of the judgment made by X is how O is behaving. X also may judge O as a person. These two assessments, the one of O and the other of O's behavior, may occur independently and yet at one time. Thus, "What you are speaks louder than what you say," and, "The doer is often better than the deed." But evaluation of O is not rated here. Where it and judgment of O's behavior both appear and differ, only the latter is counted. Actually, it cannot be assumed that young children ever distinguish evaluatively the doer from the deed, either when they judge others or when others judge them. It can be doubted, for example, that this distinction would ever get across to a five-year-old miscreant if his mother were to try to say, "I love you but not what you do." One source of equivocation is eliminated at any rate by making behavior alone the target of evaluation.

Evaluation can occur either explicitly or implicitly. X can look very sternly at O and say, "That was naughty to do," or imply minus assessment by what he says to a third person or by only being grumpy. Both explicit and implicit evaluations are rated. Thus the analyst does not look only for outright praise or blame. The manner, intimations, and innuendoes of X are considered.

It is assumed that, so long as X has an associate, the category applies; that evaluation in one form or another is always a behavioral property of X as an associate of O. This, of course, does not mean that it always is observable, for which reason a judgment of evaluation is not always possible. We believe now that the category might best be itemized to distinguish between explicit and implicit evaluation.

The model words for positive and negative evaluation are *praise* and *blame*. Verbs like blame in the records, or whose meanings are conveyed in the records by other words, include: censure, criticise, reproach, accuse, rebuke, chide, reprove, berate, reprimand, castigate, scold, upbraid, decry, deprecate, belittle, disparage, condemn, scoff at, sneer at, derogate. Verbs like praise include: esteem, admire, value, appreciate, commend, compliment, applaud, flatter.

Illustrative episodes: 28 through 30.

INTERPLAY VARIABLES

Many different kinds of social interplay are possible as consequences of differing interaction frameworks and differing modes
of action and variations in action attributes. Some of these are
treated under Interplay Type; and the level of interpersonal
harmony or disharmony is rated under Accord.

INTERPLAY TYPE

		The actions of X and 0 are:
1.	Conflict	incompatible and mutually opposed
2.	Disjunction	only incompatible
3.	Unfriendly Rivalry	incompatible and competitive
4.	Cooperation	compatible and mutually supporting
5.	Conjunction	only compatible
6.	Friendly Rivalry	compatible but competitive
7.	Juxtaposition	divergent

Interplay Type means kind of congruence or incongruence
between the actions of X and O. The items of the category are
discrete. With the exception of Juxtaposition they are based upon
the dichotomy of incompatible as against compatible actions,
and the trichotomy of mutually opposed, mutually supporting,
and competitive actions. Each kind of interplay will be defined
with reference to these basic distinctions.

X and O are engaged in compatible actions when the behavior
of each is consistent with the goal or wishes of the other. Neither
dislikes what the other does. X and O greet one another pleasantly; they exchange smiles; they converse agreeably; they walk
arm in arm; a meeting of minds occurs. Neither blames, prohibits,
opposes, or injures the other or does anything else "out of line"
with the wants of the other. Conjunction, item 5, occurs as the
type of interplay where, without being congruent in any other
sense, the actions of X and O are compatible. The behavior on
the one side need not necessarily facilitate that on the other in
conjunction; yet this may occur, as when X gratuitously helps O.
But merely conjunctive actions are never mutually supporting; X
and O do not act together and help one another.

X and O are engaged in incompatible actions when the behavior of each or of one alone is inconsistent with the momentary goal or wishes of the other. Each or either dislikes what the other does. Disjunction, item 2, occurs where, without being otherwise incongruent, the actions of X and O are incompatible. In disjunction, the action on the one side need not hinder that on the other. A unilateral opposition may occur, however, as when a mother says "stop" to her child, and the child stops. But X and O do not contend against one another. Merely disjunctive actions are never mutually opposed.

X and O are engaged in mutually opposed actions when the behavior of each hinders or counteracts the behavior of the other. X strikes and O defends himself or strikes back; X commands and O resists or counter commands; X prohibits and O defies or actively ignores. A model for interplay of this kind is a fight or a quarrel. Mutually opposed actions are always incompatible. Conflict, item 1, occurs when the actions of X and O are incompatible *and* mutually opposed. Reciprocated hindering or opposition is the essential feature of conflict. For this reason, conflict is characteristically cyclical (see Action Sequence, above). X does something O dislikes; then O opposes X; next X opposes O; and so on.

X and O are engaged in competitive actions when both elect the same or comparable things to do and each tries independently to outdo the other. To outdo here means to reach a particular goal or a higher goal from which the one person is excluded if and when the other enters the goal region. X and O try to win the same girl, get the same job, or find the same wildflower; or each tries to outrun, outwit, outspell, outwhistle, or otherwise do better than the other.

Competitive actions can be compatible or incompatible. Where they are compatible, each participant wants the other to try to outdo him. Where competitive actions are incompatible, each participant wants the other to desist from trying to outdo him. Competition is mutually invited in the one case and shunned on both sides in the other. Competitive actions are commonly compatible when "winning is its own reward," as in a game; they are often incompatible when X and O seek a goal which, like the girl, the job, or the wildflower, is valued more as an end in itself than as a mark of attainment.

Friendly Rivalry, item 6, occurs when the actions by X and O are competitive and compatible. Unfriendly Rivalry, item 3, occurs when the actions of X and O are competitive and incompatible. Rivalry, whether friendly or unfriendly, can lead to mutually opposed actions. When this holds within the course of an episode, conflict is scored.

X may compete with O under conditions such that O does not reciprocate; an interaction my be competitive on only one side. X, in other words, may try to outdo O in an activity that O undertakes without meaning to compete with X. For example, a child who is working with another on an arithmetic problem, toward which the latter shows indifference, mutters to a bystander, "I'm going to get the answer first," and clearly works hard with this intention. One can speak in such cases of *unilateral rivalry*. Unilateral rivalry can be friendly or unfriendly. It is friendly so long as the competitive action by X is not contrary to the wishes of O, i.e., so long as the action does not bring about a disjunctive type of interplay. It is unfriendly, however, if the competitive action is contrary to O's wishes, so that the form of interplay is disjunctive—as when O is annoyed or in any way displeased by the efforts of X to compete with him.

The distinction between unilateral rivalry and bilateral rivalry, while it seemed clear in the abstract, turned out to be difficult in practice. We found that it was not possible to segregate reliably the cases in which competitive action was not reciprocated, and testing indicated that the relative frequency of such cases is low. For these reasons, items to cover unilateral rivalry were at last excluded from the category.

X and O are engaged in mutually supporting actions when both elect the same thing to do, when each adopts the end of the activity as a goal held in common with the other, and when each tries to facilitate the behavior of the other toward the common goal. Mutually supporting actions generally entail some subordination of extraneous individual goals to the "joint undertaking." X and O act together and help one another in building a bird house, in carrying a load, in planning a picnic, in repairing a bicycle. Mutually supporting actions, as implied by their definition, are compatible. Cooperation, item 4, occurs when the actions of X and O are compatible *and* mutually supporting.

Cooperation can occur with rivalry, as when the members of a team, in a game or the like, cooperate with one another and yet compete with the members of an opposing team. In these cases the analyst scores the kind of interplay judged to be the more important or to have the greater weight for the subject at the time of the episode.

This leaves Juxtaposition (item 7). Here, the actions of X and O are in no sense either congruent or incongruent, but divergent; neither is behaving in relation to an action by the other person. X says, "Look at my new coat," and O says, "Pull my sled." The examples in Piaget (1926) of "collective monologue," in which children converse in such a way that each apparently disregards what the other says, are instances of juxtaposition. Juxtaposition has been found in only a negligible number of the episodes in our records, and so is not used as an item of the present category in the study of Chapter 8.

A synopsis of the principal features of each interplay type, with the exception of juxtaposition, will be given in Chapter 8. Readers may wish to refer now to this summary, which begins on page 248, in connection with the following illustrative episodes: conflict, 31; disjunction, 32; unfriendly rivalry, 33; cooperation, 35; conjunction, 34; friendly rivalry, 36.

Illustrative episodes: 31 through 36.

ACCORD

1. $- - - - -$	
2. $- - - -$	
3. $- - -$	1–5: X and O are at odds
4. $- -$	
5. $-$	
6. N	6: X and O are neither $-$ nor $+$
7. $+$	
8. $+ +$	
9. $+ + +$	7–11: X and O are at one
10. $+ + + +$	
11. $+ + + + +$	

Accord gives an overall estimation of the degree of harmony or disharmony in the interaction between subject and associate. Interplay Type tells whether the actions of X and O are compatible or incompatible, and specifies the kind of interaction. Accord brings out the *degree* of compatibility or incompatibility; it gives a generalizing measure of how well or how poorly X and O are getting along together.

The dimension is U-shaped, with maximum disharmony at one end, maximum harmony at the other, and a neutral break in which A and S cannot be considered either definitely at odds or definitely at one.

Unity of the relationship is at issue, and the degree of unity is an outcome of relationships between behavior of the associate and behavior of the subject. Thus, for example, plus affection, plus mood, and plus evaluation in both A and S are conducive to plus accord, which shifts in the direction of minus accord with every substitution of a minus for these attributes. It is on this basis that accord is an interaction product. Such interrelationships are not considered in any systematic way, however, in rating accord. On the contrary, an across-the-board estimate is made on the basis of the analyst's direct perception of the harmony or disharmony in the relationship.

Illustrative episodes: 37 and 38.

SUBJECT CONSTANTS

Only a minimal treatment of subject characteristics is provided, in line with considerations in Chapter 1.

Conventionally itemized categories on Age, Sex, and Social Group are used, as for Associate Constants, which follow.

ASSOCIATE CONSTANTS

Essential characteristics of the associate as a social behavior object are covered by associate categories on Age, Sex, Social

Group, and Role Classification, the first three of which are itemized below. The Social Group levels are defined on pages 9–10.

Age of A
1. infant
2. preschool
3. younger school
4. older school
5. adolescent
6. adult
7. mixed ch
8. ch and adol
9. ch and adult
10. adol and adult
11. ch adol adult

Sex of A
1. male
2. female
3. male and female

Social Group of A
1. I
2. II
3. III
4. I–II
5. I–III
6. II–III
7. I–II–III

The combination items in each of these categories provide for compound associates. A child speaking a piece at a school program, for example, could have as a compound associate an audience made up of children, adolescents, and adults of both sexes and all three social groups, in which case items 11, 3, and 7, respectively, under age, sex, and social group would apply.

Role classification, otherwise designated as *associate class*, refers to the common role assignment of the associate. Is the associate a mother, father, sister, brother, neighbor, teacher, grocer? The category is contingently itemized, and it allows for any role combination when the associate is compound.

APPLYING THE CATEGORIES

One rule that we have followed in applying the categories is that each episode must be studied in context. This rule requires that the whole of any episoded record must be scanned before any episode in it is analyzed, and that the analyst continually read ahead intensively as analysis of consecutive episodes proceeds. The objective in applying a category to a particular episode is to represent some aspect of the behavior or the situation within the time limits of that episode. To see clearly the characteristics of the behavior or the situation, however, it generally is necessary to use all available information on preceding and succeeding behavior and situations. This follows from the fact that every episode, although it presumably has integrity as a natural unit, is a part of a larger continuum. A geologist identifies marks on a rock as stratification lines by seeing the rock, at least in his mind's eye, as a part of a larger formation. Similarly, the target episode is only a center of focus.

The training of an analyst begins with intensive study of the categories. Three or more analysts generally worked together during this preliminary stage, reinstated from time to time with change in the analysis staff, in the instrument itself, or in methods of application. Permanently recorded ratings were preceded always by agreement checks in which, after working independently, analysts compared findings on particular episodes and resolved differences in judgment. These checks were used for both internalyst training in the method and tests of readiness to apply it.

The categories are not all alike in their demands upon an analyst. Those under Subject Constants and Associate Constants require only recording of filed information. Action Relationship, Associate Complexity, and Action Sequence require essentially that attention be paid to directly observed facts, which can be noted readily if they have been supplied by the observer. This leaves Relative Power, Social-Field Potency, the Action Modes and Attributes, Interplay Type, and Accord. Analysis by these core categories presents special problems.

Early experience led us to distinguish two differing *sets* in application of the core categories. These we have called the *rationalistic* and the *perceptual*. Both presuppose mastery of the conceptual criteria for each variable. Both presuppose accumulation through experience with the records of examples to fit the different scale points and other category items. The two approaches differ as stated below.

An Analyst Who Maintains the Rationalistic Set:	An Analyst Who Maintains the Perceptual Set:
reads the record as he would a graph or table;	reads the record as he would a serious novel;
maintains a critical detachment from the subject and his associate;	empathizes with the subject and his associate freely;
probes methodically for significant details and scrutinizes them one by one as evidence for stepwise "rational inference" (see p. 37);	maintains a sharp lookout for significant details which, however, are generally only sized up collectively as clues toward immediate "perceptual inference" (see p. 37);
makes issues of alternative interpretations and weighs exhaustively all differing possibilities;	quickly adopts the most likely one of alternative interpretations *even when this means forcing a judgment;*
strives to keep in focus strict empirical criteria for each variable;	depends upon an unformalized array of criteria from everyday social perception and from experience with the records;
exacts of himself rational grounds for every rating;	relies freely upon his hunches;
intends primarily to be logical.	intends primarily to be perceptive.

The perceptual set is by no means all negative; it is more than the absence of a methodical, critically deductive approach. It is not characteristically lax, careless, or passive. It includes on the positive side alert concentration and involvement, like that required of an effective interviewer, therapist, salesman, teacher, diplomat, social worker and, for many purposes, a good laboratory psychologist. Probably it requires more alertness and steady concentration than the rationalistic set. It has to make up with these assets for what it lacks in meticulous logic.

For better or worse we have cast our lot with the perceptual set. There is some evidence, moreover, that from the standpoint of reliability, this choice has not been for the worse but, if there is any difference, for the better. Specifications for the two sets, precisely as they are stated above, except for minor editing, were studied by three analysts who had helped to formulate them and who had been trained in all essentials of the instrument. Then, following a period of practice with first one set and then the other, agreement between independent analysts under the conditions of each was tested in an experiment that is reported later in the chapter.

As anticipated in the preceding chapter, it is impossible at the present stage of our ignorance of social behavior to draw up hard and fast empirical rules and particulars to go with variables like Social Pressure, Dominance, Nurturance, Appeal, Affection, Mood, and Evaluation. We have tried hard to do this in some cases, only to find every such effort unequal to the staggering variety of phenotypes in which differences along these dimensions, differences agreed upon by independent judges, appear in the descriptive material of specimen records. It is therefore impracticable and, we believe, confounding and a mummery to proceed—rationalistically—as if strict operational guides were now available. The observer could never state rigorously the empirical criteria for what he puts in a specimen record. No more can an analyst know rigorously the empirical criteria for what he finds in one, which means that he is up against a stone wall in holding himself to task for such knowledge. The analyst can be at best only the long arm of the observer. Both work under much the same operational limitations and both, on the other hand, are free to capitalize upon the same capacities to see what everyone must in judging the behavior of others. The main difference, perhaps, is that the observer records what he sees first-hand by using a great many relatively small words, but no numbers, while the analyst records what he sees second-hand by using a few relatively large words, to some of which numbers for scale points are attached. Fundamentally, both are observers; but the analyst's observations are the more selective, orderly, and synoptic.

It might be objected that progress toward rigorous empirical definition of behavior variables cannot be made so long as a position like the one taken here is maintained. This is a solid objection. The perceptual set, however, is not inconsistent with operational rigor; it merely sees futility, cramping restraint, and artificiality in pressing too fast to achieve it against our present lack of systematic knowledge about the kinds of phenomena that we want to describe. Another way to meet the situation, of course, would be to turn to simpler phenomena. But the variables used here seem to be about as simple as variables of molar-and-social behavior can get; for example, one cannot ask much less about a thing done by one person in relation to another than whether or not the action was aggressive. In any case, progress cannot be made by this way around the difficulties, either.

A major feature of the perceptual approach in application of the categories is its greater economy. The truth is that we would not have been led to make it explicit and to test it but for this. The Action Modes, Affection, Mood, and Interplay Type, applied as one battery, were found to require approximately 7.5 minutes per episode under the rationalistic set, maintained through a block of 105 regular social episodes, 45 analyzed before and 60 after processing of roughly 5000 episodes under the perceptual set at the rate of approximately 4 minutes per episode. The greater economy of the less methodical procedure is one of its advantages, although this alone certainly would not be enough to justify it.

RELIABILITY OF THE METHOD

PRINCIPAL FINDINGS

We shall report data from tests of agreement between independent analysts on the major categories and selection routines. The tests were so spaced as to represent all stages of the study in Chapter 8. For each, the score is an agreement percent: the percent of analyzed episodes meeting a specified criterion of agreement.

Target episodes were chosen to provide samples from all major behavior settings and from subjects distributed representatively on age, sex, social class, and disability status. The test material and the analysts were not the same throughout. Table 6.1 gives the Ns and sources of the episodes for the different categories or routines and identifies the participating analysts by letter symbols. The analysts were paired in rotation for all tests to minimize disproportionate comparisons of ratings by any two persons.

TABLE 6.1. Target Episodes and Analysts for Agreement Tests

Category or Selection Procedure	N	Episodes Source	Analysts
Sociality	380	5 Day-Records; 4M, 1D	A, B, C
Selection of Associate	234		
Episode Selection	339		
Associate Complexity Action Circuit Social-Field Potency	160	5 Day-Records; 4M, 1D	A, B, C, D
Action Sequence	106		
Relative Power Pressure Evaluation Accord	200		
Action Modes Affection Mood Interplay Type	210	11 Day-Records; 8M, 3D	E, F, G

NOTE: M, record on Midwest child; D, record on disabled child.

Full item-by-item agreement was reached on Sociality of Episode, as itemized on page 132, in 95 percent of the 380 test episodes.

The analyst must designate the particular associate of the subject in every social episode. This becomes a special problem, as indicated earlier, when the subject interacts with more than one individual during an episode, in which case two possibilities have to be weighed: a single individual with greatest influence is a simple associate, or at least two individuals form a compound associate. The data show that the same, simple or compound, associate was designated by analysts X and Y in 91 percent of the 234 social episodes. In 6 percent of these, X chose a particular simple associate while Y saw the same individual as a member of a social complex. Complete disagreement in designation of associate occurred, then, in only 3 percent of the target units.

Full agreement was reached on the general variables of Associate Complexity, Action Circuit, and Social-Field Potency, respectively, in 95, 91, and 95 percent of the test episodes. This means for social-field potency the discrimination of minimum from above minimum on the scale itemized on page 133.

In applying the categories, we have excluded from analysis beyond judging of sociality all *irregular social episodes,* each incomplete (owing usually to brief disappearance of S), or a pseudo unit of restless action (see pp. 92–93), or a unit with an acquittance issue (see p. 107). Also, we have used the categories of Sociality, Associate Complexity, Social-Field Potency, Action Circuit, and Relative Weight to select episodes for analysis by the remaining categories. Complete analysis, to summarize, is given only to *regular social episodes,* each a unit of directed action, sufficiently described, with an issue other than acquittance, in which the associate is simple, the action circuit closed, the social-field potency high, and the relative weight primary. Regular social episodes that do not meet all of these criteria are analyzed only by the categories under Subject Constants and Associate Constants in the outline on page 130. It obviously becomes important to test the reliability of this selection process. The part of the process that eliminates irregular episodes and episodes of less than primary weight falls to the episoder. As for the remaining steps, agreement between independent analysts in selecting units for complete analysis occurred in 33 percent, while agreement in the selection of units for partial analysis occurred in 58 percent of the test episodes, so that the overall percent for the main stages of the selection process was 91.

Agreement findings on Action Sequence, another general variable, are presented in Table 6.2, which reports, in addition to agreement percents, rank order correlations between the ratings of identified analysts, as seemed desirable in this case, owing to the somewhat borderline levels of the agreement measures. Note further that secondary groupings of the category items, to be found as originally itemized on page 133, are represented. The data indicate fair agreement on the distinction between initiation by S, the subject, and initiation by A, the associate, and also on cyclical versus noncyclical interaction. Rather poor item-by-item agreement was found, however, for which reason only the grosser breakdowns of the table are used in Chapter 8.

TABLE 6.2. Agreement Between Independent Analysts on Action Sequence

Paired Analysts	S Initiation Versus A Initiation		Cyclical Versus Noncyclical		Exact Discrete Rating	N
	Agreement Percent	Tb	Agreement Percent	Tb	Agreement Percent	
A:B	83	.54	76	.50	66	41
A:C	87	.75	74	.48	69	39
B:C	88	.74	81	.49	73	26

NOTE: Tb, dichotomous *tau beta* coefficient of rank correlation. See Kendall (1948).

The categories of Relative Power, Evaluation, Affection, Mood, and Accord each requires a rating on an 11-point scale. Disparity between independent analysts of no more than one scale point on these categories was as follows, with the first percent referring to the associate and the second to the subject, wherever ratings were made on both: Relative Power, 94; Evaluation, 71 and 76; Affection, 83 and 83; Mood, 86 and 81; and Accord, 84. If the criterion of substantial agreement is stretched to admit a disparity of 2 points, these values become 98 on Relative Power, 82 and 86 on Evaluation, 95 and 94 on Affection, 97 and 93 on Mood, and 96 on Accord. The Evaluation ratings show lower reliability than those on the other scales. Concerning this, a pertinent finding is that high variability is characteristic of this category, as later data will show; associates, especially, proved to be mercurial in expression of plus and minus evaluation.

Social Pressure is another continuum variable, although with a scale of only 5 points. It was rated also on virtual absence or measurable presence. Agreement on presence or absence of pressure by the subject and pressure by an associate respectively occurred in 75 and 81 percent of the test episodes. Disparity on the scale ratings no greater than one point occurred in 91 percent of these episodes, on the subject side, and in 89 percent, on the associate side.

It will be recalled that the Action Modes call for judgment as to presence or absence, and also a rating of strength. Because the strength ratings are not used in Chapter 8, only measures of agreement on presence or absence will be given here. These are, on associate and subject respectively: Dominance, 86 and 90; Aggression, 89 and 92; Resistance, 88 and 92; Avoidance, 96 and 96; Appeal, 92 and 88; Nurturance, 85 and 94; Submission, 92 and 85; Compliance, 84 and 82.

Application of the mode categories indicates that judgment errors in identifying the action modes are mostly errors of omission rather than commission. Often a particular mode is prominent in an action, or as many as three or four stand out, while others can nevertheless be detected. It is the weak mode, in the background of stronger ones, on which disagreements are most frequent. One analyst fails to note what is there but, to judge from team judgments, often reached quickly when comparisons are made, neither sees frequently what is not there. We have concluded that the mode counts probably do not tell the whole truth and yet do not often tell mistruths. It is our strong impression, also, that the frequencies on the different modes are not undershot disproportionately; we cannot pick out any kind of action that tends to be missed more than others, possibly except aggression, which has been marked by an analyst quite often, but not marked by a second who, however, has promptly seen it on having it called to his attention. If this is correct, our findings on the relative frequencies of action modes are to be trusted, although the absolute frequencies may be short of actual occurrence.

There remains one category, Interplay Type. Exact item-by-item agreement percents from three pairings of the raters are 91, 83, and 71. Agreement percents on compatible interplay (cooperation, conjunction, and friendly rivalry) versus incompatible interplay (conflict, disjunction, and unfriendly rivalry) are 96, 86, and 84. On conflict versus no conflict, the values for the three pairings are 99, 100, and 94.

RATIONALISTIC SET VERSUS PERCEPTUAL SET

Evidence on reliability under each of the two analysis sets, the rationalistic and the perceptual, will now be presented.

In each of 6 day records on subjects distributed representatively on age, sex, and social group, 20 consecutive regular social episodes were marked off. The episodes in each block of 20 were comparable in that, with minor exceptions, they occurred in the same behavior setting, most of them involved the subject in relation to the same associate, and they occurred during the same part of the day. One sample, P, of 60 episodes was formed by massing the first 10 of the 20 episodes in every block; while another sample, R, of 60 episodes was formed by massing the second 10 of the 20.

Paired analysts, working under the perceptual set, applied a battery of categories, the Action Modes, Affection, Mood, and Interplay Type, to the episodes of the P sample in processing 11 day records, including the 6 used for the present comparison. Subsequently, after all of the 5640 regular social episodes in these 11 records had been analyzed, the same analysts applied the same categories to the episodes of the R sample, which had purposely been withheld from analysis. One idea in this was to weight the rationalistic set by any advantages in experience of the analysts. Precautions were taken throughout to guarantee analysis in context of every episode in each sample. If anything, the R units were favored from this standpoint, too, because they were analyzed only after intensive reading and processing of every record concerned. The source records, blocks of target episodes, and analyst pairs are shown in Table 6.3.

Agreement percents were computed for both the P units and the R units on six of the Action Modes (Dominance, Resistance,

TABLE 6.3. Source Records, Target Episodes, and Analyst Pairs for Experiment on Reliability of Analysis Under Perceptual and Rationalistic Sets

Source Record	Target Episodes		Analyst Pair	
	P Sample	R Sample	P Sample	R Sample
JS: B,2	10	10	AB	AB
MC: G,2	10	10	AC	AC
DT: B,4	10	10	BC	BC
MR: G,5	10	10	AB	AB
VT: B,7	10	10	AC	AC
DC: B,9	10	10	BC	BC

NOTE: B, boy; G, girl. Each number following B or G gives approximate age. P, perceptual set; R, rationalistic set.

Aggression, Nurturance, Appeal, and Avoidance), the Action Attributes of Affection and Mood, and Interplay Type, with the following as agreement criteria.

Action Modes: Analysts X and Y both find the given mode absent or find it present with a strength disparity of no more than 1 scale point.

Attributes: Compared ratings by X and Y differ by no more than 1 scale point.

Interplay Type: X and Y agree on the exact item designation.

Data for the 6 modes and 2 attributes respectively, as applied to both the behavior of the associate and the behavior of the subject, were massed to give 360 ratings and 120 ratings as basic N totals. That is, each of the 6 modes was judged on each of the 60 episodes to give a total of 360 ratings; and each of the 2 attributes was judged on each of the 60 episodes to give a total of 120.

The agreement findings are presented in Table 6.4. A Chi square on significance of difference between groups, based on the Ns for agreement and disagreement, shows for each comparison that the hypothesis of no difference in reliability as between the two sets cannot be rejected. Only in the instance of Interplay Type does the obtained difference approach significance; and here the agreement percent is higher for the perceptual set. These findings are without exception consistent with results of

TABLE 6.4.   Agreement in Percent Between Independent Analysts on Action Modes, Attributes of Affection and Mood, and Interplay Type Under Perceptual and Rationalistic Sets

Categories		Perceptual Set			Rationalistic Set			Difference	
		Agreement Percent	N:E	N:R	Agreement Percent	N:E	N:R	Chi^2	P
Modes	A	88	60	360	91	60	360	.71	>.05
	S	91	60	360	91	60	360	—	—
Attributes	A	80	60	120	83	60	120	.44	>.05
	S	78	60	120	80	60	120	.10	>.05
Interplay		87	60	60	78	60	60	1.45	>.05

NOTE: A, behavior of associate; S, behavior of subject. N:E, number of episodes; N:R, number of ratings.

less formal and controlled comparisons, one of which involved P and R samples of 45 episodes each, in three day records. Wherever any appreciable difference has been found, it has suggested greater reliability of the perceptual set. Investigators of social perception and judgment might find this interesting.

The reported agreement measures are taken to indicate variable but generally satisfactory and in no case insufficient reliability of episode analysis by means of these categories. We have no direct evidence on validity. Any case for validity of the method has to rest now on meaningfulness and tenability of such results as those reported in Chapter 8.

Chapter 7

SPECIMENS OF SOCIAL BEHAVIOR AND SITUATION

SOCIAL BEHAVIOR EPISODES

This chapter has two aims. The first is to present an exhibit of social behavior in episodes of Midwest children and nearby disabled children, and the second is to define empirically the psychosocial categories. Necessarily the exhibit is small; and it is nowhere as good as the originally recorded material, because it takes episodes out of context. Yet it puts a needed bridge between the abstract definitions of the preceding chapter and the quantitative data of the one to follow.

Each episode has been chosen to represent principally a particular finding on a single category. Some illustrate findings on other categories as well, but cross-indexing is left to the reader. Episodes expressly on General Factors other than Relative Power, Strength of Motivation, and Centrality of Motivation are not included. Examples that fit the omitted categories, however, can be found readily in the exhibit. Children differing in age, sex, and other subject characteristics are sampled.

For every episode, its title, the subject, the behavior setting, the associate, the date and time of day, and the finding are given. Each subject is identified as a Midwest child, M, or a nearby disabled child, D, and placed also as to sex, social group, and age. In several instances, the original text of the source record has been abbreviated slightly to save space and, in a few cases, overlapping episodes have been eliminated. Where necessary, a brief statement is made about context.

The classification headings and category titles of the instrument are followed throughout. Associate behavior and subject behavior, where distinguished, are not both always exemplified, and the items of some categories are represented selectively.

GENERAL FACTORS

STRENGTH AND CENTRALITY OF MOTIVATION

1. *Strength of Motivation*
   Subject:[1] Dutton Thurston (M, M, 3, 3-10)
   Episode: Getting Ready to Go Outdoors
   Setting: Thurston Home, Indoors
   Associate: Mother
   Time: November 3, 1950; 7:15–7:17 P.M.
   Rating: 4

   Dutton, nicknamed Chuck, has just been given permission by his mother to go outdoors where his father is working.

Chuck slammed the door and ran back into the dining room.

He asked his mother where his gloves and jacket were. He was breathless and in a hurry to get outside.

His mother smiled and told him where to find his things.

Chuck raced to the back door, opened it and screamed as loudly as he could, "Wait a minute, Daddy."

[1] M or D: Midwest or disabled; M or F: boy or girl; 1, 2, or 3: Group; hyphenated number: age in years-months.

He tore back into the kitchen and into his bedroom. Somewhere along the way he located his jacket and gloves and cap.

He darted back into the dining room, carrying his outdoors clothes.

In a shrill, excited voice he said, "Mamma, he'll wait."

He stood in front of his mother so that she could put his jacket on him.

While Mrs. Thurston buttoned up the jacket, Chuck bounced up and down and wiggled around in an excited way.

Then he quickly turned to face her and held out his right glove.

While his mother was putting the glove on, Chuck moved his hand about to help her.

He shoved out the left glove and, while the mother put it on, wiggled around impatiently.

Mrs. Thurston chuckled and said, as if to calm Chuck down a little, "Well, he's just going out to drain the tractor."

Chuck said, "Can I go, too; can I go, too?"

This was more of a statement than a question.

As soon as he was dressed, Chuck whirled around and started on his way.

2. *Centrality of Motivation*
   Subject: Sue Dewall (D, F, 4, 7-1)
   Episode: Talking to Olivia About Letter
   Setting: Lawton Free Time, Indoors
   Associate: Olivia, Occupational Therapist
   Time: June 5, 1951; 1:27 P.M.
   Rating: 5

Olivia is reading a letter to Lila, Sue's roommate at Lawton. The letter is from Lila's parents.

Olivia noticed Sue listening intently to the letter.

Right away, looking wise and kind, Olivia pretended to read from the letter, "How is Sue?" Then Olivia paused and looked at Sue to get her reaction.

Sue smiled happily.

Olivia finished the letter and laid it on the table.

Sue, looking pleased at being mentioned in Lila's letter and wanting to talk about it, said, "Now, why did they put me in there?"

Olivia, still seated, turned around to face Sue.

Sue took two steps and threw her arms around Olivia and embraced her affectionately.

Olivia fondly put her arms around Sue and playfully slapped her on the rear once or twice.

Sue said to Olivia happily, "I didn't know I was in there." She was very pleased.

Olivia stood up and walked away.

RELATIVE POWER

3. *Relative Power: A > S*
   Subject: Margaret Reid (M, F, 3, 4-6)
   Episode: Obeying Instructions
   Setting: Vacation Church School, Kindergarten Class
   Associate: Adult Leaders (Compound A)
   Time: June 2, 1949; 9:22 A.M.
   Rating: 9

   Margaret and several other children are being lined up to practice an exercise for a program.

At this time, Mrs. Hebb, the music teacher, and some of the other leaders of the Vacation Church School, decided to sort the children, telling the shorter ones to go to either end of the row and the taller ones to stand toward the center of the line on the platform.

Margaret stood passively and watched the shuffling process.

While she watched, the adult leaders came closer and closer.

Margaret had been about fourth or fifth in line. Then, suddenly, she was switched to third from the shortest at one end.

Margaret very carefully put her toes right on the exact edge of the carpet as all the children had been instructed to do.

4. *Relative Power: S > A*
   Subject: Mary Ennis (M, F, 2, 8-7)
   Episode: Jollying Little Brother
   Setting: Ennis Home, Indoors

Associate: Timothy, her baby brother
Time: May 12, 1949; 7:59 A.M.
Rating: 3

> Mary is roaming about with a hairbrush in her hand, rather aimlessly brushing at her hair.

Mary went slowly over to her brother's crib and poked him gently, playfully, with one end of the brush.

He giggled heartily.

This made Mary laugh, so she poked him again.

Again Timothy chuckled, curling himself up into a little ball.

Mary laughed again and then said in a babyish tone of voice, as if to come down to Timothy's level, "Does that tickle you, honey?"

This tone came close to mimicking the mother's with the baby.

MODES OF ACTION

DOMINANCE

5. *Dominance: Associate*
   Subject: Douglas Crawford (M, M, 3, 9-2)
   Episode: Obeying Mother's Command
   Setting: Crawford Home, Meal
   Associate: Mother
   Time: April 18, 1949; 7:21 P.M.
   Rating: 3

> Douglas, his father, mother, and sister, Norah, are at the dining table having an animated conversation while eating supper.

Douglas stood, shoved his chair back, and marched away from the table. He was through with his meal and ready to go outside.

His mother, in no uncertain terms, commanded, "Sit down." She left absolutely no room for argument or appeal.

Douglas slowly, matter-of-factly, came back and sat down.

6. *Dominance: Subject*
   Subject: Margaret Reid (M, F, 3, 4-6)
   Episode: Ordering Mother About Bucket

Setting: Reid Home, Outdoors
Associate: Mother
Time: June 2, 1949; 8:15 P.M.
Rating: 3

Margaret has been riding in a wagon, pulled by her grandfather. Enroute she grabs up an empty bucket from the ground.

Margaret abruptly called out authoritatively, "Mother, here."

When her mother apparently paid no attention, she added impatiently, "Mother, have that ready."

As she finished talking, she threw the bucket forcefully toward her mother.

RESISTANCE

7. *Resistance: Associate*
    Subject: Margaret Reid (M, F, 3, 4-6)
    Episode: Trying to Get Permission to Go to Ellen's House
    Setting: Reid Home, Outdoors
    Associate: Mother
    Time: June 2, 1949; 1:02 P.M.
    Rating: 2

Ellen Thomas, an older neighbor girl, lives across the street from the Reids. It is Ellen's birthday. Margaret appears to like Ellen very much.

Margaret followed behind her mother.

She was suddenly intent on getting her mother's permission to go over to Ellen's house. She asked, "Mother, can I go over to Ellen's?"

The mother said flatly, with no hesitation, "No."

Margaret tried to talk her mother into letting her go by whining and arguing.

But Mrs. Reid was final and definite, answering with another, "No." Then she added, "Ellen isn't home, anyway."

Immediately, Margaret seized the opening. "Yes, she is; she's home now."

Her mother wouldn't even listen. "No, you cannot go over there now," she said, and stamped into the house.

8. *Resistance: Subject*
   Subject: Wally Wolfson (D, M, 3, 4-3)
   Episode: Protesting Being Carried to Auto Seat
   Setting: Wolfson Home, Outdoors
   Associate: Ben, six-year-old playmate
   Time: August 9, 1951; 2:57 P.M.
   Rating: 3

> Wally is playing with Jim and Ben, two older boys, in a shed
> behind the Wolfson house. Ben has just asked Wally to play
> with them on an old auto seat. Wally, note, is disabled, D.

Ben came to Wally and said shortly, "I'll carry you."

He picked Wally up by the arms and proceeded to drag him across
the debris and wire to the auto seat.

Wally squirmed and protested loudly, "I don't want over there."

He cried out repeatedly and firmly that he didn't want to go "there."

Wally's reluctance seemed to make Ben more insistent.

Ben dragged Wally over and dumped him on the end of the auto seat.

AGGRESSION

9. *Aggression: Associate*
   Subject: Margaret Reid (M, F, 3, 4-6)
   Episode: Responding to Bradley's Blow
   Setting: Reid Home, Outdoors
   Associate: Bradley, 18-month-old brother
   Time: June 2, 1949; 6:33 P.M.
   Rating: 2

> Margaret is sitting on the front porch playing rather roughly
> with a young puppy.

Bradley came from around the corner of the house. He walked deliberately over to Margaret where she sat playing with the puppy
and hit her on the head twice, just as hard as he could hit.

> It appeared that Bradley didn't like what Margaret was doing
> with the dog.

Margaret looked very surprised and annoyed. The expression on her face showed definitely that she wanted to return the blow.

10. *Aggression: Associate*
    Subject: Roy Eddy (M, M, 3, 6-2)
    Episode: Responding to Geoffrey's Blows
    Setting: Midwest Hardware and Implement Company
    Associate: Geoffrey, seven-year-old playmate
    Time: February 22, 1949; 3:43 P.M.
    Rating: 2

> Roy is playing in the Hardware store with Thomas and Geoffrey, peer playmates, both sons of employees in the store.

Geoffrey went behind the counter and got an old pair of overalls. He came up to Roy and Thomas, who stood near the counter, and swung the overalls hard against Roy.

Roy gave no sign of minding.

Geoffrey swung again, obviously to hit Roy. The expression on his face showed that he was swinging the overalls as hard as possible.

This time one of the buckles hit Roy across the hand. Roy showed irritation. He was hurt and glared at Geoffrey.

Geoffrey swung once more, hitting Thomas; and then he left rapidly. Roy stared after Geoffrey with a hurt and hostile look.

11. *Aggression: Subject*
    Subject: Wally Wolfson (D, M, 3, 4-3)
    Episode: Throwing Rock at Maud
    Setting: Wolfson Home, Outdoors
    Associate: Maud, two-year-old sister
    Time: August 9, 1951; 10:04–10:07 A.M.
    Rating: 3

> Wally has been having a brief but vigorous argument with Maud about who brought their Easter baskets, declaring that the Easter Bunny rather than Santa Claus had done so. His strong statements have reduced Maud to whimpering.

Wally cooly put the basket down. He reached down fast, picked up a large piece of gravel, and cocked his arm. His facial expression was immobile, but it struck me as coldly angry.

Maud, evidently gathering Wally's intention, ran toward the step at the north end of the porch.

> It appeared that she wanted to get inside the house to the protection of her mother before Wally threw the gravel.

Wally waited, as if stalking his prey, until Maud was near the door so that the post on the corner of the porch wouldn't be in the way.

Then, as Maud ran through the door, Walley threw the stone, which hit Maud just above her hip.

It appeared that Wally threw as hard as he could, although that actually wasn't very hard.

When the stone hit Maud, her whimpering immediately turned into loud crying. She ran on into the house where I could hear her saying something to her mother, who comforted her.

12. *Aggression: Subject*
    Subject: Margaret Reid (M, F, 3, 4-6)
    Episode: Hitting Bradley
    Setting: Reid Home, Outdoors
    Associate: Bradley, 18-month-old brother
    Time: June 2, 1949; 1:03 P.M.

> Margaret has been teasing her mother to go to the neighbors' to play; but Mrs. Reid goes into the house, having firmly refused Margaret's pleas. Bradley is wandering about the yard while Margaret and her mother argue.

Bradley picked up a tin bucket that Mrs. Reid had taken from Margaret.

He swung it, rattling a stone in the bottom of the bucket.

Margaret went over and started pounding on Bradley's legs, his back, and the back of his head.

Bradley seemed to expect this. When she came toward him, he knew what was coming. He cowered as if it were rather a regular occurrence for her to hit him.

Margaret hit Bradley again and again.

He cried a little each time she hit him and, finally, started crying seriously.

Seeing that Bradley was really going to cry in earnest, Margaret let him alone. But she taunted, "I can hit you and I can throw you."

SUBMISSION

13. *Submission: Associate*
    Subject: Mary Ennis (M, F, 2, 8-7)
    Episode: Directing Sarah in Swing
    Setting: Ennis Home, Outdoors
    Associate: Sarah, 11-year-old playmate
    Time: May 12, 1949; 4:10 P.M.
    Rating: 3

Mary abruptly suggested to Sarah that the two swing together in the long, rope swing that hung from a high branch of a tall elm tree. Sarah was easily persuaded.

Mary guided her and instructed her exactly in the position she should take in the swing.

Sarah followed Mary's instructions passively.

As Sarah sat in the swing, Mary climbed on the board so that she stood facing Sarah.

Suddenly, holding to the ropes with her hands, Mary kicked her feet straight out so that she fell, kerplunk, into Sarah's lap, practically knocking the wind out of her.

Sarah was unable to speak. She obviously wasn't very enthusiastic about this, but said nothing.

Mary showed no awareness of Sarah's disapproval. She was having a wonderful time.

Then both of the girls stood up, facing each other in the swing. They discussed the exact positions of their feet until, at the end of the discussion, Mary had both of her feet on the outside with Sarah's feet on the inside. This clearly was as Mary wanted it.

Mary maneuvered Sarah's feet, using her own to kick Sarah's out of the way until she had enough room.

Sarah did not protest in any way. As the two girls swung back and forth, Mary continued to shriek and laugh.

At last, they coasted to a stop. Sarah appeared glad to stop, and Mary too exhausted to continue. Again Mary commanded Sarah to sit down.

She was still shrieking and laughing and giggling at the top of her voice.

Sarah complied and sat down.

Again Mary climbed into the swing and abruptly sat down on Sarah's lap with all her weight.

When they came to a stop, Mary climbed vigorously right over Sarah to the ground. Looking at Sarah, she grinned and beamed, "Now, are you glad?" Then she added, "Or would you rather be murdered?"

Sarah said she was glad they had swung together. But she did say, "I'd rather be murdered." Then, she corrected herself quickly, "No, I'd rather do this."

14. *Submission: Subject*

    Subject: Wally Wolfson (D, M, 3, 4-3)
    Episode: Responding to Jim's Reprimand
    Setting: Wolfson Home, Outdoors
    Associate: Jim, eight-year-old playmate
    Time: August 9, 1951; 1:16 P.M.
    Rating: 3

    Wally is playing cars with Jim and indulging in much imaginary play and conversation about roads and cars.

Jim glanced at Wally and said sharply, "You're messing the road up." Then he ordered Wally brusquely, "You have to go back and fix 'em. Go on."

Wally obediently turned around and began to make the road more distinct and clear.

Jim commanded, "That's enough. Turn around and come back."

Wally obediently turned around and started to come back over the road.

Jim admonished him, "Don't go too fast. You'll get your leg in it again." Hardly stopping, he said, "There, you did get your leg in it again," as Wally's foot touched a side of the road.

Wally carefully lifted his leg over the road without touching any more of it. He said reassuringly, "I'll fix it up."

NURTURANCE

15. *Nurturance: Associate*
    Subject: Verne Trennell (D, M, 3, 7-5)
    Episode: Letting Father Dress Him for Bed
    Setting: Trennell Home, Indoors
    Associate: Father
    Time: June 21, 1951; 9:14 P.M.
    Rating: 3

> Verne has just been bathed and dried by his father. The urinal bag worn by Verne in the daytime has been removed. This bag has to be replaced by absorbent diapers for night wear.

Verne's father got two diapers from the drawer in the same cupboard in the bathroom where the towels were. He wrapped a towel around Verne, picked him up in his arms, and carried him out to the bedroom and laid him on his bed.

Verne lay passively on the bed with the towel wrapped around his shoulders.

His father went to a chest of drawers behind Verne and took out a can of talcum powder. He returned to the bed and powdered Verne's genitals. Then he placed the diapers under Verne and fastened them, using safety pins.

Verne passively permitted his father to do this.

> Throughout, Verne seemed to play the role of an infant and his father treated him like one.

The father turned around and straightened the light woolen blanket on Verne's bed.

> Verne slept in a crib with iron sides on it. The side away from the wall was lowered; the side next to the wall was raised.

Mr. Trennell turned back to Verne. He picked up the tops of a pair of pajamas that were on the bed and asked Verne kindly, "You want to put these on?"

Verne sat up and helped his father put the tops of the pajamas on him by lifting his arms and pulling his hands through the sleeves.

16. *Nurturance: Subject*
    Subject: Maud Pintner (M, F, 1, 5-0)
    Episode: Responding to Fred's Fall
    Setting: Pintner Home, Outdoors
    Associate: Fred, 20-month-old brother
    Time: December 11, 1950; 11:06 A.M.
    Rating: 3

> Maud and Otto, a four-and-one-half-year-old playmate, are swinging, with Maud doing the pushing. Fred, Maud's young brother, is wandering about near the porch swing.

Fred accidentally skidded on the floor so that he fell with his body partially under the swing as it swooped back from the library doors. He yelled, "Whoops," and then lay still when he saw the swing coming back over him.

Maud noticed his fall and at once gripped the swing chain tightly, halting it as quickly as possible. Her face showed real concern about her brother as she held firmly to the chain of the swing until he could get out from under it.

As soon as the swing stopped, Otto got out to check on Fred's welfare.

APPEAL

17. *Appeal: Associate*
    Subject: Douglas Crawford (M, M, 3, 9-2)
    Episode: Responding to Blake's Coaxing
    Setting: Eddy's Home, Outdoors
    Associate: Blake, six-year-old playmate
    Time: April 18, 1949; 6:24 P.M.
    Rating: 2

> Douglas and Blake are playing Indians.

Douglas picked up his bow and arrow and then started to get ready as though he were going to shoot it.

In a wheedling tone of voice, Blake said, "I'd like to shoot it."
There was no response.

"Can I shoot it once? Please?" Blake sounded even more wheedling.
He coaxed again, "Please, can I shoot it just once?"

Graciously, although not very promptly, Douglas handed the bow to
Blake.

> I thought that Douglas was going to give it to him all along,
> but that he enjoyed being asked, and having someone else
> want so much to shoot it.

18. *Appeal: Subject*

    Subject: Maud Pintner (M, F, 1, 5-0)
    Episode: Questioning Mother about Going to Game
    Setting: Pintner Home, Indoors
    Associate: Mother
    Time: December 11, 1950; 3:51 P.M.
    Rating: 3

> Maud is apparently intensely occupied with coloring as she
> kneels on the floor and bends over a coloring book.

Maud suddenly jumped to her feet and raced to the breakfast room
where her mother was ironing.

She said in a rather plaintive tone, "Mom, are we going to the ball
game?"

Her mother answered rather vaguely, "I don't know. You can ask your
daddy. But you didn't get any rest, so I don't know."

Maud said, "I'll lay down now."

Her mother continued, "Well, I don't know about daddy, either; he's
awfully busy. Maybe not tonight."

Maud kept on, "Well, if I just closed my eyes, could I go?"

The mother said, more firmly, "Well, we'll go to some game but not
tonight. We don't have a good team this year. Let's go to a good
game."

Maud asked plaintively, "Well, when is basketball going to come?"

Her mother replied, "Well, this is a basketball game tonight."

Then Maud began to squeal and cry.

She said, between squeals, "Well, I want to go to a basketball game; that's what I want to go to."

AVOIDANCE

19. *Avoidance: Associate*
    Subject: Douglas Crawford (M, M, 3, 9-2)
    Episode: Teasing Charlotte
    Setting: School, Third Grade Classroom
    Associate: Charlotte, classmate
    Time: April 18, 1941; 8:58 A.M.
    Rating: 2

> Douglas has just come to school and is sitting at his desk gazing rather idly about the room.

He called to Charlotte as she came in the door, "Hey, Charlotte."

Charlotte ignored him.

Douglas watched her while she walked all the way back to the back seat in the front row, which was just at my right.

Charlotte sat down and another girl, Shirley Vey, sat on her desk and began to talk to her.

Douglas called back, "Did you wear them pigtails yesterday?"

Charlotte said something to Shirley Vey, another classmate, that sounded like, "I'm not listening to him."

Douglas kept on saying, "Those are like tails off pigs—tails off pigs—tails off pigs," to no one in particular, but making sure that it was loud enough that Charlotte could hear him. He definitely was teasing.

ATTRIBUTES OF ACTION

PRESSURE

20. *Pressure: Associate*
    Subject: Douglas Crawford (M, M, 3, 9-2)
    Episode: Resisting Out-of-Bed Demand
    Setting: Crawford Home, Indoors
    Associate: Mother
    Time: April 18, 1949; 7:30 A.M.
    Rating: 4

Douglas lay asleep on one of the two cots in his room.

Douglas' mother walked casually into the room.

She turned to Douglas and straightened out the covers, which were somewhat tumbled, and began shaking him, saying in a rather sharp voice with an urgent tone, "Douglas, Douglas."

She repeated his name several times, loudly, and then said, "Wake up, wake up," in the same pressing tone of voice.

Douglas did not respond.

After another urging by his mother, Douglas grunted a very sleepy, but full, "Uh."

He lay still; he was lying on his face.

He wiggled a little as his mother called his name again.

Douglas said, "Well, all right," in a very grumpy, sleepy, reluctant tone.

Mrs. Crawford said, "Get up," three times, with a commanding, sharp, but not angry expression.

She said, "Wake up, Douglas, it's time to go to school." Her voice was more pleasant.

Douglas continued to lie still. After a few seconds he began wiggling around.

He slid down in his bed.

He slipped his head from the pillow.

He gradually rose on his knees.

He said, "I'm getting up," in a grumpy, sleepy voice, as though really reluctant to part with his slumber.

When she saw that Douglas was really aroused, Mrs. Crawford left the room.

21. *Pressure: Subject*

Subject: Mary Chaco (M, F, 2, 1-10)
Episode: Getting Salad
Setting: Chaco Home, Meal
Associate: Father
Time: October 10, 1950; 12:10 P.M.
Rating: 4

The family is seated around the kitchen table eating the noon-day meal. Mary has been eating heartily.

Mary indicated that she wanted something else to eat by a string of words apparently unintelligible to her parents.

She pointed toward the table, raising her voice slightly as she spoke.

Her father started to give her some meat.

She became more upset than before. The meat definitely was not what Mary had in mind.

Her voice changed to a whine. She kicked her feet against the foot rest on the highchair. She was demanding and impatient.

By lifting each dish in turn, Mr. and Mrs. Chaco found it was jello salad that Mary wanted.

Her father immediately gave her a helping of salad.

Mary seemed pleased, but took this as a matter of course.

AFFECTION

22. *Minus Affection: Associate*
    Subject: Verne Trennell (D, M, 3, 7-5)
    Episode: Taking Reprimand from Marilyn
    Setting: Lawton, Rest Period
    Associate: Marilyn, Aide
    Time: June 21, 1951; 1:00 P.M.
    Rating: 2

Verne has earlier been ordered by Marilyn to lie still and nap.

Verne picked up his crutch and inspected it busily from top to bottom. He held the crutch high in front of his face.

Marilyn walked into the room just at that moment and shouted to him sternly, "Verne, will you put that down and leave it alone?"

Verne obediently dropped the crutch immediately, a momentary trace of fear in his expression.

Marilyn walked over and picked up both of Verne's crutches. She placed them out of his reach, then turned around and walked away.

As she disappeared, Verne's right foot moved sharply and briskly as if he were kicking something hard in anger. His lips moved quickly.

He frowned. Verne appeared to be very angry. He closed his eyes as if wanting to shut out the world. Then he opened them again. He muttered to himself angrily. He made a fist with his right hand.

23. *Minus Affection: Subject*
    Subject: Wally Wolfson (D, M, 3, 4-3)
    Episode: Protesting Ben's Tipping Wagon
    Setting: Wolfson Home, Outdoors
    Associate: Ben, six-year-old playmate
    Time: August 9, 1951; 2:55 P.M.
    Rating: 2

> Wally is sitting in his wagon on the walk in front of his home. Ben ambles into the Wolfson's yard from his home next door.

Ben turned his attention to Wally. He purposely lifted the wagon high up in front, pulling the handle up so that Wally almost fell out.

Wally held on tightly to the wagon. He said heatedly, "Stop, goddam it, stop."

Ben continued to tip the wagon. He was teasing.

Wally protested, "Quit, Ben," in a plaintive complaining tone.

Mrs. Wolfson called from the kitchen, from which she could see through a front window, "Ben, be careful."

Wally called a final, annoyed, "Goddam it," at Ben.

24. *Plus Affection: Associate and Subject*
    Subject: Jimmy Sexton (M, M, 2, 1-11)
    Episode: Responding to Father's Attention
    Setting: Sexton Home, Indoors
    Associate: Father
    Time: February 8, 1951; 7:10 P.M.
    Rating: 10

> Jimmy and his father are in the Sexton's living room where Mr. Sexton has been reading and Jimmy has been playing about the room.

Mr. Sexton gazed fondly at Jimmy; in fact, he had been doing so for some time, although Jimmy had seemed unaware of the attention.

Suddenly Jimmy turned his face toward his father and looked at him with contentment and satisfaction.

As though unable to contain his admiration any longer, Mr. Sexton picked Jimmy up and held him close on his lap. Then, laughing in a playful way, he turned Jimmy face down across his knees.

Grinning with pleasure, Jimmy wiggled himself off his father's lap and landed with feet flat on the floor.

25. *Plus Affection: Subject*
    Subject: Sue Dewall (D, F, 4, 7-1)
    Episode: Whispering to Celeste
    Setting: Lawton, Time to Eat
    Associate: Celeste Beloit, Director of Lawton
    Time: June 5, 1951; 10:04 A.M.
    Rating: 10

> Between lessons in the schoolroom is a brief refreshment period. Celeste Beloit passes through the room, stopping for a moment to drink a glass of water.

Celeste walked past Sue, set her glass down on a nearby table and then came back past Sue again.

Sue looked up at her and all of a sudden impulsively held out her arms, with a happy smile on her face.

Celeste leaned down, putting her head close to Sue's lips.

Sue whispered something into Celeste's ear.

Celeste smiled companionably.

Sue laughed quietly about the secret. She looked very pleased.

MOOD

26. *Minus Mood: Subject*
    Subject: Sue Dewall (D, F, 4, 7-1)
    Episode: Responding to Theresa's Teasing
    Setting: Lawton, Younger Children's Classroom
    Associate: Theresa, older classmate
    Time: June 5, 1951; 1:32 P.M.
    Rating: 2

> A kind of a gap has been reached in the regimen of the day.

Sue has been alternating between acting sleepy, sober, happy, and grumpy since lunchtime. She is seated now among her classmates at a table in the schoolroom, apparently awaiting the next period in the day's schedule.

Theresa, sitting next to Sue, reached over and ran her hands through Sue's hair in a teasing way.

Sue said crossly, "Don't, Theresa."

Theresa continued as before.

Once again Sue said, with more firmness and irritation, "Don't, Theresa."

Theresa persisted tenaciously.

Sue almost cried. She was obviously unhappy and upset.

She protested once again, "Don't, Theresa," and this time raised her head and turned it from side to side, trying to evade Theresa's overtures.

Then Theresa took her hand away, smiling broadly.

Sue remained sitting at the table and looked around the room with a very forlorn expression on her face.

27. *Plus Mood: Subject*

    Subject: Dutton Thurston (M, M, 3, 3-10)
    Episode: Making Noises in Truck
    Setting   Thurston Home, Outdoors
    Associate: Father
    Time: November 3, 1950; 7:30 P.M.
    Rating: 10

Chuck is "working" in the yard with his father, who has turned on the motor of the truck.

Chuck apparently enjoyed the noise of the motor for he squealed with delight. He let out several squeals in quick succession, seeming to enjoy both process and result.

He did quite a bit of jabbering which I could not understand; Chuck was making noise rather than communicating.

He squealed again, in the same tone of voice as before.

I had the impression that he was really enjoying himself.

He combined a real laugh with a squeal, throwing back his head in a quick, abandoned movement.

EVALUATION

28. *Minus Evaluation: Associate*
    Subject: Margaret Reid (M, F, 3, 4-6)
    Episode: "Painting" Porch Pillar[2]
    Setting: Reid Home, Outdoors
    Associate: Mother
    Time: June 2, 1949; 11:37 A.M.
    Rating: 1

> Using a small branch with leaves on it as a brush, Margaret has just finished "painting" a tree trunk, using dirty water in a bucket as paint. Her mother, taking a very unfavorable view of this, has scolded Margaret for it.

Mrs. Reid brushed some dirt from Margaret's dress, slapping her hands down the skirt. Bradley, the baby brother, started howling in an abandoned way, for "Mommy." His mother was too busy to go to him. Instead she scolded Margaret for getting dirty.

Margaret hopped onto the porch with her pail and "brush."

She started painting the porch pillar in a flustered way, wildly and carelessly daubing with the branch.

> I felt that Margaret painted on the pillar partly because of what her mother had said about painting the tree. Margaret knew, I think, that spreading ditch water on the pillar would make her mother crosser than if she painted on the tree trunk.

With the baby still howling, the mother scolded loudly again, "Don't do that on the porch. Do it on the tree if you have to, but do it on the tree."

---

[2] This rather long episode strikes us as some kind of a classic in child-and-mother behavior. Readers probably will agree that there is much more in it than minus evaluation by the associate.

This was a modification of her first command, which was to desist from all painting.

The baby cried so hard that the mother's attention finally turned to him. While Bradley continued to cry, Mrs. Reid tried to get Margaret to hush him. "Why do you always paint? Why don't you play with Bradley?" she asked petulantly.

But at last she went inside the house as if giving up.

Bradley kept on crying loudly.

Margaret calmly painted the porch pillar, giving no indication of disturbance.

Mrs. Reid came out in answer to Bradley's cries, but ignored him after a brief look.

She said to Margaret, "I don't *want* you to paint there. *Stop it!*" She was definitely giving an order.

Margaret did not stop. She painted on, putting on an air of unconcern.

The mother tried another tactic. She said, "I bet daddy won't like what you're doing when I tell him." Then she paused, apparently expecting Margaret to obey at last.

Margaret brushed her wet, muddy hands over the pillar.

This action, I thought, was more purposeful naughtiness, directed at the mother.

"Don't wipe your hands all over the porch," the mother insisted with exasperation.

Margaret kept right on painting the porch pillar, poker-faced, but a little jittery in her movements.

"Why can't you play with your dolls and let that go?" her mother asked with much disgust.

Margaret kept on painting the pillar as before, neither looking at her mother nor answering her.

"Listen, Margaret, don't you go to that ditch and get any more water. You hear?" Mrs. Reid spoke emphatically, thoroughly aroused.

Margaret nodded affirmatively this time, meaning apparently to acknowledge the query, "You hear?"

The mother said, "O.K., you said you wouldn't and now you mustn't," and went back into the house.

Bradley still howled.

Margaret muttered half under her breath, with great determination, "Well, I'll have to get done with this, anyway."

> In other words, she simply was not going to stop just because her mother wanted her to stop.

She said, "Well, I have to get this much done."

> She seemed to be speaking to herself, but at the same time about her mother's command.

After a time she crouched down so that she could scrape and stir around in the bucket.

Then she went right on, alternately dipping the twig brush and painting the pillar. She was very much involved in this and was enjoying herself thoroughly.

> I took it that she found pleasure in this activity for two reasons: The play itself was fun, and going counter to orders was fun.

She spoke to herself, saying approximately these words, "No, don't you touch this, 'cause you'll get it on your hands."

After a while she said, "It's a long time before I paint."

> I couldn't tell from her sentence or her manner whether she meant that it had been a long time since she had painted or that it would be a long time before she would paint again.

Then she added, "I'm going to get done forever again."

> I think she meant that she was going to keep on painting and painting and painting, never stopping. She spoke from the bottom of her heart, as if she simply was never going to stop painting, and I did feel that this was a direct answer to her mother's command not to paint.

She poured some water onto the porch with a very pleased expression on her face.

She said, "This is dry, maybe," and gingerly poked at the freshly "painted" porch floor.

Then she said, "That'll dry," and poked another place on the porch with an experimenting finger. She repeated, "That'll dry."

"This stuff," she said, and paused as if inhibiting her thoughts. Then her voice took on emphasis as she continued under her breath, "This stuff will be dirty for a hundred days."

She sounded very pleased.

29. *Plus Evaluation: Associate*

    Subject: Verne Trennell (D, M, 3, 7-5)
    Episode: Keeping Up with Tommy
    Setting: Neighbor's Home, Outdoors
    Associate: Tommy, eight-year-old playmate
    Time: June 21, 1951; 6:07 P.M.
    Rating: 11

    Verne and Tommy have been playing in Tommy's front yard, near the front porch.

Tommy dashed up the steps and ran to the far end of the porch.

With a beaming face, Verne hurried after Tommy on his crutches as if nothing in the world could be more important than keeping up with Tommy.

He managed, by hanging onto the porch post and supporting himself partially on the step in front of him, to drag himself up the steps to the porch floor.

Verne's face showed some surprise, evidently at the speed with which he navigated the steps.

Tommy apparently had the same idea, for he stopped short in his cavortings and said, "Why, Verne, you can walk *pretty good.*"

This was an entirely spontaneous remark and Verne's expression showed that he took it as acclaim.

Standing close to the porch pillar, Verne asked Tommy in all seriousness, "Does it hurt when you fall off?"

He looked down at the grass before him and seemed to measure the distance from the porch to the ground in a tentative way as if he were tempted to fall off as Tommy earlier had done.

30. *Plus Evaluation: Subject*
    Subject: Sue Dewall (D, F, 4, 7-1)
    Episode: Complimenting Theresa
    Setting: Lawton, Trafficways, Downstairs
    Associate: Theresa, older classmate
    Time: June 5, 1951; 12:11 P.M.
    Rating: 10

    Sue is watching while Theresa, a child who walks with difficulty by using two canes, goes slowly and patiently to the schoolroom.

Sue said to Theresa in an adult-like fashion, patronizingly, yet in a very complimentary tone, "That's a girl!"

Sue continued in the same tone, "I'm proud of you, Theresa."

INTERACTION PRODUCTS

INTERPLAY TYPE

31. *Interplay Type: Conflict*
    Subject: Roy Eddy (M, M, 3, 6-2)
    Episode: Responding to Boy's Teasing
    Setting: Trafficways
    Associate: Douglas Herne, 11-year-old playmate
    Time: February 22, 1949; 3:34 P.M.

    Roy and Thomas have just come out of the Midwest Hardware Store.

The boys met Douglas Herne walking past the hardware store.

Without apparent provocation, Douglas reached out antagonistically and ruffled Roy's hair. There had been no preliminary conversation, nor any action which might have led to hostility.

Roy seemed to take this very seriously. He squared off angrily at big, redheaded Douglas.

Douglas backed off a little, although he obviously had nothing to fear. Despite his retreat, he seemed to be threatening Roy.

Roy held his ground and didn't give an inch.

Although he did not attack, he stood alert, cautiously prepared for any eventuality.

Even though Roy remained poised and prepared for action, the older boy turned and left; and that was all.

32. *Interplay Type: Disjunction*
     Subject: Wally Wolfson (D, M, 3, 4-3)
     Episode: Saying "Hi" to Jim
     Setting: Wolfson Home, Outdoors
     Associate: Jim, eight-year-old playmate
     Time: August 9, 1951; 1:08 p.m.

     Wally is playing in his yard with small cars, running them on the ground. Jim lives next door.

Jim came over.

Wally said in a friendly manner, "Hi, Jim."

Jim didn't reply.

Wally repeated insistently, "Hi, Jim."

Jim still didn't answer.

Wally said, "Hi, Jimmy," once more, but he seemed to understand that Jim was not going to play with him.

Jim picked up the bike that was lying on the ground nearby and rode away.

33. *Interplay Type: Unfriendly Rivalry*
     Subject: Roy Eddy (M, M, 3, 6-2)
     Episode: Retrieving Chair
     Setting: School, First Grade Classroom
     Associate: Seven-year-old Jimmy Vey, eight-year-old
                 Betty Reeves, schoolmates
     Time: February 22, 1949; 12:29 p.m.

     The children are free to do almost anything they please after they have eaten their lunches. Roy is seated at a long, low table modeling with clay. Children are roughhousing all around him but he seems to be concentrating on his clay modeling.

Jimmy Vey suddenly pulled the chair on which Roy was sitting out from under him.

Roy quickly reached out to get the chair back. Grabbing hold of it, he pulled hard.

Jimmy at last gave in, but Betty Reeves took hold of the chair, saying she did not have one.

Roy, determination, not hostility, in his face, would not give in one bit. He battled over the chair with Betty for a moment.

Roy won. He took the chair, placed it firmly and with satisfaction where it had been, and sat down.

He had been quiet but persistent and a little annoyed at the interference.

34. *Interplay Type: Conjunction*
    Subject: Jimmy Sexton (M, M, 2, 1-11)
    Episode: Looking at Book
    Setting: Sexton Home, Indoors
    Associate: Father
    Time: February 8, 1951; 4:23–4:25 P.M.

    Jimmy is looking for his own small book and suddenly spies it on the arm of a chair. His father is reading in a nearby chair.

Picking up his book, Jimmy ran quickly to the davenport.

    I had the impression that for the past few minutes he had been looking for his book so he could read, too, like his daddy.

He made a very contented little sound as he opened and leafed through the book.

Suddenly, Jimmy sneezed loudly.

He caught his daddy's eye as he sneezed.

Jimmy and his father grinned happily although neither spoke.

Jimmy immediately returned his glance to his book.

35. *Interplay Type: Cooperation*
    Subject: Claire Graves (M, F, 3, 10-9)
    Episode: Making Bed with Sister
    Setting: Graves' Home, Indoors

Associate: Frances, nine-year-old sister
Time: January 28, 1949; 8:06–8:08 A.M.

Claire is standing in the front near the stove while her sister, Frances, is in the kitchen.

Claire went to the doorway and called pleasantly to Frances, "Come on, Frances, let's go and make our bed."

Frances went into the bedroom, followed by Claire.

They started to make the bed together, talking as they worked, with Claire on one side and Frances on the other.

Claire took the leading role momentarily.

She said, "Now, this cover." She went on, working all the while, "Now, that one. Let's smooth out that one; here is a bumpy place."

She chatted along pleasantly with Frances.

Claire smoothed the covers out with both hands and was very professional about putting the spread on.

Frances breathed heavily to see her breath in the cold room.

The room was quite cold, for the door to the front room, the only heat source, was closed.

Claire and Frances proceeded to put on the spread and Claire said, "Oh, it goes this way," after looking at it. She was directing Frances and helping her at the same time.

Frances didn't mind Claire's direction. Rather, they cooperated on this project.

They got the spread on and smoothed it out.

36. *Interplay Type: Friendly Rivalry*
   Subject: Dutton Thurston (M, M, 3, 3-10)
   Episode: Having Play Fight with Brother
   Setting: Thurston Home, Indoors
   Associate: Al, 18-year-old brother
   Time: November 3, 1950; 6:42 P.M.

Chuck is just back in the house after going out on the porch with Shirley to feed the kitten.

Chuck dashed through the kitchen into the dining room to Al who was seated on the divan.

Chuck ran into Al's legs and pounded playfully, yet hard, on them.

Al ordered Chuck with mock sternness, "Cut that out," as he stood to defend himself, assuming a boxer's pose.

Grinning, Chuck backed away.

He extended his left hand in front of him as if he were going to take a haymaker swing at Al.

With mock ferociousness Chuck acted as though he would kick Al on the leg.

Al warned him playfully that he had better not kick him, only to give Chuck further incentive.

Chuck gamely tried to kick Al on the leg.

He finally slipped close enough to kick Al but didn't kick as hard as he might have; he was being entirely playful.

Al made out that he was greatly offended. He seized Chuck by the arms and briefly lifted him off the floor.

As Al put him down, Chuck landed on his hands and feet.

Al playfully kicked Chuck in the seat of the pants. Both were enjoying the game a great deal.

Still playful, Al tried to seize Chuck.

Chuck fled into the kitchen as fast as he could go.

Then Al sat down in a rocking chair.

Chuck sauntered back into the dining room, mockingly nonchalant.

He circled around Al, showing that he had dared to come back.

ACCORD

37. *Minus Accord*

    Subject: Ben Hutchings (M, M, 1, 7-4)
    Episode: Quarreling about Rules
    Setting: Hutchings' Home, Indoors
    Associate: Morris, six-year-old playmate
    Time: November 23, 1948; 4:30 P.M.
    Rating: 2

Ben and Morris are playing with toy soldiers, having a pretend battle. Ann, Morris' sister, is seated nearby looking at a book. One rule that Ben has made is that no plane may go up without a man in it.

Then Ben said, "Let's stay in our places; let's not move the other soldiers around. Move the airplanes."

Morris objected, "Heck, no. I'm going to send up planes without men."

Ben countered, his voice raised, "Not with my men." (Meaning, not while you're playing with my toys.)

Morris stated loudly, "These aren't yours."

Ben yelled, "Yes, they are; these are Sarah's," referring to the ones he was playing with, and "those are mine—you aren't going to take a plane up with my men."

Suddenly both boys were rolling around on the floor. They fought quietly.

Morris reached out and knocked Ben's soldiers all over the floor.

Ben knocked Morris' men helter-skelter.

Ben got the upper hand and sat on top of Morris.

Morris almost began to cry.

Ann left the kitchen hastily and went to find Mrs. Hutchings.

Mrs. Hutchings came in and said, "What's the matter here?" She spoke with curiosity, showing little concern.

Ben got off Morris very slowly; he didn't jump up as if he were frightened.

38. *Plus Accord*

Subject: Claire Graves (M, F, 3, 10-9)
Episode: Joking about "John"
Setting: Graves' Home, Indoors
Associate: Frances, nine-year-old sister; Stanley, teenage brother
Time: January 28, 1949; 4:40 P.M.
Rating: 11

Frances and Claire are warming up in front of a glowing base burner after coming from school. Stanley enters, stamping off snow, after shoveling a narrow path, and is preparing to warm himself before going back to more work on the path. Charles, the four-year-old brother, also is on hand. The air outdoors is sharp.

Stanley, Frances, and Claire gathered about the stove, while Charles stood upon a chair near the telephone.

Stanley and Charles began talking about a person or thing called "John." It was evidently something they had a secret about. Frances and Claire were trying to discover who or what "John" was. There was a great deal of joking.

Claire said teasingly, "Who is John?"

Stanley said, "Don't you tell, Charles."

Claire looked merry.

> The merriment was not extreme, but there was a comfortable family feeling about the whole situation. Stanley and Charles lined up against Frances and Claire and everybody recognized this. I had the feeling that it was all done for Charles' benefit.

Charles became quite boisterous. He laughed as if he were getting a big kick out of it all.

The two girls smiled broadly. They giggled.

Then Claire and Frances began to wheedle Charles, trying to get him to tell.

Stanley interrupted to say, "Don't tell; don't you dare tell, Charles."

Frances suddenly walked over and picked Charles up and whirled him around as best she could and both she and he giggled and walked into the kitchen.

This left Stanley and Claire standing contentedly by the fire.

CONCLUSION

These episodes answer some questions about the social habitat and behavior of the children. But they also raise a number of questions.

How common among Midwest mothers with their children is

dominance, such as Mrs. Crawford's when she ordered Douglas to sit down? How often do the children submit to someone as Douglas did to her? How frequent is aggressive behavior like Geoffrey's against Roy, with the overalls as a whip? As far as we know, nothing of this kind has been counted, episode by episode. How often does evaluation by a mother or anyone, such as Mrs. Reid's disapproval of Margaret's "painting," fall on a Midwest child? And how often in a day do Midwest children resist pressure from others, as Margaret did in resolving to paint on? Is social conflict, like that between Roy and Douglas in front of the store, common in Midwest? And how much of the time is everything agreeable between children of Midwest and their associates, as between Claire, Stanley, Frances, and Charles, before the fire?

What of relationships between social behavior and age in Midwest, and of differences between the physically normal Midwest children and the disabled children? Easier questions also are raised by the material. We wished to know how frequently the children get involved with others, who these others are, and how large a part different kinds of individuals play in the social lives of the children.

Questions like these started the present line of study, and will serve to introduce the following chapter. We have gone to pains in belief that answers based on a few days of a few children should be instructive.

Chapter 8

A QUANTITATIVE VIEW OF CHILDREN WITH OTHERS

PROBLEM AND MATERIAL

The categories of Chapter 6 have been applied to 10,406 episodes of 11 day records whose subjects are eight children of Midwest and three nearby disabled children. The total episode populations for the Midwest and disabled children respectively are 7751 and 2655. Below, in Table 8.1, with the number of episodes from each record and with information on every child, are the 11 subjects.

The eight Midwest records give a balanced sample on age, sex, and social group. There are four preschool children and four of school age. Boys and girls are equally represented, as they are approximately in the total child population of Midwest, while also a boy and a girl are paired at the younger and older preschool levels, and at the younger and older school levels. The children are equally divided between social Groups II

TABLE 8.1. Subjects of the Psychosocial Study

| | Midwest Children | | | |
	Episodes	Sex	Group	Age
Mary Chaco (MC)	1103	F	II	1-10
Jimmy Sexton (JS)	1027	M	II	1-11
Dutton Thurston (DT)	1159	M	III	3-10
Margaret Reid (MR)	1059	F	III	4-6
Raymond Birch (RB)	1000	M	II	7-4
Mary Ennis (ME)	969	F	II	8-7
Douglas Crawford (DC)	940	M	III	9-2
Claire Graves (CG)	494	F	III	10-9
	Disabled Children			
	Episodes	Sex	Group	Age
Wally Wolfson (WW)	907	M	III	4-3
Sue Dewall (SD)	771	F	IV	7-1
Verne Trennell (VT)	977	M	III	7-5

and III, which account for 88 percent of the Midwest child population.

Wally Wolfson, Sue Dewall, and Verne Trennell have been identified earlier as children with severe orthopedic disabilities. For particulars on the behavior settings unique to these children when their records were made, and also for comparable information on the Midwest children, readers are referred again to the biographical sketches of the Appendix.

The assignment before us is to describe some aspects of social behavior and situation in episodes of the 11 records on these children. The relation between child and associate is basic in all of the description. Relationships between age of the Midwest subjects and different aspects of their social behavior and its conditions are to be explored; and so are differences between the Midwest and disabled children, although we shall be concerned most with the children of Midwest.

Readers will recall that sex and social group are among Subject Constants of the instrument and that the eight Midwest children are equally divided on both. Attention will be confined, however, to relationships with age as a subject variable. This simplifies a crowded picture and leaves for later special study the social group and sex of the subjects as social behavior correlates.

SURVEY OF EPISODES

We begin with a survey to determine the relative frequency of social and potentially social episodes, to identify associates of the children, and to get background information about some basic characteristics of the recorded situations and social relationships. This survey also will select for extended analysis social episodes with significant common features. The data will be presented in some detail in a series of tables, followed by a summary of the main findings.

Note on Statistics. Inspection of the data indicates that certain of the distributions are not normal and that the variances are in many instances heterogeneous. Therefore, and also because the maximum N is 11 (Midwest children: 8; disabled children: 3), nonparametric methods have been used throughout.

We shall be concerned at several points with differences for each subject between measures X and Y. In every such case, the number of differences in each of the possible directions, $X > Y$ and $Y > X$, was determined, and the probability that a split of the observed magnitude could occur by chance was computed by expanding the binomial $(P + Q)^n$. Following Walker and Lev (1953), we have ignored ties in getting this statistic.

Various relationships with age are reported in rank order correlations. The coefficient, as in Chapter 5, is Tau (Kendall, 1948).

All probability values are two-tailed.

Additional statistics required by special problems are left for comment where they are used.

FREQUENCY OF SOCIAL UNITS

In what degree did other individuals play their parts in the days of the children?

Table 8.2 answers with a sociality breakdown of the total episode population. It shows the percent of social, potentially

TABLE 8.2. Percent of Social, Potentially Social, and Nonsocial Episodes in Records of Midwest and Disabled Children

		MC	JS	DT	MR	RB	ME	DC	CG	Mdn	WW	SD	VT	Mdn
						Midwest							Disabled	
SOCIAL	Standard R	64	53	54	66	52	51	45	54	54	62	62	66	62
	Standard I	2	2	6	3	7	6	4	8	5	4	8	4	4
	Standard T	66	55	60	69	59	57	49	62	61	66	70	70	70
	Observer R	15	18	18	16	17	23	31	21	18	11	13	18	13
	Observer I	1	0	2	2	3	2	2	3	2	2	4	2	2
	Observer T	16	18	20	18	20	25	33	24	20	13	17	20	17
	All	82	73	80	87	79	82	82	86	85	79	87	90	87
Potentially Social		18	26	19	12	16	16	17	14	16	21	12	10	12
Nonsocial		0	1	1	1	5	2	1	0	1	0	1	0	0
Total N		1103	1027	1159	1059	1000	969	940	494	7751	907	771	977	2655

NOTE: R, regular episode; I, irregular episode; T, total (R + I).

social, and nonsocial episodes respectively in each day, with regular and irregular standard and observer units distinguished among social episodes. It will often be convenient to call individuals in the standard units *participant associates*. The standard and observer episodes are defined on page 132, the regular and irregular on page 162, above.

ASSOCIATE COMPLEXITY

There were 4286 regular standard social episodes in the Midwest days, 1689 in the days of the disabled children. Table 8.3 shows for every record the percent of these episodes with simple and compound associates.

For the Midwest children, there is a positive relationship between percent of standard episodes with compound associates and age, as shown by a rank order correlation of .82, significant beyond .01.

Social episodes with compound associates are to be eliminated from this point forward. They are relatively infrequent, as Table 8.3 shows. Also, they are not uniformly comparable; the associate can be a couple in one, a trio of friends in another, or an audience in a third, so that an indiscriminate sample of such episodes lacks precise meaning. It would be interesting to study episodes with different types of compound associates, but considerable experimenting has shown that the available material does not justify analysis that refined.

The elimination of units with compound associates leaves a total of 5272 regular standard social episodes in which the associate was a single individual, and our next problem is to sort these persons.

PRINCIPAL ASSOCIATES

Table 8.4 shows the percent of standard units in which specified individuals or classes of individuals were associates of the subjects. Some of these data are represented graphically in Figure 8.1.

TABLE 8.3. Percent of Standard and Observer Episodes with Simple and Compound Associates

Episodes		MC	JS	DT	MR	Midwest RB	ME	DC	CG	Mdn	WW	Disabled SD	VT	Mdn	All Mdn
Std	Simple	96	96	86	90	82	84	84	79	85	86	85	92	86	86
	Compound	4	4	13	9	17	16	15	21	14	14	14	7	14	14
	Total N	704	538	629	705	520	498	424	267	4286	566	479	644	1689	5975
Obs	Simple	92	96	98	96	92	98	92	85	94	94	93	94	94	94
	Compound	8	4	2	4	8	2	8	15	6	6	7	6	6	6
	Total N	166	188	207	167	170	219	292	103	1512	102	97	176	375	1887

NOTE: Std, standard episodes; Obs, observer episodes. Any residue from 100 percent in any column is the percent of indeterminate episodes.

		Midwest									Disabled			
	Associates	MC	JS	DT	MR	RB	ME	DC	CG	Mdn	WW	SD	VT	Mdn
ADULTS	Mothers	70	52	42	51	13	25	11	20	34	24	0	15	15
	Fathers	11	38	13	3	7	3	3	0	5	3	0	10	3
	Relatives	+	1	0	4	0	0	0	0	0	2	0	0	0
	Teachers	0	0	0	5	24	16	18	21	10	0	19	14	14
	Friends	3	1	13	3	5	4	21	5	4	1	0	2	1
	L Guardian	—	—	—	—	—	—	—	—	—	—	14	0	
	L Director	—	—	—	—	—	—	—	—	—	—	3	0	
	L Aide	—	—	—	—	—	—	—	—	—	—	21	9	9
	All	84	92	68	66	49	48	53	46	59	30	57	50	50
ADO	Friends	0	0	0	2	+	7	2	1	2	+	14	3	3
	Siblings	0	0	21	0	0	0	0	7	0	0	0	0	0
	All	0	0	21	2	+	7	2	7	2	+	14	3	3
CHILDREN FRIENDS	Infant	0	0	0	+	1	0	0	0	0	0	0	0	0
	Preschool	0	0	0	8	3	4	0	0	0	2	0	1	1
	Younger School	0	7	0	4	30	24	22	3	6	56	7	30	30
	Older School	0	+	0	9	11	9	13	17	9	+	20	9	9
	All	0	7	0	21	45	37	35	20	21	58	27	40	40
CHILDREN SIBS	Younger	0	0	0	8	0	3	7	27	2	7	0	4	4
	Older	14	0	0	0	0	0	0	0	0	0	0	0	0
	All	14	0	0	8	0	3	7	27	6	7	0	4	4
	All	14	7	0	29	45	40	42	47	34	65	27	44	44
	Male	25	39	36	19	43	24	35	21	30	63	13	46	46
	Female	73	60	53	78	51	71	62	79	67	33	86	51	51
	ANIMALS	2	1	11	3	5	3	2	0	3	3	+	3	3
	INDETERMINATE	+	0	0	0	0	2	1	0	0	1	1	0	1
		681	517	540	632	429	419	355	211	3784	484	409	595	1488

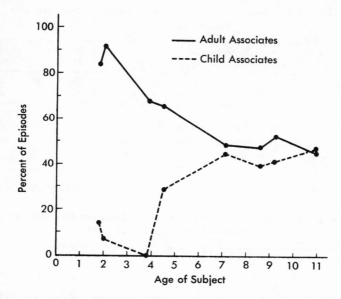

Fig. 8.1. Percent of regular standard episodes in Midwest with adult and child associates.

An adult friend is any grownup other than a parent or other relative, a teacher, or, for the records on Sue and Verne, any member of the Lawton staff. Guardian refers to a supervisor of Lawton who was made a mother surrogate to Sue. An adolescent friend is any adolescent or young adult other than a sibling. A child friend is any child under 12 other than a sibling; in Midwest or at Lawton, if you are not a relative, you are a friend.

Figure 8.1 abstracts from Table 8.4 a representation of the relationship between age of the Midwest child and the relative frequency among his associates of adults and children.

ACTION CIRCUIT AND POTENCY

Table 8.5 shows for each record the percent of standard and observer units with a closed rather than open circuit.

TABLE 8.5.   Percent of Standard and Observer Episodes with Closed Action Circuit

					Midwest						Disabled			All
Episodes	MC	JS	DT	MR	RB	ME	DC	CG	Mdn	WW	SD	VT	Mdn	Mdn
Standard	89	75	78	86	81	80	87	80	80	88	76	83	83	83
Observer	64	22	41	87	58	62	88	53	60	74	58	78	74	62

Table 8.6 shows for each record the percent of standard and observer episodes in which potency of the social field was superior. It answers to the question of how often, relatively, transactions with social habitat objects in an episode were of greater importance to the child than transactions with nonsocial habitat

TABLE 8.6.   Percent of Standard and Observer Episodes with Superior Potency of Social Field

					Midwest						Disabled			All
Episodes	MC	JS	DT	MR	RB	ME	DC	CG	Mdn	WW	SD	VT	Mdn	Mdn
Standard	95	96	94	94	96	92	88	90	94	94	94	97	94	94
Observer	96	98	97	93	97	93	96	97	96	98	93	99	98	97

objects. This leaves for consideration the basic weighting of the social action units in the days of the children, concerning which Table 8.7 gives for each record the percent of standard

TABLE 8.7.   Percent of Standard and Observer Episodes with Primary Relative Weight

					Midwest						Disabled			All
Episodes	MC	JS	DT	MR	RB	ME	DC	CG	Mdn	WW	SD	VT	Mdn	Mdn
Standard	92	93	86	94	84	83	88	84	87	89	86	84	86	86
Observer	74	88	56	90	64	55	86	68	71	72	70	83	72	72

units and observer units with a primary weight rating. The percent of the former with primary weight may be seen to range from 83 to 94. This means that a large majority of the episodes involving the children in relationships with participant associates either stood alone, with no others overlapping with them, or outranked overlapping units in potency. The table shows that social episodes were preponderantly of first order potency even when observers were the associates. But the percent of primary observer units is lower for each of the 11 days, with the median of the actual differences 16 percent. Data not tabled here indicate further that nonsocial or only potentially social episodes are not consistently higher or lower, but more variable, in potency than social episodes, with observers or Midwesterners as associates. At all events, the social units were characteristically preemptive.

SUMMARY OF THE EPISODE SURVEY

Excluding observers as associates, and assuming validity of the ratings and judgments, we draw from the foregoing a number of generalizations about the social situations and behavior of the Midwest children.

The episodes were preponderantly social. A substantial majority of them involved the children with interacting individuals, and most of the remaining episodes occurred in behavior settings that made social behavior objects available.

Much more often than not, others became associates of the children one at a time, although groupings of two or more individuals did occur as compound associates in 4 to 21 percent of all social episodes in the different days. The percent of episodes in which behavior was transacted with these complex social units increased with age of the children.

Single individuals as associates included mothers, fathers, teachers, relatives in addition to parents, grownups exclusive of all relatives and teachers, pets, and other children. Above all, the associates were adults. Among adults, mothers participated in the largest number of episodes, teachers in the next to the largest. Teachers had a part in more episodes than mothers for three children among the four of school age. Fathers were associates much less frequently than mothers and, for the four older children, much less frequently than teachers. Although parents and teachers account for a large majority of the children's transactions with adults, while relatives who were not parents formed a small minority of associates, other Midwest grownups entered some episodes of every child. There remain chiefly other children as associates. The four younger subjects had few child associates. Episodes with other children increased, however, as the children grew older. At the same time, episodes with adult associates were most frequent among the younger children. In general, the younger were reared more by adults, the older more by peers. The child associates themselves were about equally divided among older, same age, and younger children, the older decreasing and the younger increasing in frequency with age of the subjects.

The children behaved in one way or another in relation to all of their associates, by definition. But the other person did not always reciprocate. Action in only the one direction occurred in approximately one fifth of the episodes. In those remaining, the action circuit, opened either by the child or an associate, was closed, with behavior occurring on both sides. Thus, in something like four out of every five episodes, an associate and the child completed a social interchange.

Beyond being extensive, the social activity of the children was also intensive in two ways. First, the parts of their social episodes involving the children with associates generally were superior to the nonsocial parts in potency. Things and relations with things were subordinated to individuals and relations with individuals in roughly 9 of 10 episodes in the day of every child. Second, in a ratio near nine to one, the social episodes themselves either occurred alone with no other action units intersecting with them or outranked overlapping episodes in relative importance; the social units of each day were not often crowded out by other units or left subordinate to others in relative weight.

Observers became associates of the children in 16 to 33 percent of all social and extrasocial episodes. There are indications, however, that involvement of observers with the children was quite restricted and shallow. Most notably, the action circuits of episodes with observers were much less frequently closed than those of episodes with participant associates in six of the eight days, and the frequency of observer episodes with high relative weight was lower in each day. The relative potency of the social field was consistently greater with observers as associates, but this can be attributed to restriction of action by the observer to mainly verbal behavior, short of participation with the child in activities involving nonsocial behavior objects.

The disabled children differ in important ways from the Midwest children in the composition of their associate realm. Despite this and the additional fact of their physical limitations, consistent differences between them and the Midwest children in other variables of the survey do not appear. There is no evidence that physical disability and its immediate consequences in social behavior settings and objects influence habitat and behavior on this basic level.

INTERACTION EPISODES OF THE SURVEY

Gains made in selection of social action units for analysis can now be consolidated.

We began with 10,406 episodes of 11 specimen day records. These have been sorted by the categories of Associate Complexity, Action Circuit, Potency of the Social Field, and Relative Weight. Below, expressed in percents based upon pooled standard and observer episodes of all 11 records, are data that represent the main steps of the sorting process and redistill its findings.

1. Eighty-two percent of these episodes are social, in that they involved the children with associates.
2. Of these social episodes, 92 percent are regular, i.e., adequately recorded and substantial units.
3. Ninety percent of the regular social episodes involved the child with single individuals, called simple associates, rather than groupings of individuals, called compound associates.
4. Of the regular social episodes with simple associates: (a) 77 percent are marked by social action on both sides of the relationship between associate and child; (b) 95 percent are

characterized by superior importance of social as against non-social habitat objects; and (c) 84 percent are of first order relative weight.

One more step shows that 4661, or 66 percent, of the regular social episodes with simple associates have in common the features of closed action circuit, superior potency of the social field, and primary importance in relation to simultaneously occurring episodes. This is to say that these units are comparable in fundamental ways. They alone have been analyzed by categories remaining in the descriptive scheme, and attention will be confined to them in all that follows. For study of the social habitat and behavior of these children, their most important common feature is two-sidedness of action relationship, for which reason we shall call them *interaction episodes*.

Table 8.8 presents a breakdown of these units into standard and observer episodes of the Midwest and disabled children. The N counts in this table give the major totals upon which all results to follow are based. Note that the totals range from 225

TABLE 8.8.   Number of Standard and Observer Interaction Episodes of Midwest and Disabled Children

Episodes	Midwest	Disabled	Total
Standard	2696	1065	3761
Observer	675	225	900
Total	3371	1290	4661

for observer episodes of the disabled children to 2696 for standard episodes of Midwest children. Episodes with observers as associates make up 19 percent of the total for all subjects, 20 percent for Midwest children, and 17 percent for disabled children. Comparison of these values with those of Table 8.2 shows that they are of the same order of magnitude as the percent of all social units with observers as associates among both social and extrasocial episodes in each record.

Table 8.9 lists the different associate classes common to the

TABLE 8.9. Number of Interaction Episodes with Specified Associates

				Midwest							Disabled			All
Associates	MC	JS	DT	MR	RB	ME	DC	CG	All	WW	SD	VT	All	All
PARTICIPANT ADULTS														
Mothers	378	184	164	289	40	75	25	30	1185	83	48	69	200	1385
Fathers	69	135	40	16	22	9	9	–	300	11	–	41	52	352
Teachers	–	–	–	25	77	47	35	32	216	–	53	61	114	330
All	458	327	235	369	152	136	124	62	1863	102	168	212	482	2345
PARTICIPANT CHILDREN														
Friends	–	20	–	88	121	101	103	21	454	221	70	172	463	917
Siblings	68	–	82	24	–	6	17	33	230	27	–	16	43	273
All	68	20	–	112	121	107	120	54	602	248	70	188	506	1108
All	533	348	359	501	293	281	252	129	2696	368	280	417	1065	3761
Observer	76	35	66	121	63	73	206	35	675	60	46	119	225	900

NOTE: The entries opposite All are not in every case column totals, for the reason that the associate classes represented in the table are not all-inclusive.

children in numbers of episodes large enough for statistical purposes. Here are the principal groupings of individual Midwest people, Lawton residents, and others who interacted with the children in episodes of high social potency and primary relative weight.

Every grownup is included among *all* adults in the total associate realm of the subjects, not just mothers, fathers, and teachers. Similarly, *all* participant associates include every individual, all mothers, fathers, teachers, brothers, sisters, schoolmates, neighbors, store clerks, pets, and others.

Study of the data shows that the essential findings of the survey of associates in standard social episodes, as reported on pages 202–211, hold also for the interaction episodes of Table 8.9. This appears to be true at any rate of findings with pertinence for the data to follow. It holds with unimportant qualification for the proportions of adult and child associates, for the proportion of adult friends among adult associates en masse, and for the relative frequency of younger children, children of the same age, and older children among child associates. For these reasons, a special associate survey of the standard interaction episodes will not be reported. We present only the data of Table 8.9 to show the N totals upon which later analysis is based.

Gaps in Table 8.9 will be noted; certain associate classes are not represented in some of the records. Most of those missing are accounted for in the sketches on children prepared in connection with their day records and presented in the Appendix. Concerning this it is mentioned further that, since the basic N for all of the comparisons and correlations (with age) is the number of subjects, these gaps count against findings beyond chance expectation. The same holds, of course, for classes of associates that are in some cases meagerly represented, as in the instance of the father for Mary Ennis and Douglas Crawford.

A few of the entries in Table 8.9 call for brief comment.

As anticipated, in the episodes of Sue Dewall with "mothers," the associate was an aide at Lawton who, in view of the role she filled in relation to Sue, was considered a mother equivalent.

The total number of sibling associates was relatively low; and it may be seen that for Jimmy Sexton and Raymond Birch, both only children, and for Sue Dewall, who had no contacts with family members on the day of her record, associates of this class were lacking. Furthermore, the siblings remaining differ so greatly as to age and sex that, for many purposes, it becomes questionable to group them. Yet, for other purposes, we have thought it worthwhile to compare the sibling episodes with those involving other associates, as in asking whether the brothers and sisters of these children differed from their parents in frequency of nurturant behavior. For the reasons indicated, this grouping will be given separate consideration only in special cases. Special attention is called to the 82 sibling episodes in the day of Dutton Thurston which are entered in Table 8.9 in italics to set them apart from others of this class. In all of these, the sibling was a brother or a sister, both of whom we have classified in Table 8.4 with adolescents, although the brother was a young adult. These episodes are excluded from those in the total for child associates en masse. For purposes to be represented later, however, it has seemed profitable to group them with episodes in which the sibling associates were children.

We are confronted by the upshot of this sorting process with a defined population of social action units in which the Midwest and disabled children interacted with social habitat objects of a defined associate realm. Thus far, however, nothing has been said about the nature and development of the person-to-person relationship between associate and child. Some basic elements of this relationship are now to be considered.

POWER AND SEQUENCE RELATIONS

RELATIVE POWER

Figure 8.2 presents a graph based on the ratio scale for measurement of Relative Power. It shows for each child in relation to his total realm of participant associates the median and inter-quartile range of all ratings on this dimension.

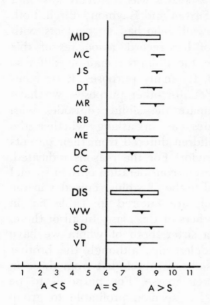

Fig. 8.2. Relative power of Midwest and disabled children in relation to all associates. *A* designates power of associates, *S* power of subjects. The vertical line is erected on the middlemost point of the power scale, represented by the base line. It stands for equality of power between *A* and *S*. The individual children of the Midwest (*MID*) and disabled (*DIS*) groups are listed in the order of their ages to the left of this line. Each horizontal bar extends through the interquartile range of the power ratings for a single child or for one of the two groupings of children. The mean rating in each case is indicated by an arrowhead extending downward from the bar.

The data show that these children lived the social parts of their days in action relationships with individuals generally more powerful than they, i.e., with persons whose rated ability at the time to change the behavior of the child usually exceeded his ability to change theirs. This may be the fate of children everywhere, which is not to say that there are no substantial differences across communities and cultures in the relative power of children. For the record, in any case, the median of our ratings on the 11-point scale is 8.4 and 8.1 for the Midwest and disabled children.

Age and power in Midwest are related in two ways. First, the older the child, the greater his relative power, as shown by a correlation of .93, significant beyond .01. Second, the older the child, the more variable his relative power. Evidence of continuous increase with age in power fluctuation is no better than a correlation of .57, with a p of .10. But inspection of Figure 8.2 leaves no doubt that the power relations of the four younger, preschool children were more stable than those of the four older, school children; and no doubt is left either that greater power was held by the older.

As we have seen, the power ratings were guided by an expectation that, given a child C, his power with an associate A generally will depend in part, though not entirely, upon how much bigger or smaller, stronger or weaker, and higher or lower in enduring status position A is than C (see p. 135). Thus, earlier tables that identify associates of the different children as to age and role classification anticipate these data; and so also do earlier findings on the Midwest children of increase with age in frequency of child associates and decrease with age in frequency of adult associates. The older child subjects interacted more with children and less with adults; therefore, their relative power was greater. The older children divided their interactions more between children and adults; therefore, their relative power was less stable.

Dependence of the associate to child ratio of power upon difference in maturity level between child and associate is confirmed by Figure 8.3. Note first the graph on the left. Its medians and measures of dispersion show that, with adults, the Midwest and disabled children were in a greatly inferior power position that varied little from episode to episode. Surprisingly enough, this position varied scarcely at all from child to child; the medians from Mary through Verne form a nearly straight vertical line. Generalized, these data would say, among other things, that neither growing up from 2 to 11 nor being physically normal within this age range will gain you anything in power relations with adults in Midwest or its vicinity.

The graph on the right states a quite different case about children with children. The medians here do show a gain in power with age, confirmed by a rank correlation of $-.71$, significant beyond .05,[1] between age of subject and power of as-

---

[1] The magnitude and significance of this coefficient are reduced by loss of a case owing to Dutton's day without child associates.

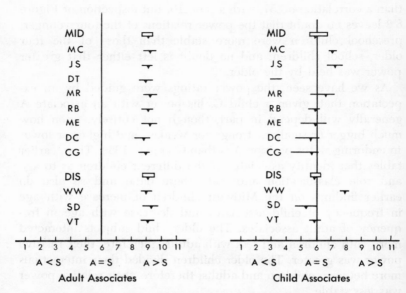

Fig. 8.3. Relative power of Midwest and disabled children in relation to adult associates and child associates. (Cf. Fig. 8.2.)

sociate. The quartile deviations appear to be similarly related with age, although the coefficient in this case (.57, with a *p* of .10) is low and of doubtful significance. It obviously is pertinent to both of these age relationships that growing up necessarily carries with it a gain in the person-anchored correlates of power in relation to a constantly increasing number of children.

Comparison of the graphs in Figure 8.3 shows that each of the children had higher relative power in interactions with children than in interactions with adults. The median of the actual differences is 3.2 scale points for the Midwest subjects. There is a correlation of .67, significant beyond .05, between these differences and age, which means that the degree in which power with other children outranks power with adult associates increases with age.

A canvass of likely power differences as between different

principal associates shows that in their relations with the children, (a) mothers had greater power than child friends, (b) mothers had greater power than siblings, and (c) adults en masse had greater power than observers, according to the ratings. The first two of these differences has a p of .05, and the third a p of .01. A tendency toward greater power on the part of teachers than child associates is suggested by a p of .10.

Outstanding among these differences is the evidence of relatively low power of observers as compared with other adults. Observers, no less than these other mature persons, had many characteristic power traits that go with maturity. Yet they evidently managed to place and keep themselves in relatively powerless positions, as it was their aim to do. This fact goes to show that adulthood in itself was not the only factor in the higher relative power of adults.

No consistent differences in the power ratings are evident as between the Midwest and disabled children. The main findings on the power relations of the children will be noted again at later points in the description.

ACTION SEQUENCE

We are concerned here with two questions about the sequential character of the interaction between associate and child: Who started it? And how far did it go? Answers to each of these questions will be considered separately.

INITIATION BY SUBJECT VERSUS INITIATION BY ASSOCIATE. Table 8.10 records for every day the percent of standard and

TABLE 8.10. Percent of Standard and Observer Interaction Episodes in Which Interaction Was Initiated by the Subject

| Episodes | Midwest | | | | | | | | | Disabled | | | | All |
	MC	JS	DT	MR	RB	ME	DC	CG	Mdn	WW	SD	VT	Mdn	Mdn
Standard	50	56	52	50	40	51	56	46	50	50	54	47	50	50
Observer	77	82	83	85	76	82	91	62	82	93	89	85	89	85

observer episodes in which interaction was initiated by subjects rather than associates. It shows that, for both the Midwest children and the disabled children, "starting it" in relations with participant associates occurred about half of the time. One might have predicted from the data on relative power a quite different result. It seems reasonable to expect from greatly superior power on the side of participant associates that they would outdo the children in taking the lead. For these children, however, initiation of interplay evidently has nothing to do with relative power, or at least, with the use of it. Apparently, too, initiation, unlike power, has nothing to do with age. There is no evidence either that it depends upon differences between the Midwest and disabled children, or that it varies with differences between different classes of associates.

But all of this applies only to participant associates; the observer is again in a class by himself. In no case does the percent of observer episodes in which interaction was initiated by the child fall below 62; it reaches 93 for disabled Wally, with the median 82 for the Midwest children, and 85 for the three disabled children. The main thing to be said about this, we think, is that the observers apparently stood rather well by their policy of noninterference, leaving it to the child to take the greater initiative.

CYCLICAL VERSUS NONCYCLICAL INTERACTION.   In a noncyclical interaction, again, X does something, Y reacts—and that is all; whereas, in a cyclical interaction, there occurs in addition at least an action by X in response to the reaction by Y. If only in total amount of social behavior, cyclical interplay is the more complex.

Table 8.11 gives for all records the percent of standard and observer episodes in which cyclical interaction occurred. It shows first that, for every Midwest child but one, and for the three disabled children, action relationships with participant associates were preponderantly cyclical, with the median percents for the Midwest and disabled children respectively 62 and 64. Continuance of interaction with participant associates beyond one act and a response occurred, then, substantially more often than not.

TABLE 8.11.   Percent of Standard and Observer Interaction Episodes in Which Interaction Was Cyclical

| Episodes | Midwest | | | | | | | | | Disabled | | | | All |
	MC	JS	DT	MR	RB	ME	DC	CG	Mdn	WW	SD	VT	Mdn	Mdn
Standard	64	72	65	57	62	62	50	56	62	70	65	70	70	64
Observer	60	39	57	40	54	57	40	32	47	47	58	62	58	54

The range for the Midwest children extends from 50 to 72, and variation within this range is age related as shown by a rank order correlation of $-.68$, with a p value of .05, between age and percent of cyclical interactions. This indication was surprising to us. Why should the relative frequency of the seemingly more complex interactions go down with age? Toward an answer, we have run correlations between age and percent of cyclical interactions with different classes of associates, to find that: the negative relationship holds only for adults; there is no correlation between age and relative frequency of cyclical interactions with other children en masse or with other children of any associate class. For adult associates, the coefficient is $-.93$, significant at .01. For mothers only, it is $-.54$, with a p of .10; for fathers, $-.52$, with a p of .15. Generalized, these data would mean that, for whatever reasons, the more adult in point of age Midwest children become, the more noncyclical are their interactions with adults. Here is an episode from our record on Claire Graves—the oldest child of the study—who has been helping Mrs. Graves get breakfast.

Claire said to her mother, "Did you forget about the cocoa?"
Her mother said pleasantly, "You know, I haven't forgotten, but I guess it should be moved," and she then took the cocoa off the fire.

The following is an episode from the record on Douglas Crawford, next to the oldest child, who is reading in the living room of his home.

Mrs. Crawford came into the room and said, "Well, you found your *Ben Hur* book."

"Oh, no," Douglas said, while he went on reading, "I'm not looking at that."

These X, Y rather than X, Y, X . . . exchanges are typical of noncyclical interactions with adults that occur increasingly with advance in the maturity of the children, and now that we look at them on the child side, they seem rather adult.

Noncyclical interaction may be more common among mature persons than its simplicity at first suggests. Much social intercourse between adults is of the noncyclical variety; and it could be argued that this is often both a result and a requirement of social efficiency, if not of sociability, as when a conductor says, "Your ticket, please," and a passenger only hands over the ticket. On the other hand, much social behavior of very young children with adults is protractedly cyclical, sometimes owing to the child's wish to socialize, as in saying, "Goodnight, mother" 20 times running, and frequently, because of social inefficiency, as when, in episode 21 of Chapter 7, two-year-old Mary Chaco wound her parents up with her in a tedious effort to identify a wanted dish of salad, whereas an older child might well have asked for and received the salad in an easy noncyclical transaction. One could not use frequency of noncyclical interaction in an unqualified way as a measure of maturity; obviously, extended social give-and-take is characteristic of mature persons under some conditions, as in examination of a witness, whereas one *give* followed by no more than one *take* is characteristic of immature persons under other conditions. Special study of the conditions under which cyclical and noncyclical interactions occur at different age levels could be interesting.

The percent of cyclical interactions with observers is consistently below the same with participant associates. The percents for observer episodes vary greatly from child to child, but they do not turn out to be related with age. Also, there are no significant differences in this variable as between different classes of associates.

ACTION BY ASSOCIATE AND CHILD

Except for information to identify associates, everything reported to this point on the social behavior and situations of the children has been concerned most with formal characteristics of person-to-person relations within episodes. Qualitative characteristics of the behavior in the interactions between associate and child have been left out of account. Helping, attacking, resisting, submitting, praising, blaming, and other distinctive kinds of social behavior occurred on both sides in these interactions, as we have learned from episodes of the foregoing chapter, and our problem now is to quantify such phenomena.

As anticipated by the categories on page 130, action by associates and subjects will be described under two headings, Modes of Action and Attributes of Action. Episodes of the Midwest children with participant associates are to get first and most notice, but episodes with observers and differences between the Midwest and disabled children also will be considered.

MODES OF ACTION

BEHAVIOR OF ASSOCIATES

RELATIVE FREQUENCY OF ACTION MODES. We begin here with the relative frequency of different modes of action by participant associates en masse of the Midwest children. Figure 8.4 serves the purpose.

All action modes were ranked in order on the basis of the percent of units in which they occurred in the standard interaction episodes of every record. Each bar of the figure shows the mean of the ranks for a given mode, and the median percent appears in each case beneath the bar. Probability values are reported as explained in the caption of the figure.

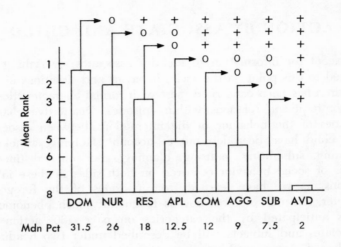

Fig. 8.4. Relative frequency of different modes of action by all participant associates of the Midwest children. Names of the modes are abbreviated as follows: *DOM*, dominance; *NUR*, nurturance; *RES*, resistance; *APL*, appeal; *COM*, compliance; *AGG*, aggression; *SUB*, submission; *AVD*, avoidance. Each mode is represented by a bar whose height expresses the mean of the ranks established by first determining for each record the percent of standard interaction episodes in which the given mode was judged to occur, and then arranging the obtained percents in order of magnitude. For every mode the median percent (*Mdn Pct*) is entered under the appropriate bar. Attention is called to the symbols, + and 0, and to their placement in relation to the bars and arrows. A plus (+) over one bar and opposite the arrow extending from another denotes a difference in mean rank significant beyond the 5 percent level between the modes represented by the two bars. For example, the + over *RES* and opposite the arrow extending from *DOM* shows that dominance significantly outranks resistance with the *p* value of this difference beyond .05, while the 0 over *NUR* and opposite the arrow extending from *DOM* shows that nurturance and dominance do not differ significantly in rank.

The array of ranks here and in similar presentations to follow raises the question of how consistent the frequency pattern is from child to child. We have computed in answer the coefficient of concordance, W, for each array. W is .81, with a p of .01 in the present case; and although the coefficient is considerably lower in some instances, it is significant beyond .01 for all of the other distributions as well.

It may be seen that among the modes of action by associates, in toto, dominance, nurturance, and resistance rank highest, and avoidance lowest, with appeal, compliance, aggression, and submission of relatively low and insignificantly differing rank. Dominance of the children was found in nearly one third of their episodes with persons other than observers. But note also that the median percent on nurturance is 26, and that dominance does not exceed nurturance consistently; evidently, although others applied much authoritarian pressure, they tended about as strongly to benefit the children. Resistance is nevertheless prominent in the picture. This kind of behavior is outranked significantly only by dominance, and it ranks consistently above every other mode but nurturance and appeal. Avoidance is all but out of the pattern.

Aggression is notably low on the list, and some readers may find this surprising. They may recall in any case that our aim throughout is to describe social action, not social motivation, above the threshold for perception of behavior by the children themselves.

Modes of action by adults, represented in Figure 8.5, may be seen at once to differ little from the same by associates en masse. Adults got into the social episodes of the children more often than others, as Table 8.4 has shown. But it is now clear also that they were far from being neutral agents. Near identity of Figures 8.4 and 8.5 suggests that, instead, adults put their stamp on the ways in which all others treated the children.

Only one difference between the frequency pattern for all associates and the one for adults alone is apparent. Resistance ranks lower in the latter. It consistently exceeds avoidance only in the adult array, whereas it significantly outranks compliance,

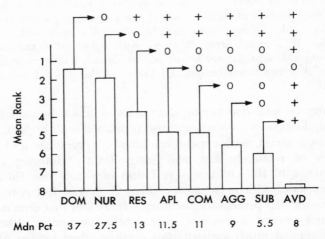

Fig. 8.5. Relative frequency of different modes of action by all participant adult associates of the Midwest children. (Cf. Fig. 8.4.)

aggression, submission, and avoidance in the one for all associates. Yet it cannot be said that adults steered clear of contention with the children. Contention in the more pushing form of dominance is rivalled only by nurturance as a kind of social action by adults.

Figure 8.6 shows the rankings for child associates. Resistance here outranks all other ways of behaving. Its rate exceeds significantly that of appeal, submission, aggression, and avoidance. Nurturance follows next, although it consistently exceeds only compliance and avoidance. Other divergencies of child associates from adults in mean rank of the modes will be noted. There is no further evidence, however, that any one of the kinds of behavior by other children, dominance, appeal, submission, aggression, or avoidance, occurred more or less often than another with consistency among the eight subjects. Dominance is in the foreground; it is next to nurturance in mean rank, and the median percent of episodes, 15, in which it was found is relatively high.

DIFFERENCES BETWEEN CLASSES OF PARTICIPANT ASSOCIATES. Comparison of Figures 8.5 and 8.6 raises the question of dissimilarity between different classes of associates. Actually, only one difference between all adult and all child associates is significant beyond .05, namely, one showing more frequent dominance by adults. But breakdowns reveal, in differences significant beyond .05, dominance by mothers more frequent than by child friends, and avoidance by child friends more frequent than by mothers.

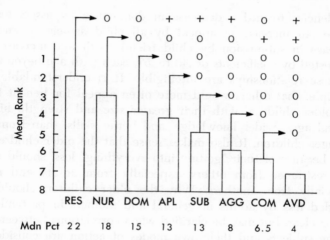

Fig. 8.6. Relative frequency of different modes of action by all child associates of the Midwest children. (Cf. Fig. 8.4.)

The evidence that mothers shunned the subject less frequently than other children fits the adage about a boy's best friend. But we are impressed more by the greater prominence among mothers of dominative behavior. However one looks at the data, this directive, ruling kind of social action stands out in the behavior of Midwest adults with the children, although the high rank of nurturance among the same adults should be kept in view.

AGE RELATIONSHIPS. Does age of the children make a difference to kind of social behavior with the child? There is evidence that it does for appeal, resistance, and avoidance. Correlations show that, with increase in age of the children:

appeal by associates en masse *increases* (.82, $p < .01$);
appeal by all adults *increases* (.68, $p < .05$);
resistance by all adults *decreases* ($-.61, p < .05$);
resistance by mothers in particular *decreases* ($-.71, p < .05$);
avoidance by all adults *decreases* ($-.71, p < .05$);
avoidance by mothers *decreases* ($-.71, p < .05$).

Tendencies toward a decrease in dominance by associates en masse, an increase in appeal by all child associates, and an increase in submission by child friends with age increase are suggested by coefficients of .46 to .57, each with a p beyond .10.

These relationships are intelligible. It is understandable, for example, that others would more often appeal for benefit from the older children, with their greater size and strength, higher mental ages, wider knowledge, and better skills, than from the younger children. It also makes sense that the older children, if only because of their "getting into everything" less, should meet less resistance from others, especially from adults and more especially from mothers. Why the older children should be avoided less by adults in general and mothers in particular is not so clear, but may be clarified when correlations between age of the subjects and their own modes of action are considered. Meanwhile, these age relationships contribute to a developmental psychology of the social environment in Midwest.

One cannot help but note kinds of action by adult associates that do not change with age of the children. This holds arrestingly for nurturance and dominance, both of which have appeared above as the most frequent kinds of adult behavior with the children. There is no evidence that, as might be expected, nurturance by adults declines with age; and there is no evidence that, as some might expect and be pleased to discover, dominance by adults declines with age. Through the whole child span of years 2 to 11, these two ways of adult behaving are found in the raw data to be remarkably constant at the levels shown by the median percents of Figure 8.5.

So much for modes of action on the associate side.

BEHAVIOR OF SUBJECTS

Figure 8.7 represents the relative frequency of the action modes on the child side, and it tells a different story.

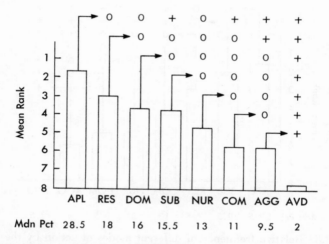

Fig. 8.7. Relative frequency of different modes of action by the Midwest children in relation to all participant associates. (Cf. Fig. 8.4.)

Appeal is the most prominent kind of social behavior by the children. The median percent of interaction episodes in which it was scored is 28.5, and it significantly outranks all other modes but resistance, dominance, and nurturance. Resistance is the nearest in frequency to appeal, but the only kinds of behavior that it consistently outranks are avoidance and aggression. Avoidance is again near zero, relatively, and it is significantly less frequent than every other mode. This leaves dominance, submission, nurturance, compliance, and aggression, no one of which occurred relatively more or less often than another.

Modes of action by the children with adults alone are represented in Figure 8.8. As indicated by both the median percents and the mean ranks, appeal remains at the top, and avoidance at the bottom, of the hierarchy. Submission, however, replaces resistance as the mode nearest to the top, with its frequency near that of appeal. Yet resistance, the opposite of submission,

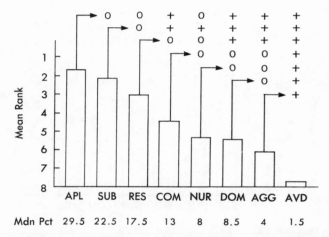

Fig. 8.8. Relative frequency of different modes of action by the Midwest children in relation to all participant adult associates. (Cf. Fig. 8.4.)

is next in order, although this kind of action with adults does fall below submission in the number of other modes that it consistently outranks. Again, nothing can be said with confidence about the relative frequency of nurturance, compliance, dominance, and aggression.

In short, then, soliciting benefit, giving in to pressure, and holding out against pressure are the preponderant varieties of behavior by the children with adults; and we shall later give

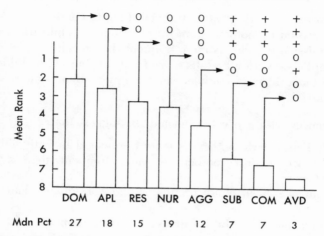

Fig. 8.9. Relative frequency of different modes of action by the Midwest children in relation to all child associates. (Cf. Fig. 8.4.)

special attention to the second of these, submission, and the first, appeal.

Figure 8.9, which shows modes of action by the children with children, makes two points especially, when it is compared with the graph for the children with adults. First, whereas submission is one of the most frequent kinds of behavior by the children with adults, it is one of the least frequent by the children with children. Second, whereas dominance is one of the least frequent by the children with adults, it is one of the most frequent by the children with children. Giving in to adults, but dominating peers, would seem to have been a common rule.

In actions by the children with child associates, dominance, appeal, and resistance all rank significantly above submission, compliance, and avoidance, with the last again the least frequent.

DIFFERENCES IN BEHAVIOR TOWARD DIFFERENT CLASSES OF ASSOCIATES.   All possible comparisons across associate classes on every action mode reveal differences, significant beyond .05, that show the following.

submission to adults *more* frequent than to children;
submission to mothers *more* frequent than to child friends;
submission to mothers *more* frequent than to siblings;
compliance with all adults *more* frequent than with children;
resistance against mothers *more* frequent than against child friends.

Differences with a p value beyond .10 suggest that:

compliance with mothers is *more* frequent than with siblings;
resistance against mothers is *more* frequent than against teachers;
dominance over child friends is *more* frequent than over mothers;
dominance over child friends is *more* frequent than over teachers;
aggression against mothers is *more* frequent than against teachers;
nurturance of siblings is *more* frequent than that of mothers.

These comparisons are consistent with the differences found when modes of action by different classes of associates were compared. More frequent dominance by adults than by children is complemented now by more frequent submission to adults, and by more frequent compliance with them, especially with mothers as associates. On the other hand, as if to balance accounts with adults by subjugating peers, the children evidently dominated child friends more than mothers, who so often dominated them, and also more than teachers. Teachers evoked more than mothers a kind of "tread easy" policy, to judge from indications of comparatively low resistance and aggression against them. That the children were bolder in resisting mothers than child friends is against the drift of the data. But this holds only for mothers, not for any other class of adults, and not for adults en masse. Mothers may generally learn not to expect returns on their nurturant behavior. Yet they might be surprised by our evidence that the children acted less often to benefit mothers than to benefit brothers and sisters.

AGE RELATIONSHIPS. Correlations show that, with increase in age of the children:

appeal to all associates *decreases* $(-.61, p < .05)$;
compliance with all associates *increases* $(.67, p < .05)$;
compliance with all adult associates *increases* $(.71, p < .05)$;
nurturance of all associates *increases* $(.64, p < .05)$;
nurturance of all adult associates *increases* $(.64, p < .05)$;
nurturance of all child associates *increases* $(.67, p < .05)$.

Tendencies toward an increase in nurturance of mothers, an increase in dominance over siblings, a decrease in resistance against teachers, and an increase in submission to adults with increase in age are suggested by coefficients from .51 to .80, all with a p beyond .10.

These are measurements of social maturing in terms which, at least in Midwest, are widely recognized and endorsed as signs of growing up. Midwest adults to whom we have shown the data say that they do expect children to ask for benefit from others less as they grow older, to comply more with requests, especially when these are made by adults, to help, protect, or give things to others more, to resist their teachers less, by all means, and also to submit to adults more. Some of them express surprise that we do not find aggression decreasing with age of the children. In general, however, there is congruence between the data and expectation norms of Midwest.

Yet certain relationships with age of the children are again conspicuous by their absence or lack of strength. This is true especially for two prominent modes: resistance and submission. Resistance against associates in general, against adults en masse, against mothers, fathers, child friends, and siblings varies little in frequency through the age span; it stands in the records of all subjects near the median percents in Figures 8.7 through 8.9. The same holds for submission to all associates, to mothers, to fathers, and to teachers. There is indeed some indication that, in relating themselves to adults, the older children submitted even more often than the younger. To say the least, with increasing age of the children, submission does not go down; nor does resistance change at all.

ASSOCIATE BEHAVIOR VERSUS SUBJECT BEHAVIOR

Having considered action by associates and action by the children, we turn to direct comparison of associate behavior with subject behavior in Figure 8.10, where the bars show the median

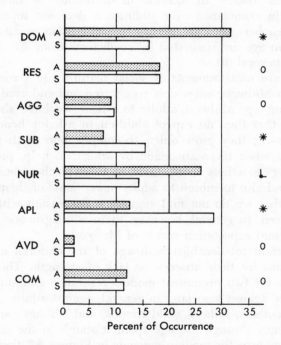

Fig. 8.10. Modes of action by all associates versus modes of action by the Midwest children. A denotes action by associate; S action by subject. The symbols on the right refer to significance levels of the represented differences as follows: ∗, P < .01; ⌐, p < .10; 0, no significant difference.

percents of all standard interaction episodes on each side in the social exchange.

Greater frequency of dominance by associates, of submission by the subjects, and of appeal by the subjects appear, with more nurturance by associates. Otherwise, there are no consistent dissimilarities between the children and the generality of others.

All possible comparisons of action by associates of subordinate classes with action by the children show or suggest that:

dominance by subjects is *less* frequent than by
adults en masse ($p < .01$),
mothers ($p < .05$),
fathers ($p < .05$),
teachers ($p < .10$);

submission by subjects is *more* frequent than by
adults ($p < .01$),
mothers ($p < .01$),
fathers ($p < .05$),
teachers ($p < .10$);

appeal by subjects is *more* frequent than by
adults ($p < .01$),
mothers ($p < .05$),
fathers ($p < .05$);

nurturance by subjects is *less* frequent than by
adults ($p < .10$),
mothers ($p < .01$),
fathers ($p < .05$),
teachers ($p < .10$);

resistance by subjects is *more* frequent than by
adults ($p < .10$),
mothers ($p < .10$),
all child associates ($p < .05$),
child friends ($p < .05$).

This breakdown still leaves dominance, submission, and appeal in the foreground as kinds of behavior in which the children differed from individuals with whom they interacted. But it also points in each case to adults on the associate side. The children evidently got from adults, and most of all from parents, a good deal more than they gave in dominative behavior, and gave the more in submissive behavior and dependent asking behavior. Not to be overlooked here is the evidence of more frequent nurturance by associates, adults in particular, and parents above others. Finally, there is the evidence of more frequent resistance by the subjects in their relations with adults, especially mothers, and, more consistently, in their relations with other children.

PATTERNING OF THE ACTION MODES

The data reported thus far on action modes may now be applied to description of the general habitat-and-behavior pattern of the children with others in Midwest.

Clues to a nuclear part of the pattern are in complementary relationships between the behavior of the children and behavior of their adult associates. In examining these and other relationships, we shall make some inferences about reciprocity of action, i.e., about how the children behaved when adults behaved thus and so. The idea is to approach understanding of action interdependencies from straight analysis of, first, associate behavior and, then, child behavior, in the episode population.

Frequent appeal by the children complements frequent nurturance by adults. It was the part of the children to ask and about equally often the part of adults to give. Here a dependency relation is evident, with the child as solicitor, petitioner, supplicant, and the adult as grantor, helper, protector. Frequent submission by the children complements frequent dominance by adults. Adults directed, and the children deferred only a little less often than they appealed; and, in this, there appears a control relation. These two relations of dependency and control seem fundamental in action relationships involving the children with adults.

With qualifications shortly to be stated, this much plus earlier findings on child power versus adult power suggests that the children lived with adults in a benevolent authoritarian regimen with the common features of superior power to benefit and dominate at work in actual beneficence and directiveness, on one side, and of inferior power and dependence realized in submission and appeal, on the other. This regimen had also the characteristic authoritarian feature of centralization, chiefly in mothers and next in teachers, of power actually used in nurturance and dominance. So it appears to have been with these children; and any to whom the main outline of the pattern looks strange must live a long way from Midwest. Evidently Midwest adults are on a pipeline of authoritarianism in child rearing that runs through a much wider culture.

The system did not hold the children in close subjection. Its machinery for managing, regulating, supervising, and settling things, for prohibiting and restraining, and for imposing conditions and requirements ran smoothly much of the time; for adults often achieved control, as we know from the high count on submission to them. Yet there was much resistance; the children held out against adults only a little less frequently than they gave in to them, especially in relations with mothers, who dominated them most. Resistance against the "leader," however, also is a common trait of the authoritarian social system, as experimental studies have shown (cf. Lippitt, 1940).

There is evidence that the pattern was not highly conflictive, as more autocratic social arrangements are sometimes found to be. Resistance complements dominance in a negative sense; as what you do to reciprocate if someone else dominates you first, it is in social principle a kind of equivalent to dominance. But contention with adults in the more positive form of dominance itself rarely occurred; the control relation evidently was too restraining for the children to tell their elders often what or what not to do. In any case, because dominance on the child side was relatively infrequent, interactions between grownups and the children were less conflictive than they would otherwise have been.

The pattern was not narrowly restrictive, muzzling, or oppressive. The considerable resistance by the children implies as much, and there is more direct evidence in the same direction, under

Action Sequence, in data to show that the children started things with others as often as their associates in every grouping, including adults.

Baldwin, Kalhorn, and Breese (1941, 1949) have disclosed different types of autocracy in adult-to-child relations. They distinguish especially family autocracies in which indulgence, hostility, and rejection are prominent. Evidently the Midwest pattern was not characteristically indulgent, hostile, or rejective, to judge from the high frequencies of both resistance and nurturance and the almost negligible frequency of avoidance in the behavior of adults with the children.

Some core features of the pattern changed little with increase in age of the children, while other quite central parts of it were altered by developmental forces.

The children did not outgrow essentials of the control relation in gaining nine years on adults.[2] Dominance by grownups did not go down during these years, and neither did submission to them; nor did resistance by the children against adults go up. Claire Graves at 10 years, 9 months was ordered and directed by grownups as much, while at the same time she gave in to them as much, as Mary Chaco at 1 year, 10 months; nor did Claire resist adults more. Resistance on the adult side did decrease with age of the children. We cannot say whether this was because the older children ran counter to adults less or because adults let them get away with more. There is indicated here in either case something of an increase in the liberality of adult control as the children matured, although the basic control relation evidently held firm through the nine years of growth.

There remains the dependency relation with its complementary elements of nurturance by adults and appeal to them. Increase in maturity evidently did not alter it on the associate side; for adult help, gratuities, and protection were extended to the older children no less than to the younger. But asking behavior of the children did yield to developmental change. While adults sustained fully their nurturant role with increase in age of the children, appeal to them by the children diminished. It appears that

[2] We suppose that it can do no harm here to write for convenience as if the study had been a longitudinal one.

the older children got more than they asked for; that adults kept saying in effect, "You need what we give you," while the children were telling them, by not appealing as often as earlier, "We can now get along better without you." Meanwhile, as they gained in maturity, the children gave more to adults instead of asking more from them. Their actions apparently began to say as they grew older, "You are still too big for us to boss you, but we can now benefit you." Let alone being receptive to this kind of behavior, the grownups on their side appealed increasingly to the children, evidently recognizing growth in ability to benefit them, as in getting dishes washed and having things put away.

How is the pattern affected by substitution of children for adults as associates? The situation of children with children cannot be represented sufficiently without quite exact specifications, not permitted by the data, of differences in age between child and child associate. But certain general characteristics of the interactions between the subjects and their child associates do appear.

In the first place, a control relation is not found in the situation of children with children. Dominance ranked high on both sides, but it was not complemented by frequent submission. Instead, on *each* side of the child to child relation, it was nearly matched in frequency by resistance. So the children did not give in to other children; they resisted them, or met dominance with dominance. There is no relation of control by other children over the subjects, or of the subjects over other children. But there is a well defined social relation nevertheless, namely, one of conflict.

High dominance in the pattern free of adults is arresting. It is as if the children took the dominance they got from adults and passed it on to their peers, who acted upon an equally fair chance to return it or resist it. There is some indication that the subjects resisted other children more than adults, perhaps because they controlled other children less, with the further consequence that other children tried to dominate them more.

The pattern involving the children with children does show the dependency relation, with its reciprocals of nurturance and appeal; there is frequent appeal by the children and comparably frequent nurturance by their child associates. Our best guess is that the older nurture the younger while the younger appeal to the older. Again, however, we are not now prepared to examine relations between children differing in age.

MIDWEST VERSUS DISABLED CHILDREN

The Festinger method (1946) was used to test the consistency of differences between the Midwest and disabled children in percent of episodes scored on each mode for subjects and associates.

Differences significant beyond .05 show that, in relative frequency, mothers of the disabled children were more nurturant, while child friends of the disabled were more aggressive and child friends of the Midwest children were more avoidant. Equally consistent differences show that, on their side, the disabled children appealed more frequently than the Midwest subjects for benefit from mothers, as also from adults in general, and that the disabled were more frequently aggressive and resisting, yet more often submissive with child associates. These differences are generally substantial, as indicated by the median percents of Table 8.12, which restates the comparisons.

Relatively great dependence of the disabled subjects appears in more frequent action by mothers to aid or protect them and in their own more frequent appeals to mothers and other adults. The data in Table 8.12 indicate further that Wally, Sue, and Verne did not get along with other children as well as the physically normal subjects of Midwest. They attacked and were attacked by other children, resisted them, and yet gave in to them more frequently. All of the child associates of Sue were disabled, all in Wally's day were physically normal, and Verne's were about equally divided between normal and disabled associates. These comparisons invite more study.

ACTION MODES AND THE OBSERVER

What modes of action were characteristic of observers in relations with the subjects? And vice versa? We will use here only data from the Midwest children.

TABLE 8.12.   Percent of Interaction Episodes of Midwest and Disabled Children in which Designated Modes of Action Occurred

Action by Associates	Nurturance by Mothers	Midwest	32
		Disabled	52
	Aggression by Child Friends	Midwest	6
		Disabled	20
	Avoidance by Child Friends	Midwest	5
		Disabled	2
Action by Subject	Appeal to Mothers	Midwest	34
		Disabled	54
	Appeal to Adults	Midwest	30
		Disabled	44
	Aggression Against Child Associates	Midwest	12
		Disabled	19
	Resistance Against Child Associates	Midwest	15
		Disabled	24
	Submission to Child Associates	Midwest	7
		Disabled	12

Figure 8.11 shows the relative frequency pattern for action by observers. In mean rank, nurturance is above all other modes, whereas it was second for participant adults. Compliance ranks second, whereas it outranked avoidance only for participant adults. Dominance is one of the three least frequent modes, whereas it was most frequent for the regular Midwest grownups.

The frequencies for action by the subjects toward observers are in Figure 8.12. Appeal holds the top position, as it did for behavior toward participant adults, and resistance is again third in mean rank. But there are two conspicuous differences. First, whereas submission ranked next to the top for action toward other adults, here it ranks last. Second, whereas nurturance ranked near the bottom for action toward other adults, here it is next to the top.

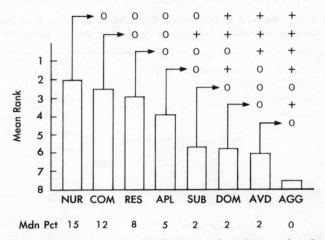

Fig. 8.11. Relative frequency of different modes of action by observers in relation to the Midwest children. (Cf. Fig. 8.4.)

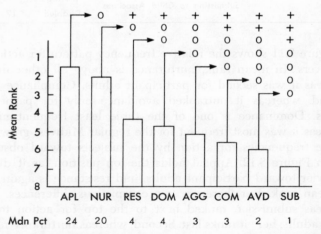

Fig. 8.12. Relative frequency of different modes of action by the Midwest children in relation to observers. (Cf. Fig. 8.4.)

The dependency relation evidently occurred in interactions with observers in that appeal and nurturance were most frequent for the children and the observers respectively. But the control relation breaks down; observers rarely dominated the children and the children rarely submitted to observers. The high place of dominance for the permanent residents is taken by compliance for observers, which suggests more control of observers by the children than the reverse. At the same time, frequent submission to participant adults is displaced by frequent action to benefit observers. The children tended more to be helpful and beneficent to observers, who dominated them little, than to participant adults, who dominated them much.

Comparisons a mode at a time of action by observers with action by participant adults shows that:

dominance by observers is *less* frequent ($p < .01$);
nurturance by observers is *less* frequent ($p < .01$);
resistance by observers is *less* frequent ($p < .05$);
aggression by observers is *less* frequent ($p < .01$);
avoidance by observers is *less* frequent ($p < .05$).

Comparisons on the subject side show that:

resistance against observers is *less* frequent ($p < .01$);
compliance with observers is *less* frequent ($p < .05$);
submission to observers is *less* frequent ($p < .01$).

In general, the differences of the present section fit the role that the observers aimed to play.

A canvass of possible correlations between age of the subjects and either action by or action toward observers reveals no relationships that differentiate observers from participant associates. Also, only one dissimilarity appears when observer episodes of the Midwest children and disabled children are compared: appeal to an observer was found more often in the episodes of the disabled children. Greater dependency of the physically handicapped children upon others apparently extended even to their relations with the observer, whose place in their situations we now know to have been peripheral.

ATTRIBUTES OF ACTION

AFFECTION, MOOD, AND EVALUATION

The analysis scheme defines affection, mood, and evaluation as dimensions of all social behavior that vary independently of the action modes. Each goes with aggressive, submissive, or nurturant action, or any other kind of interpersonal behavior. Findings on the attributes will be used to expand and qualify the description from the mode analysis. We shall consider the three variables together, first on the associate side and then on the child side, in the Midwest and disabled children's days.

BEHAVIOR OF ASSOCIATES. As explained more fully in Chapter 6, each attribute poses negative, neutral, and positive behavior on a U-shaped continuum, scaled with 11 points. Figure 8.13 shows for each of the Midwest and disabled children the median and interquartile range of the ratings on each variable in the behavior of all participant associates. It shows chiefly that associates en masse gravitated generally in their relations with the children to high positive affection, mood, and evaluation: individuals by and large with whom the subjects interacted evidently were given more to feeling for than to feeling against the children, more to happiness than to unhappiness, and more to approval than to disapproval of the children's conduct. For none of the variables does the median rating fall even to the neutral part of the continuum. Only for evaluation, moreover, do we find values of the interquartile range in the minus part of the scale, and this occurs in only 4 of the 11 days. Evaluation shows generally greater variability than affection or mood, apparent from inspection for all of the disabled children. The same difference among the Midwest children is significant beyond .01 for the comparison with mood, and beyond the .05 for the comparison with affection. It appears, then, that associates of the children were more steady in affective attitude and in general feeling tone than in approval or disapproval of what the children did.

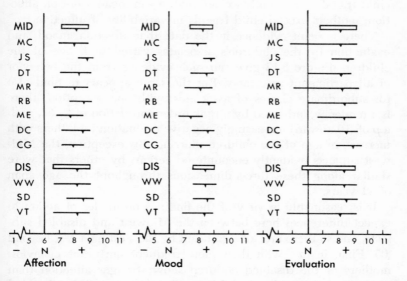

Fig. 8.13. Affection, mood, and evaluation on the part of participant associates en masse in relation to the Midwest and disabled children. The scales used to measure these attributes of action are represented by the baselines of the three graphs. Points *1* through *5* extend through the negative part, while points *7* through *11* extend through the positive part of each continuum. The vertical line erected on point *6*, the middlemost value of each scale, stands for behavior classified as neutral with respect to the given variable. The individual children of the Midwest (*MID*) and disabled (*DIS*) groups are listed in the order of their ages to the left of this line. Every horizontal bar of each graph extends through the interquartile range of the ratings for a single child or for one of the two groupings of children, with the median rating denoted by an arrowhead that points downward from the bar.

For the Midwest subjects, the graphs of Figure 8.13 are closely representative of the ratings on different classes of participant associates. All possible comparisons as between different associate classes reveal only two differences, both significant beyond .05:

child friends consistently exceed mothers in mean score on affection; mothers exceed child friends in variability of affection.

There is scant evidence in the data that affection, mood, and evaluation by the children's associates varied with age of the children; Figure 8.13 gives no such evidence from the behavior of all participant associates. But the same appears to hold also for subordinate classes of associates, with one exception; there is a tendency, indicated by a rank order correlation of —.62, with a p of .10, toward increasingly negative evaluation by fathers with increase in age of the children. Barring this exception, the Midwest subjects evidently encountered actions by others that were similar along these three dimensions throughout the age span of 11 years.

It is reasonable in view of the findings on modes of action to expect differences here between the Midwest and disabled subjects; and so there are, all significant by the Festinger test beyond .05. First, in line with their more frequent nurturant behavior, mothers of the disabled children show stronger affection than mothers of the Midwest children. Also, mothers of the disabled children show more highly positive mood. Stronger approval of conduct holds for child friends of the Midwest subjects, and child friends of the disabled display greater variability in affection.

BEHAVIOR OF SUBJECTS.   The children balanced accounts with participant associates in affection, mood, and evaluation, according to Figure 8.14. The dispersion values on affection and mood appear to be larger than on the associate side, and they are for two (Wally and Verne) of the three disabled children; but there is no consistent difference in this direction for the Midwest subjects. Variability of evaluation is lower than on the associate side.

We found in the behavior of associates greater affection for the Midwest children by child friends than by their mothers. A reciprocal to this now appears in greater affection by the children for child friends than for their mothers, significant at .05. Furthermore, differences at the same p level show more happiness with other children than with adults, and greater happiness with fathers than with mothers.

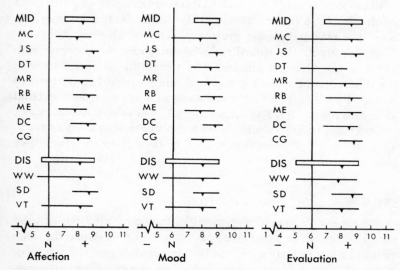

Fig. 8.14. Affection, mood, and evaluation on the part of the Midwest and disabled children in relation to participant associates en masse. (Cf. Fig. 8.13.)

Feeling for child associates goes down with age: the older the child the lower the mean rating on affection for other children, as shown by a correlation of —.60, which has a *p* of .05. A correlation of —.62, with a *p* of .10, suggests also a decline with age in positive evaluation of fathers' behavior, which reciprocates the tendency noted above toward decrease with age in favorable evaluation by fathers of the children's behavior.

Again, there are differences, significant beyond .05, between the Midwest and disabled children. This holds, however, only for episodes with other children. The disabled subjects, like their child associates, show greater variability in affection for other children than the Midwest subjects. Also, they show in episodes with other children greater fluctuation in both mood and evaluation. Further, the Midwest subjects stand higher than the disabled in plus evaluation of conduct by their friends.

RELATIONS WITH OBSERVERS.   Observers differ from participant adult associates on affection, mood, and evaluation in only one way: the ratings indicate greater stability of observer behavior. Comparisons of the quartile deviations show for observer episodes of the Midwest children less variability in affection, with the difference significant beyond .01, and suggest like differences in mood and evaluation. Much the same appears on the child side with the p .10 for affection and .01 for evaluation and mood.

Observers tried to maintain with the subjects an even relationship, free of affective extremes, and the data show something like this.

PRESSURE

Pressure is a summarizing variable. Including all kinds of used social power, it expresses the total amount of influence that one person brings to bear upon another. In what degree did the associates of the children act, whether by commanding, denying, begging, suggesting, cajoling, arguing, teasing, or tempting, to change the children's behavior? And in what degree did the children act to change the behavior of their associates? Both of these questions have been answered by episode ratings on a scale of five points, plus a zero for pressure not detectable; and the answers should help to consolidate some earlier data. Readers should keep in mind that pressure need not be authoritarian. It can be the opposite, as in begging, or take any form, so long as social influence is wielded in some way.

Figure 8.15 presents for the individual Midwest and disabled children the mean and percent of the ratings above zero on pressure exerted by all participant associates. It shows pressure from the associate side in 45 percent of the Midwest episodes, with the individual percents ranging from 38 through 59. It shows also that, for episodes with rated pressure greater than zero, the mean rating is 2.4, with the means ranging from 1.4 through 2.5. Corresponding values of similar size hold for the disabled children. The data show that at least minimum pressure was exerted by an associate in not far under half of the interaction episodes per day.

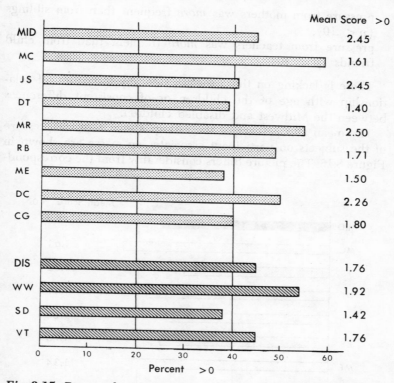

Fig. 8.15. Pressure by participant associates en masse on the Midwest and disabled children. *MID*, Midwest children; *DIS*, disabled children.

We have compared different classes of participant associates on percent of episodes in which pressure was applied by an associate, to find that:

pressure from adults was *more* frequent than from children ($p < .05$);

pressure from mothers was *more* frequent than from child friends ($p < .05$);

pressure from mothers was *less* frequent than from teachers ($p < .10$);

pressure from mothers was *more* frequent than from siblings ($p < .10$);

pressure from teachers was *more* frequent than from child friends ($p < .10$).

There is lacking on the associate side any indication of relationship with age of the children or of consistent differences between the Midwest and disabled children.

The mean and percent of the ratings above zero for pressure of the subjects on participant associates en masse are shown in Figure 8.16. The picture differs considerably from the correspond-

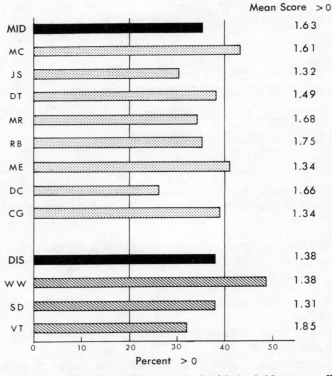

Fig. 8.16. Pressure by Midwest and disabled children on all participant associates. *MID*, Midwest children; *DIS*, disabled children.

ing one of behavior by associates. For the Midwest subjects, the mean pressure rating is 1.6, against 2.4 on the associate side. Comparisons in terms of the percent of episodes in which pressure was judged to occur show that:

> **pressure** from all associates is *more* frequent than pressure by the children upon all associates ($p < .01$);
>
> **pressure** from all adults is *more* frequent than pressure upon all adults ($p < .01$);
>
> **pressure** from mothers is *more* frequent than pressure upon mothers ($p < .01$);
>
> **pressure** from fathers is *more* frequent than pressure upon fathers ($p < .05$);
>
> **pressure** from teachers is *more* frequent than pressure upon teachers ($p < .10$).

On the subject side, no consistent differences are found from one to another class of associates in pressure exerted by the child as compared with all others. Again, there are no relationships with age of the children, and there are no differences between the Midwest and disabled subjects. A difference significant at .01 shows that observers put less pressure than other adults upon the children. There is no evidence that the children exerted either more or less pressure upon observers than upon other associates of any class. A difference significant again at .01 does indicate, however, more pressure by the subjects upon observers than by observers upon the subjects, whereas we have seen the reverse for all classes of participant adults. The bystander position of the observer is demonstrated as clearly here as at any point.

SOCIAL INTERPLAY

With what relative frequency did the children become involved with their associates in different types of *inter*action proper?

INTERPLAY TYPE

Our types of interplay may be summarized as follows from discussion in Chapter 6. Where associate and child are involved in conflict   the action of each disagrees with the wants of the other, and the two actions are mutually opposed;

disjunction   the action of each or of either is contrary to the wants of the other, but the two actions are not mutually opposed;

unfriendly rivalry   both jointly elect the same activity or comparable activities, each tries to outdo the other, and the action of each disagrees with the other's wants, so that neither wishes the other to compete;

cooperation   both jointly elect the same activity, each adopts the end of this activity as a common goal, both play down other goals, and the action of each agrees with the wants of the other, with the total effect that the two actions tend to be mutually supporting;

conjunction   the action of each agrees with the wants of the other, and the action of one may, yet need not, support that of the other (as in gratuitous helping), but the two actions are not mutually supporting;

friendly rivalry   both elect the same activity or comparable activities, each tries to outdo the other, and the action of each agrees with the wants of the other in such a way that each wants the other to compete.

There are incompatible actions in conflict, disjunction, and unfriendly rivalry as against compatible actions in cooperation, conjunction, and friendly rivalry. The different forms of rivalry are combined in Figure 8.17 because the frequency of each is too low for the more refined breakdown.

Figure 8.17 shows the relative frequency of the interplay types

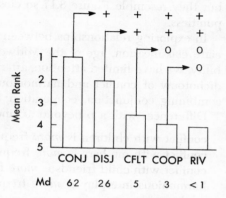

Fig. 8.17. Kinds of interplay between Midwest children and all participant associates. CONJ, conjunction; DISJ, disjunction; CFLT, conflict; COOP, cooperation. (See Fig. 8.4 for other conventions.)

in all interaction episodes of the Midwest children. The total frequency array is quite consistent from child to child, as shown by a W coefficient of .88, significant beyond .01.

Conjunction is foremost among the different kinds of interaction. This ordinary social intercourse without joint activity, but with "a meeting of minds," ranks first in frequency in all of the eight days, and the median percent of episodes in which the analysts found it is 62. Disjunction ranks second, with the median percent down to 26, while conflict ranks third, with a median percent of only 5. Cooperation follows in mean rank, although it is not exceeded consistently by conflict. Rivalry, last in order, accounts for less than 1 percent of all interactions involving the Midwest children.

Episodes in which the actions of Midwest associate and child were compatible greatly exceeded in percent those in which the contrary was true. Added, the percents for conjunction, cooperation, and friendly rivalry show that approximately two-thirds of all standard interaction episodes in the days of the Midwest subjects were judged to involve the children in compatible action relationships. Yet there are the episodes of the remaining near one-third, more than 100 per recorded day, in which incompatible actions were found.

We have drawn pictures like that of Figure 8.17 for the Midwest children with adults and for their interactions with children, but they resemble Figure 8.17 so closely that presenting them is pointless.

In exploring relationships between kind of interplay and associate classification, age of the Midwest child, and physical disability, we have limited attention, after some experimenting, to the dichotomy of conflict and harmonious interplay, with the latter combining conjunction, cooperation, and friendly rivalry.

Differences with a *p* beyond .05 indicate that:

conflict with children is *more* frequent than with adults;
conflict with mothers is *more* frequent than with teachers;
conflict with child friends is *more* frequent than with teachers;
harmonious interplay is *more* frequent with fathers than with mothers.

The data on modes of action anticipate those on conflict. One could expect greater frequency of conflict with adults than with children from the evidence for more frequent counterdominance and less frequent submission by the subjects in their relations with child associates. One could expect greater frequency of conflict with mothers than with teachers from the evidence for more frequent aggression and resistance against mothers than against teachers; and the less frequent conflict with teachers than with child friends is interpretable on similar grounds. The greater frequency of harmonious interplay with fathers than with mothers also is consistent with earlier data.

There is a clear case in a rank order correlation of —1 for decrease in conflict with child associates as age of the Midwest children increases. Also, a correlation of —.57, with a *p* of .10, suggests a decline with age in conflict between the children and adults. These data agree with earlier evidence, especially in the data on action modes, for greater social maturity of the older children.

When the Midwest and disabled children are compared, greater frequency of harmonious interplay with child associates appears among the former. This difference, significant beyond .05, strengthens evidence from the mode data that the Midwest subjects got along better with other children.

One would expect relatively little conflict and at least hope for comparatively harmonious relations between observers and the children, and so it turns out consistently. Differences significant beyond .01 show less frequent conflict and more frequent harmonious interplay in observer episodes than in episodes with participant adults. In five of the eight Midwest days, conflict with observers did not occur at all, and in no case did it occur in more than 3 percent of the interaction episodes. The median percent of harmonious interactions with observers was 88.

ACCORD

Accord gives a synoptic measure in an 11-point scale that extends from maximum disharmony through a neutral point to maximum harmony.

Figure 8.18 shows the mean and interquartile range of the ratings on accord with all participant associates for each of the Midwest and disabled children. The mean ratings, which do not

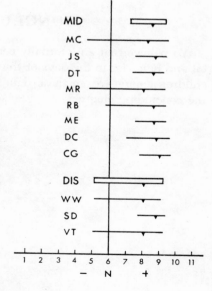

Fig. 8.18. Level of accord on the part of Midwest and disabled subjects with all participant associates. *N*, neutral relationship; —, minus accord (subject and associate at odds); +, plus accord (subject and associate at one). (See Fig. 8.2 for other conventions.)

fall below 8 on the scale or rise above 9, refine the evidence just seen for predominantly harmonious interaction, and indicate high uniformity among the children in average level of accord. Spread of the ratings into the minus part of the scale is conspicuous for 5 of the 11 subjects, 2 of whom are disabled children. One finds on turning back to Figures 8.13 and 8.14 that a similar spread on both evaluation by associates and evaluation by the child hold for each of the same 5 subjects.

No significant differences appear on comparison of associate classes in terms of this variable. However, a rank order correlation of .61, significant beyond .05, indicates increasingly harmonious interaction with child friends with increase in age of the Midwest subjects. Also, a difference with a p of .05 points to more harmonious interaction with child friends in the episodes of the Midwest children than in the episodes of the disabled. These findings are in agreement with those on harmonious interplay and conflict reported under interplay type, and so are parallel comparisons of observers with participant associates.

CONCLUSION

We believe that an internally consistent picture of social habitat and behavior in the days of the Midwest and nearby disabled children emerges from these data, which are drawn together in the concluding chapter.

Chapter 9

THE PRESENT YIELD
OF THE METHOD:
A DIGEST

... sleep in the minutes, let and come chociction. The behavior ... communications often than the ... recovered only of normal ... ... direct major to coordinate very rapid. Most ... ... stand occasion of the one half to over 30 percent of the ... ... in the children ... ...

SYNOPSIS

We have collected specimen behavior records from individual children who lived during the middle years of this century in the American town of Midwest, and from disabled children of neighboring communities. Each record is a detailed, sequential narrative of behavior and psychological living conditions as seen by skilled observers. The records have been divided into integral units of molar behavior and situation. These units, called episodes, have been studied in their relations with one another as elements of behavior structure. Characteristics of the social situations and behavior of the children have been examined and quantified, episode by episode.

These procedures identify the way to record and analyze child behavior that has been presented in this book. We shall not retrace the steps of the procedures or review the efforts to ground and connect them conceptually. We shall instead try to represent the method pragmatically by summarizing the results of its application to the behavior streams of the children.

THE STRUCTURE OF INDIVIDUAL BEHAVIOR

The findings on the structure of individual behavior as revealed by interrelations between behavior-situation episodes are based on data for 12 Midwest children from 2 to 11 years old and 4 disabled children within this age range. We shall begin with the children of Midwest.

Each of these children was seen to engage in a multitude of episodes; the number of things a child did in a day, according to our criteria, varied approximately from 500 to 1300. Duration of the episodes ranged from a few seconds to 121 minutes, with more than 70 percent of them shorter than 2 minutes.

Most of the episodes did not occur in isolation. The behavior continuum was often like the interwoven strands of a cord in that its molar units often overlapped. More than one behavior strand occurred at one time in half to over 80 percent of the episodes in the different records. The strands were limited in number when the behavior was cord-like in this way. Only about 10 percent of the overlapping episodes included more than two strands. Most of the overlapping involved intersection of an entire short episode with a relatively small part of a longer one.

The behavior was cord-like, too, in the sense that overlapping episodes often did not terminate at the same time, but formed an interwoven merging continuum. On the average, the transitions of more than half of the episodes were of this kind. Sequences of structurally interrelated episodes, called linkages, averaged about 400 per day. They included up to 81 episodes each, with the median number 2.3.

The episodes were not always continuous from beginning to end. Three percent or less of all in a day were interrupted at some point and later resumed after interpolation of one or more episodes. Not more than 9 percent of the episodes in any record were interpolated between segments of discontinuous units.

Episodes that appeared to start spontaneously and episodes initiated by external events were about equal in frequency. For every child, however, spontaneous termination of episodes exceeded termination brought about by outside forces.

The children completed more than 70 percent of their episodes, assumedly with some release of tension in every such case. Definitely "good" endings (attainment, gratification, or success) occurred in 4 to 19 percent of the episodes of every record, and episodes with "bad" endings (nonattainment, frustration, or failure) occurred in less than 10 percent.

The structure of behavior changed with increasing age. The younger children tended to shift from one action to another, to do things sequentially, one at a time, and to quit episodes before completing them more frequently than the older children; and the latter tended to engage more often in actions of longer duration, to carry on more than one action at a given time, and to complete a higher proportion of their episodes. We have found it surprising that the frequency of success, failure, and frustration was not related in any way to age among the children, and that age and the spontaneity of episode initiation and termination were not positively related.

Another surprise to us is the absence of unequivocal evidence that the physically disabled children differed appreciably from the normal Midwest children in behavior structure. There are only suggestions that more interpolated episodes and more instigated initiations and terminations may have occurred in the days of the disabled children. The second of these indications may be attributable to the more adult-permeated living conditions under which most of the disabled children lived.

Many structural characteristics of behavior vary widely from subject to subject; here is an area of great individual differences. In some characteristics, however, the differences are small, despite a wide range in age and physical status. The absence of clear differences between the normal and disabled children, particularly in completion of episodes and in success, failure, frustration, and gratification, seems to carry two important implications: (a) the structure of behavior as an episode complex is centrally, not peripherally, determined; and (b) the outcome of behavior episodes in terms of success, failure, and frustration is in children virtually unrelated to motor and intellectual abilities. The fact that the 2-year-olds and the 10-year-olds, the physically disabled and the normal children evidently experienced much the same episode outcomes raises the possibility that some governing apparatus functions to protect the weak and disabled from too injurious psychological consequences of their limitations.

SOCIAL ACTION AND INTERACTION

Analysis of the social components in behavior episodes of eight Midwest children, divided equally as to sex and social group, and distributed in age from 2 years through 10, has provided a variegated description of social action and interaction in the lives of the children. A day of episodes in the life of each child was studied, with the number in a day ranging from 494 to 1159. The number of analyzed units varied for different stages of the analysis, as Chapter 8 will here be left to explain.

The habitats of the children were predominantly social in that 73 to 87 percent of the episodes in a day involved the child with an associate. The social parts of these episodes, moreover, generally outranked the nonsocial in potency and, where social and nonsocial episodes overlapped, the former were almost always of greater relative weight. Hence the target days were both extensively and intensively social. The associate was a single individual rather than a grouping of individuals in some 90 percent of the social episodes. Observers became associates in about 20 percent. But the data indicate that, as intended, the observers characteristically were bystanders, with low output as initiators, evaluators, dominators, aggressors, resistors, and benefactors, with neutral affection and mood—in episodes of low weight. Roughly, overall, adults made up 60, children 35, adolescents 2, and pets or other animals 3 percent of the "regular" Midwest associates. Mothers were most frequent among adults, with teachers second; and mothers exceeded fathers about 7 to 1.

A complete interaction occurred in about 80 percent of the social units; and from here on only *interaction episodes* that involved the child with a single regular Midwest inhabitant enter into the review. Observers will be left out of account in view of their chiefly methodological significance.

Greater rated power of associates was a generally prevailing rule of the children's social situations. Frequent exceptions occurred only when the associate was a child of an age equal or under that of the subjects; the rule held best for interactions with adults, who consistently far outweighed the children in power. Yet the children did not characteristically wait for associates of any class to take the lead. All of them initiated about half of their behavior transactions with others of every associate class. Interaction between associate and child, however started, continued beyond a single act and a response much more often than not; involvement of the children with others was cyclical in this sense in about two of every three interaction episodes.

Data on modes of action in behavior of the children and their associates are summarized in Tables 9.1 and 9.2, which list prototypic verbalizations of the different action modes. Table 9.1 represents the frequency of each mode of action by, and of the children toward, adult associates; and Table 9.2 does the same for child associates. The asterisks show the number of occurrences of each mode on the average in every 50 episodes. Several generalizations are raised for review by these schematic approximations.

It appears that the children lived their days with adults in a benevolent autocracy. Evidence for this is in salient complementary relationships between adult behavior and child behavior. Adults were often dominative, while the children often submitted to adults. Grownups, then, frequently controlled the children in an authoritarian way. The children often appealed to adults while adults were often nurturant. Thus, grownups frequently acted to benefit the children who, at the same time,

TABLE 9.1.   Modes of Action by Midwest Children and their Adult Associates

Mode of Action		Associate Side	Child Side
Dominance:	Quiet! Quiet!	******************	****
Nurturance:	Let me help you	**************	****
Resistance:	No	*******	********
Appeal:	Please	*****	***************
Compliance:	I will	*****	******
Aggression:	Take that!	***	***
Submission:	I give in	**	***********
Avoidance:	You repel me		*

NOTE: Each row of symbols represents the number of occurrences of a mode in every 50 episodes. For example, the row of symbols on the child side and opposite dominance shows that in 4 episodes of every 50 dominance occurred in behavior of the children with adult associates. The data are based upon analysis of episodes in eight specimen day records.

showed dependence by their frequent solicitation of benefit. The regimen of the children with adults had also the common authoritarian feature of centralization, most of all in mothers, and next in teachers, of power used in dominance and nurturance; the autocracy was matriarchal.

This benevolent autocracy was not characteristically subjugative, for the children resisted adults only a little less often than they submitted to them, even in interactions with mothers, who dominated them most. Further, in some episodes the children did attack or act to dominate grownups; aggression, dominance, *and* resistance occurred singly, in pairs, or in a bold triad in 30 percent of the interactions with adults. Also, by initiating roughly every other interaction with a grownup, the children showed freedom to approach and call upon their elders, to lead off, speak up, and have a say with them. Adults did not cow the children.

The autocracy was not characteristically indulgent, for adult resistance ranked just below adult action to benefit. Nor was it hostile, as the high frequency of nurturance and the rarity of aggression by adults imply, to say nothing of evidence that the children got from grownups much more approval and plus affection than disapproval and minus affection. Neither was the adult-over-child situation characteristically rejective, to judge from the virtual absence of avoidance by adults. Nor was it conflictive in the particular sense that the children frequently met dominance with counterdominance. Also, there was little outright aggression on either side.

Turning now in Table 9.2 to action of the children with children, we note first that it does not show an authoritarian control relation. Child associates were quite often dominative. But the children were by no means commensurately submissive. On the other hand, they were frequently resisting. And they showed even somewhat more dominance than their friends and siblings. Thus, instead of submitting to peers, the children held out against them or countered their dominative behavior. The children got into contention with other children much more than with adults, who were more powerful; dominance, aggression, and resistance occurred in 54 percent of the episodes with other children. This could mean that impulses to contend against strong authority were transferred to weaker associates. Something of a dependency relation does appear in action involving the children with children; for frequent appeal by the subjects complements frequent nurturance by child associates. Differences in age between child and child associates may account for this relationship, but episode by episode data on these differences are not now available.

We have seen that the mode-of-action picture, while it does show adult control and child dependence, also reveals beneficence in the social situation of the children with adults. Rounding out this picture, data on affection, mood, and evaluation as attributes of all social behavior disclose a characteristically friendly, pleasant, and approving situation with grownups, and others as well. These data also show that the children generally gave what they got from all others in affection, mood, and evaluation. Although much more often approving than disapproving, evaluation of the children by their associates, and vice versa, varied a great deal more than affection and mood of both associate and child. Social pressure, as a fourth basic attribute of social action, was exerted on the children by their associates in 45 percent of the interaction episodes, but on associates by the children in only about 35 percent of these episodes. This one might easily expect from the findings on relative power.

**TABLE 9.2.   Modes of Action by Midwest Children and their
Child Associates**

Mode of Action		Associate Side	Child Side
Dominance:	Quiet! Quiet!	*******	************
Nurturance:	Let me help you	**********	*********
Resistance:	No	*************	********
Appeal:	Please	******	*********
Compliance:	I will	***	***
Aggression:	Take that!	****	******
Submission:	I give in	******	***
Avoidance:	You repel me	**	*

NOTE: See legend under Table 9.1.

Also, in line with the power findings, adults outdid child associates, while mothers and teachers surpassed associates of every other class, in bringing pressure to bear upon the children.

This leaves interaction per se as a social process. Harmonious types of interaction (conjunction, cooperation, and friendly rivalry) outnumbered disharmonious types (disjunction, conflict, and unfriendly rivalry) about 2 to 1. The most frequent single kind of social interplay was conjunction, defined as friendly interaction short of cooperation, which occurred in 3 of every 5 interaction episodes; and the type next in frequency was disjunction, or discord short of conflict, which occurred in 1 interaction episode of every 4. In only 5 interactions per 100 did the children get into outright conflict with associates. On the other hand, full-fledged cooperation occurred in but 3 interactions per 100. Friendly and unfriendly rivalry together account for just 1 interaction per 100. On the whole, the Midwest children got along quite impressively well with others. This fact is summed up by the finding that, on a scale, for *accord,* of 11 points, which extends from extremely disharmonious to extremely harmonious social relations, the mean rating on every child falls between 8 and 9.

Some of the ways in which the psychosocial habitat and behavior of the children differed according to class of associate have been mentioned. But several other such differences remain.

Adults surpassed all child associates, mothers exceeded both child friends and siblings, while teachers surpassed child friends, in power over the children as well as in frequency of measurable pressure put upon them. Further, teachers exerted pressure at a higher rate than mothers. Pressure from associates en masse, from adults, from mothers in particular, and from fathers was more frequent than pressure by the children upon each of these.

As for modes of action, adult associates exceeded child associates, and mothers exceeded child friends, in frequency of dominance. At the same time, the children submitted more often to adult than to child associates, and to mothers more often than to child friends. Also, the children understandably gave in to mothers more frequently than to siblings. Child friends avoided the children more often than did mothers. The children complied with adults more frequently than with other children, and yet resisted mothers more often than child friends.

Direct comparison of associate behavior with behavior of the children on action modes shows *dominance* by the children less frequent than by adults en masse, mothers, or fathers; *submission* by the children *more* frequent than by adults en masse, mothers, or fathers; *appeal* by the children also more frequent than by all adults or either parent; *nurturance* by the children less frequent than by either parent; and *resistance* by the children more frequent than by child associates.

Child friends of the children displayed greater and more stable affection for them than did their mothers while, as if to reciprocate, the children showed greater affection for peers than for their mothers. Yet they got into conflict with child associates more frequently than with adults in general. Also, they got into conflict with mothers and child friends more often than with teachers. They were happier, too, with child friends than with adults in general. They were happier with fathers than with mothers; and their social interplay was more often harmonious with fathers than with mothers.

Some of the variables in this analysis of social action were related to the age of the child. With increase in age of the children there occurred: a gain in the complexity of social partners as shown by an increase in groupings of two or more individuals as associates; a decrease in the frequency of adults and especially of parents as associates; an increase in child associates among whom, moreover, the proportion of children younger than the subjects rose; an increase in amount of power and in fluctuation of power from episode to episode in relations with associates en masse; a definite power gain in interactions with other children; a decline in the frequency of cyclical interplay with adults; a decline in resistance against the children by grownups in general and mothers in particular; a change in the relation of dependency upon adults, marked by a decline in appeal to grownups without loss, however, in nurturance of the children by grownups; a gain in action to benefit adults and also a gain in appeal by adults to the children; an increase in action by the children to benefit child associates; an increase in compliance with associates en masse and with adults in particular; a decrease in avoidance of adults and especially of mothers; a gain in momentary liking for other children; an increase in harmonious relations and a decrease in conflict with other children, and a decrease in conflict with adults. Psychologists have known that development brings change in social situation and behavior; and here are intelligible measures of such change under naturally occurring conditions.

Comparisons of findings from the records on disabled children with those on the Midwest children disclosed some noteworthy differences.

Relatively great dependency of the disabled appeared in more frequent nurturance by their mothers and more frequent appeal to them and to the generality of adults. Mothers of the disabled children displayed greater affection and better mood than mothers of the Midwest children.

Child friends of the disabled subjects were more often aggressive, while the disabled subjects themselves also were more often aggressive and resisting, yet also more frequently submissive with all child associates. Child friends of the disabled were less approving and less steadfastly affectionate. The disabled children, in their relations with child associates, showed greater variability in affection, mood, and evaluation and, like their child friends, less approval of action by the other person. Conflict with child friends occurred more often, and interaction with other children was generally less harmonious in the episodes of the disabled children. In general, child associates were storm centers for the disabled and their mothers were forts of relief from stress. Our data do not go to show that the serious physical disabilities of these children had consequences for the other psychosocial variables of the study.

POSTSCRIPT

When we look back over the report on the Midwest children and their situations and behavior, much of it sounds like American children almost anywhere, as far as one can tell by living in some different parts of the country, by reading novels and short stories about American children, by going to American movies, by visiting American schools, by having an American family. But some of it probably is unique to Midwest. How much, we do not know. We have found little direct aggression by and against Midwest children. Is there more in Chicago? Perhaps children of English villages do not start as many as half of their social episodes. Do mothers of Park Avenue in New York spend as much time with their children as mothers of Midwest?

No kind of casual observing can answer such questions. But systematic observing can. It is hoped that these and other ecological uses of observational methods in psychology will be stimulated by these and other beginnings, with belief that the resulting store of knowledge cannot but be of practical and theoretical value.

REFERENCES

Adams, D. K. A restatement of the problem of learning. *British J. of Psychol.*, 1931–1932, **22**, 150–178.

Allport, G. W. The use of personal documents in psychological science. *Social Science Research Council Bull.*, 1942, No. 49.

Anderson, H. H. The measurement of domination and of socially integrative behavior in teachers' contacts with children. *Child Develpm.*, 1939, **10**, 73–89.

Andrus, Ruth. A tentative inventory of the habits of children from two to four years of age. *Teach. Coll. Contr. Educ.*, 1924, No. 160.

Baldwin, A. L. *Psychological development in childhood.* New York: Holt, Rinehart and Winston, 1955.

Baldwin, A. L., Kalhorn, Joan, and Breese, F. H. Variables of parent behavior. *J. abnorm. soc. Psychol.*, 1941, **30**, 525–542.

Baldwin, A. L., Kalhorn, Joan, & Breese, F. H. The appraisal of parent behavior. *Psychol. Monogr.*, 1949, **63**, No. 4.

Barker, R. G. Ecology and motivation. In M. R. Jones (Ed.), *Nebraska symposium on motivation.* Lincoln: Univer. Nebraska Press, 1960. Pp. 1–49.

Barker, R. G. (Ed.) *The stream of behavior.* New York: Appleton-Century-Crofts, 1963.

Barker, R. G. Explorations in ecological psychology. *Amer. Psychologist*, 1965, **20**, 1–14.

Barker, R. G., & Barker, Louise S. Behavior units for the comparative study of cultures. In B. Kaplan (Ed.), *Studying personality cross-culturally.* New York: Harper & Row, 1961. Pp. 457–476.

Barker, R. G., & Gump, P. V. *Big school, small school.* Stanford: Stanford Univer. Press., 1964.

Barker, R. G., & Wright, H. F. Psychological ecology and the problem of psychosocial development. *Child Develpm.*, 1949, **20**, 131–143.

Barker, R. G., & Wright, H. F. *One boy's day.* New York: Harper & Row, 1951.

Barker, R. G. & Wright, H. F. *Midwest and its children: the psychological ecology of an American town.* New York: Harper & Row, 1955.

Barker, R. G., Dembo, Tamara, & Lewin, K. Frustration and regression: a study of young children. *Univer. of Iowa Stud. Child Welf.*, 1941, **18**, No. 1.

Barker, R. G., Wright, H. F., & Koppe, W. A. The psychological ecology of a small town. In Wayne Dennis (Ed.), *Readings in child psychology.* Englewood Cliffs, N.J.: Prentice-Hall, 1951. Pp. 552–566.

Barker, R. G., Wright, H. F., Barker, Louise S., & Schoggen, Maxine. *Specimen records of American and English children.* Lawrence, Kan.: Univer. of Kansas Press, 1961.

Barnes, R. M. *Motion and time study.* New York: Wiley, 1958.

Biber, Barbara, Murphy, Lois B., Woodcock, Louise P., & Black, Irma S. *Child life in school: a study of a seven-year-old group.* New York: Dutton, 1942.

Bingham, H. C. Selective transportation by chimpanzees. *Psychol. Monogr.*, 1929, **5**, No. 26.

Dawe, Helen C. An analysis of two hundred quarrels of preschool children. *Child Develpm.*, 1934, **5**, 139–157.

Dennis, W. A biography of baby biographies. *Child Develpm.*, 1936, **7**, 71–73.

Dresslar, F. B. A morning's observation of a baby. *Pedagogical Sem.* 1901, **8**, 469–481.

Festinger, L. The significance of difference between means without reference to the frequency distribution function. *Psychometrics*, 1946, **11**, 97–105.

Fite, M. D. Aggressive behavior in young children and children's attitudes toward aggression. *Genet. Psychol. Monogr.*, 1940, **22**, 151–319.

Frank, L. K. Time perspectives. *J. soc. Phil.*, 1939, **4**, 293–312.

Gellert, Elizabeth. Systematic observation: a method of child study. *Harvard Educ. Rev.*, 1955, **25**, 179–195.

Gingerelli, J. A. The principle of maxima and minima in animal learning. *J. comp. Psychol.*, 1930, **11**, 193–236.

Goldstein, K. *The organism: a holistic approach to biology derived from pathological data on man*, Vol. II. New York: American Book Company, 1939.

Guthrie, E. R. *The psychology of learning.* New York: Harper & Row, 1935.

Hartley, Ruth E., Frank, L. K., & Goldenson, R. N. *Understanding children's play.* New York: Columbia Univer. Press, 1952.

Heider, F. *Ding und medium.* Symposion, 1927, **1**, 109–157. Trans.: J. Psychol. Issues, **I**, No. 3. 1959.

Heider, F. Social perception and phenomenal causality. *Psychol. Rev.*, 1944, **51**, 358–374.

Heyns, R. W., & Lippitt, R. Systematic observational techniques. In G. Lindzey (Ed.), *Handbook of social psychology*, Vol. I. Cambridge: Addison-Wesley, 1954, 370–404.

Isaacs, Susan. *Intellectual growth of young children.* New York: Harcourt, Brace & World, 1930.

Isaacs, Susan. *Social development in young children.* New York: Harcourt, Brace & World, 1933.

Jersild, A. T., & Meigs, M. F. Direct observation as a research method. *Rev. of educ. Res.*, 1939, **9**, 472–482.

Kendall, M. *Rank correlation methods.* London: Griffin, 1948.

Köhler, W. *Mentality of apes.* Translated by E. Winter. New York: Harcourt, Brace & World, 1925.

Koppe, W. A. A study in psychological ecology: a survey of the behavior settings of Midwest. Unpublished doctoral dissertation. Univer. of Kansas, 1954.

Kounin, J. S. Intellectual development and rigidity. In R. G. Barker, J. S. Kounin, & H. F. Wright (Eds.), *Child behavior and development.* New York: McGraw-Hill, 1943.

Lafore, Gertrude G. *Practices of parents in dealing with preschool children.* New York: Teach. Coll. Contr. Educ., 1945.

Lewin, K. *Dynamic theory of personality.* Translated by D. K. Adams & K. E. Zener. New York: McGraw-Hill, 1935.

Lewin, K. *Principles of topological psychology.* New York: McGraw-Hill, 1936.

Lewin, K. *The conceptual representation and the measurement of psychological forces.* Durham, N.C.: Duke Univer. Press, *Contributions to psychological theory,* 1938, **1**, No. 4.

Lippitt, R. An experimental study of the effect of democratic and authoritarian group atmospheres. Studies in topological and vector psychology, *Univer. of Iowa Stud. in Child Welf.,* 1940, **16**, No. 3.

Littman, R. A., & Rosen, E. Molar and molecular. *Psychol. Rev.,* 1950, **57**, 58–65.

McDougall, W. *Outline of psychology.* New York: Scribner, 1923.

McFarland, Margaret B. Relationships between young sisters as revealed in their overt responses. *Child Devel. Monogr.,* 1938, No. 23.

Muchow, Martha & Muchow, H. *Der Lebensraum des Grosstadtkindes.* From the monograph series: Der Ertrag der Hamburger Erziehungsbewegung, 1935. No. 2, Hamburg: Martin Riegel.

Muenzinger, K. F. *Psychology: the science of behavior.* New York: Harper & Row, 1942.

Murray, H. A. *Explorations in personality.* New York: Oxford Univer. Press, 1938.

Muse, Marianne. Time expenditures in homemaking activities in 183 Vermont farm homes. *Vermont Agricultural Experiment Station Bull.,* 1946, No. 530.

Novikoff, A. B. The concept of integrative levels and biology. *Science,* 1945, **101**, 209–215.

Piaget, J. *The language and thought of the child.* New York: Harcourt, Brace & World, 1926.

Raush, H. L. On the locus of behavior-observations in multiple settings within residential treatment. *Amer. J. Orthopsychiat.,* 1959, **29**, 235–243.

Raush, H. L., Dittmann, A. T., & Taylor, T. J. The interpersonal behavior of children in residential treatment. *J. abnorm. soc. Psychol.,* 1959a, **58**, 9–27.

Raush, H. L., Dittmann, A. T., & Taylor, T. J. Person, setting, and change in social interaction. *Human Relat.,* 1959b, **12**, No. 4, 361–378.

Raush, H. L., Dittmann, A. T., & Taylor, T. J. Person, setting, and change in social interaction: II. A normal control study. *Human Relat.*, 1960, **13**, 305–332.

Rickers-Ovsiankina, Marika. Die Wiederaufnahme unterbrockener Handlungen. *Psychologische Forschung*, 1928, **11**, 302–379.

Schoggen, P. H. Structural properties of children's behavior based on sixteen day-long specimen records. Unpublished doctoral dissertation. Univer. of Kansas, 1954.

Schoggen, P. H. A device for electronic recording of behavior specimens. Unpublished report, 1961.

Sherman, M. The differentiation of emotional responses. *J. comp. Psychol.*, 1927, **7**, 265–284.

Sorokin, P. & Berger, C. Q. *Time-budgets of human behavior.* Cambridge: Harvard Univer. Press, 1939.

Tolman, E. C. *Purposive behavior in animals and men.* New York: Appleton-Century-Crofts, 1932.

Walker, Helen M., & Lev, J. *Statistical inference.* New York: Holt, Rinehart and Winston, 1953.

Warner, W. L., Meeker, Marchia, & Eells, K. *Social class in America.* Chicago: Science Research Associates, 1949.

Watson, J. B. *Behaviorism.* New York: The People's Institute Publishing Co., 1924.

Weick, K. E. Systematic observational methods. In G. Lindzey, and E. Aronson (Eds.), *Handbook of social psychology.* Rev. ed. Reading, Mass.: Addison-Wesley. In press.

Wheeler, R. & Perkins, T. *Principles of mental development.* New York: Crowell, 1932.

White, R. W. *Lives in progress.* New York: Holt, Rinehart and Winston, 1952.

Wright, H. F. Psychological development in Midwest. *Child Devel.*, 1956, **27**, 265–286.

Wright, H. F. Observational child study. In P. H. Mussen (Ed.), *Handbook of research methods in child development.* New York: Wiley, 1960. Pp. 71–139.

Wright, H. F. The city-town project: a study of children in communities differing in size. Department of Psychology, Univer. of Kansas, 1961.

Wright, H. F. *Community size and child behavior.* In preparation. 1966.

Wright, H. F., & Barker, R. G. *Methods in psychological ecology*. Lawrence, Kan.: Department of Psychology, Univer. of Kansas, 1950.

Wright, H. F., Barker, R. G., Nall, J., & Schoggen, P. H. Toward a psychological ecology of the classroom. *J. of educ. Res.*, 1951, **45**, 187–200.

Zeigarnik, B. Uber das Behalten von erledigten und unerledigten Handlungen. *Psychologische Forschung*, 1927, **9**, 1–85.

APPENDIX

Sketches that outline identifying characteristics and circumstances of the children who served as subjects for specimen day records are subjoined.[1] Introductory comment about the children is on pages 9 and 10.

The sketches are in order by ages of the children, for each of whom conventional notations of sex, age, and social group follow the code name of the child.

All of the records were made between November 23, 1948, and February 8, 1951. The date and time span of the record on each child is entered beneath his or her code name.

CHILDREN OF MIDWEST

PRESCHOOL CHILDREN

Mary Chaco: F, 1-10, II
October 10, 1950: 7:00 A.M.–9:45 P.M.

Mary was pert, small-boned, blond, and brown-eyed. Much of her ready chatter was understandable.

Mary's family consisted of her father and mother and her brother, Otto, a lively four-year-old. The father owned and operated a service station and car repair business. He was active in the American Legion and one of the youngest members of the local Rotary Club. Mary's mother belonged to the Homemaker's Club and was president of the American Legion Auxiliary. Mrs. Chaco's mother and father, two sisters, and a younger brother, lived in Midwest. The Chaco children often were cared for by their grandmother and two aunts.

[1] Louise Barker, Maxine Schoggen, and Lorene Wright prepared the original sketches.

The family rented a small, neat, frame house near the service station. A single bedroom held Mary's crib, Otto's roll-away bed, and the parents' bed. The kitchen and bathroom were modern and well equipped, and the living room was attractively furnished. The dining room served as a sewing-play space most of the time. The back yard, approximately 40×50 feet, blended imperceptibly with the yards of the two neighbors, with both of whom Mary was on visiting terms.

James Sexton: M, 1-11, II
February 8, 1951: 7:20 A.M.–8:10 P.M.

Jimmy Sexton was a rosy-cheeked, blond boy with sparkling, brown eyes. He was an only child. Jimmy talked a lot, often in understandable sentences. He was skillful at manipulating things.

Jimmy's father was the operator of two farms near town. He and his wife sponsored the Methodist Youth Fellowship, and he was active in the American Legion and the Masonic Lodge. The mother participated energetically in Methodist Church groups, the Eastern Star, the Homemaker's Club, and the American Legion Auxiliary. She also was a leader of the Brownie Scout Troop. A docile Scottie dog was prominent in the immediate family circle. Jimmy's paternal grandfather and an aunt lived in Midwest, and his maternal grandparents lived a few miles out of town on a farm.

The family rented a white, frame bungalow set toward the front of a large corner lot. A living room, dining room, kitchen, two bedrooms, and a bathroom were all comfortably furnished. The dining room served as a sewing space for Mrs. Sexton and a playroom for Jimmy.

Lewis Hope: M, 2-11, II
November 21, 1950: 7:00 A.M.–9:15 P.M.

Lewis, better known as "Chuck," was the third in a family of four children. He was a robust, sturdy child with an unusually friendly, winning style. He spoke clearly and expressed himself well.

Chuck's father was an instructor in the Veterans Administration Vocational Farm Training Program in Midwest. He belonged to the American Legion, the Farm Bureau, and the Presbyterian Church Choir. His wife had graduated from the State University and taught English in a high school for several years before her children were born. She was an active member of the Homemaker's Club, the

American Legion Auxiliary, the Home Demonstration Unit, the Eastern Star, the PTA., and the Presbyterian Church. Stanton, the eldest son, was 10 years old and in the fourth grade. Alma, the only girl in the family, was 8 years old and in the second grade. Ben, the baby, was 11 months old. The Hopes had, in addition to a large, yellow cat and a dog, three calves and a milk cow, housed in a small barn on their lot and pastured on a neighboring five acres. One calf was proudly claimed by Chuck.

The Hope family had lived in Midwest for only a year. They owned a five-room, one-story, white, frame house which had been modernized. The surrounding yard provided shaded areas for play.

Dutton Thurston: M, 3-10, III
November 3, 1950: 7:06 A.M.–9:16 P.M.

Dutton, nicknamed "Chuck," was the youngest in a family of three children. He was well-coordinated and remarkably energetic.

Mr. Thurston worked at the Midwest Hardware and Implement Store as a mechanic, and Mrs. Thurston worked on Friday mornings and all day Saturdays in Cabell's Department Store. She was president of the PTA and a member of the Homemaker's Club. Alfred, an older brother, had graduated from Midwest High School in 1950. He lived at home and worked with his father at the hardware store. Shirley, a 14-year-old, was a sophomore in high school. A large dog and a small kitten were the family pets. The maternal grandparents lived in Midwest and the paternal grandparents had a home on a farm about six miles out of town.

The Thurstons rented a large farm house at the edge of Midwest on something over 60 acres of pasture land, where they kept several dairy cows and some horses, pigs, and chickens. The house had electricity but no running water, and its heat was provided by a miscellany of stoves that burned kerosene, wood, and oil.

Margaret Reid: F, 4-6, III
June 2, 1949: 8:00 A.M.–10:17 P.M.

Margaret was a daintily-built child of average height for her age. She was animated and alert.

Margaret's father worked in Kerr's Grocery. His chief hobbies were raising dogs and hunting with them. Margaret's mother possessed a beautiful voice, and her singing was often in demand at church and community affairs. She was active in Methodist Church groups and attended the Methodist Sunday School with Margaret and 18-month-old Bradley. Both maternal and paternal grandparents lived in Midwest and were frequent visitors at the Reid home. Tiny, a fox terrier puppy, was the pet of the family.

The Reids owned their one-story, white, frame house, which contained a living room, dining room, kitchen, two bedrooms, and a bathroom. The yard offered plenty of shade and play space.

Maud Pintner: F, 5-0, I
December 5, 1950: 8:26 A.M.–7:44 P.M.

Maud was a blond, blue-eyed girl of small, wiry build with more than average agility and pertness. She often enlivened Sunday School and Ladies' Aid programs with a recitation or song.

Maud's family included her father and mother, her 20-month-old brother, Frederick, and her maternal grandmother. The father was part owner and the manager of an abstract business. He belonged to the American Legion and sang in the Presbyterian Church Choir. Mrs. Pintner, a native of Midwest, had worked as a stenographer before her marriage. She belonged to the Eastern Star, the Presbyterian Church Choir, the American Legion Auxiliary, and Women's Club I. Kemo, a huge, long-haired dog, was a long-suffering playmate of the children.

The Pintners lived in a modern, white, frame house that belonged to the grandmother. It consisted of a living room, music room, dining room, kitchen, dinette, four bedrooms, and a bathroom, all on one floor. The furnishings, many of them antiques, were attractive and tastefully arranged. Many full bookshelves, a record player, and a grand piano were all in regular use. The yard surrounding the house was well landscaped.

SCHOOL-AGE CHILDREN

Roy Eddy: M, 6-2, III
February 22, 1949: 7:00 A.M.–8:31 P.M.

Roy was of about average height and weight for his age, and quite robust. He was in the first grade in school and attended the Presbyterian Sunday School, in which he had won a perfect attendance award.

Roy lived with his father, mother, two older sisters, and one older brother. The father worked on the county road crew and was one of the advisors for the 4-H group. Roy's mother worked as a cook in a local cafe, which she helped to manage. Yet she spent a good deal of time with her children, especially in working with them on their 4-H projects. Mrs. Eddy belonged to the Presbyterian Church and the PTA. The entire family, except Roy, contributed to the family income. The oldest sister, Lola, a junior in high school, worked at Poole's Grocery after school. Mollie, a freshman in high school, was responsible for the housekeeping at home. Vernon, a 12-year-old, was raising two calves for market besides milking the family cow. He delivered the weekly advertising sheet for Kane's Grocery. A cocker spaniel was often a central part of the family group.

The Eddys rented a one-story, white, frame house with two bedrooms, a dining room, a living room, a large kitchen, and a bathroom. All meals were served in the kitchen, leaving the dining space for Roy and Vernon as a sleeping room. The furnishings throughout the house were sturdy and worn. The floors were covered with linoleum rugs and the house was heated by gas stoves.

Raymond Birch: M, 7-4, II

April 26, 1947: 7:00 A.M.—8:33 P.M.

Raymond was a sturdy child, slightly shorter and heavier than the average boy of his age. He was the youngest among the second graders in the Midwest school.

Raymond was an only child. The Birches had no relatives in Midwest, but both the maternal and paternal grandparents lived on nearby farms, and Raymond was a frequent visitor in their homes. The father held a position with the Midwest Hardware and Implement Company, and Mrs. Birch worked in the office of the County Clerk. Honey, a fat, old, fox terrier, was the family pet.

The Birch family rented an apartment in a white, frame house, which, although more than 60 years old, was well-preserved and modernized. The apartment was on the ground floor and had a living room, dining room, kitchen, two bedrooms, and a bathroom. The Birches were responsible for the care of the premises, which included a tall barn, a double garage, a place for a vegetable garden, and a well-kept lawn. The whole place looked neat and comfortable.

Benjamin Hutchings: M, 7-4, I

November 23, 1948: 7:33 A.M.—8:00 P.M.

Benjamin was a slender, dark-haired, sober-faced second grader. He was quiet and seemed to be preoccupied a good deal of the time, but this was offset by his alertness and sparkle when entertained or aroused. He was taller than the average boy of his age group.

Ben's father had a law office over the Midwest bank. He held a law degree from the State University and had been established in Midwest for five years. The mother worked part time as secretary in her husband's office. Both Mr. and Mrs. Hutchings were active in the Methodist Church. She was the president of the Methodist Ladies' Aid and he was the chairman of the church governing board. The Hutchings were active also in community and social circles, with memberships between them in bridge clubs, Women's Club I, the Rotary Club, and the PTA. Ben's sister, Sarah, was 10 years old and in the fifth grade. The children shared two pet dogs and a cat.

The Hutchings lived in their own home, a roomy, two-story, white, frame house on a spacious corner lot. The house had a living room, dining room, and kitchen downstairs, and three bedrooms and a bathroom upstairs. Books were in ample supply for the children.

Mary Ennis: F, 8-7, II

May 12, 1949: 7:00 A.M.–9:25 P.M.

Mary was blond, blue-eyed, small-boned, and dainty. She was in the third grade, took piano lessons, sang in the Junior Choir, belonged to the Brownie Scouts, and attended the Methodist Sunday School.

Mr. Ennis, a civil engineer employed by the federal government, was in charge of a county-wide project. He was a member of the Rotary Club, taught an adult Sunday School Class, and sang in the Methodist Choir and a male quartet. Mary's mother, besides being a good housekeeper, was a mainstay in a number of community groups. She directed the church choir, was president of the Methodist Women's Evening Guild, belonged to Women's Club I, the Rotary Anns, and the American Legion Auxiliary. She was in demand as an accompanist or soloist at musical functions. Timothy, the second child, was a happy, healthy, seven-month-old boy. The family dog, Chico, a large, white shepherd, was much beloved by Mary and her brother.

The Ennis family had lived in Midwest for three years. They had bought their home and done much to make it efficient and attractive. The living room, dining room, two bedrooms, modern kitchen, bathroom, and large, screened porch were all on one floor. A spinet piano added to the charm of the living room, and a new gas furnace to the comfort of the house. The Ennis home was catercorner from the Hutching's.

Douglas Crawford: M, 9-2, II
April 18, 1949: 7:28 A.M.–9:45 P.M.

Douglas was in the third grade. Larger than any other child in the third and fourth grade room, he was well built, weighed about 90 pounds, and had an enviable reputation for strength, toughness, and physical prowess. He wore glasses and was greatly bothered by them at play. Douglas had a lively interest in hunting and fishing, and also was interested in rocks, fossils, flowers, and animals.

The immediate family included his father and mother, an older brother, Thomas, and a younger sister, Norah. The maternal grandparents, who lived on a farm about a mile south of Midwest, were very important to the family. Thomas lived with his grandparents much of the time, to help his grandfather with the chores, and Douglas sometimes helped on the land by driving a tractor. Douglas' father was a graduate of the local high school. He kept some cows to milk, raised pigs, and tilled 40 acres of land adjoining the maternal grandfather's farm. He also did farm labor and sawed timber with a motor-driven saw. Mrs. Crawford, who belonged to an old Midwest family, attended the Presbyterian Church and was secretary of the Ladies' Aid and a member of the Missionary Society. Thomas was a husky, six-foot-tall, eighth grader, and Norah a sociable, independent, six-year-old. All of the family attended the Presbyterian Sunday School, where Douglas was well on toward his seventh year of perfect attendance.

The Crawfords lived in a large, old, white, two-story house on about an acre of land. The house had electricity and running water, but no bathroom. Gas stoves were used for heat. A living room, dining room, kitchen, parents' bedroom and a utility room were on the first floor. Norah and the boys had bedrooms upstairs. A large lawn separated the Crawford's house from the one next door. A number of miscellaneous sheds, chicken yards, and fenced-in areas were scattered near the house. The Crawfords planted a large vegetable garden, and Douglas helped to care for it and the animals.

Claire Graves: F, 10-9, III
January 28, 1949: 7:20 A.M.–9:40 P.M.

Claire Graves, a fifth grader, was a slight child with dark eyes and curly, black hair. She was vividly pretty when animated. Her height was about medium for her age although she looked rather less mature than many of her classmates. Claire belonged to the Girl Scouts and attended the Methodist Church, where she sang in the Junior Choir. She had regular duties at home, and she sometimes helped her older brothers with their paper route.

Claire's parents had come from Midwest County families. Mr. Graves worked in a neighboring city, where he did construction work in the yards of a railway. He was often away from home. Mrs. Graves was the president of the Homemaker's Club, which she had helped to organize. She also belonged to the PTA and the Methodist Church. Other children of the family were Wendell, a high school junior, Ruth, a sophomore in high school, Stanley, an eighth grader, Frances, a fourth grader, and Charles, who was four years old and not yet in school. The family had a big dog and several cats.

The large living room and the kitchen of the Graves' one-story, frame house were centers of the family activities, particularly in winter, when coal stoves kept the house comfortably warm. There was a bedroom for the girls, one for the older boys, and one for Charles and his parents. The kitchen had cold running water and a gas cooking stove. There was no bathroom in the house. The large yard provided plenty of play space, room for a generous vegetable garden, and a chicken yard.

DISABLED CHILDREN OF COMMUNITIES NEAR MIDWEST

Sue Dewall: F, 7-1, IV
June 6, 1951: 6:30 A.M.–8:08 P.M.

Sue Dewall was in the first and second grade room of the Lawton School, a special school for handicapped children in Capitol City, which had a population of approximately 100,000. She was a slight, small-boned, fair-skinned girl with straight, taffy-blond hair. She usually wore clean, cotton school dresses, orthopedic shoes, and anklets; she also wore plastic-framed glasses to help correct a severe myopia. Her manner was intent, frequently serious, and vigorous. The impression of serious intensity derived in part, at least, from the way she bent her head close to whatever she was doing.

Sue had been diagnosed as having cerebral palsy of the spastic type. She was 45 inches tall and weighed just under 50 pounds. She had less than average strength, yet stood out at the school as one of its more active children. Although unmistakably handicapped, she could do almost anything expected of a normal child. She walked on the balls of her feet, and held her arms akimbo as she hurried along. She ran with an unsteady, tripping flurry, not as fast as a normal child, but with as much energy.

Soon after Sue's birth her mother died, and she had been raised by an older, married sister until her admittance to Lawton at five years of age. She was described, at the time of her admission to the school, as having few social graces. The staff members mentioned such things as disorderliness and destructiveness with her own clothes and toys. During her two years at Lawton she had learned to keep herself and her things neat and clean.

Sue was the youngest of seven children, all of whom lived with their father, except Sue and the married sister. The father worked intermittently as a day laborer.

Verne Trennell: M, 7-5, III
June 21, 1951: 7:00 A.M.–9:32 P.M.

Verne was a day student at Lawton, a pleasant-featured boy with unusually rosy cheeks. He wore plastic-framed glasses to remedy crossed eyes. He walked with Canadian-type crutches, and his gait with them was fascinating. Rather than placing the two crutches on the ground and swinging his body between them, Verne used the crutches as extensions of his arms and walked with a four-legged gait, chopping along with surprising speed when he hurried.

A report of a general physical examination of Verne read: "Neurogenic bladder, probably of hypotonic type, resulting from the congenital anomaly *spina bifida*." Verne was slightly hydrocephalic, and his eyesight was impaired by an internal strabismus. Examination of his heart had revealed a grade-two systolic murmur and, owing to neural damage, his legs were partially paralyzed. He had no bladder control, and was obliged, therefore, to wear a rubber urinal strapped to his right leg. His general health had been good, aside from the usual childhood diseases: measles, chickenpox, and scarlet fever.

On week days, Verne attended the Lawton School from 8:30 A.M. to 3:30 P.M. On Sundays he went with his parents to the Lutheran Church and Sunday School, from which he had received a perfect attendance pin. Verne had two older sisters and a younger sister. Mr. Trennell worked as an inspector in an industrial plant of Capitol

City. He was a member of his union's Executive Council and the chief steward of the union at the plant. He belonged to the school board of the Lutheran School Association, and was superintendent of the Lutheran Sunday School. He encouraged Verne to help him with the family car, to fix things about the house, and to be as independent as possible. Verne's mother did her own housework, sewed for the girls, and canned fruits and vegetables from the garden. She was active in the Lutheran Church, where she was a member of the choir and taught a Sunday School class. Mrs. Trennell and her husband had worked closely together in their effort to give Verne the care his handicap demanded. Verne's oldest sister, Sarah, worked as a carhop at a drive-in cafe in the afternoons and evenings. He played with Saralee, the youngest sister and, less often, with Sherlyne, aged nine. Cuddles, a fox terrier, belonged to Verne and was his close companion.

The Trennells owned their house, which was quite far back from a dirt road in a section where the houses were spaced rather far apart. It was a one-story, white, frame house containing a living room, bedroom, kitchen, and bathroom. An additional room was being repaired to become the girls' bedroom; meanwhile their bed was in the living room. Like almost every other home in the neighborhood, the Trennell's had a vegetable garden and a large play space in the yard.

Wally Wolfson: M, 4-3, III
July 9, 1951: 8:00 A.M.–7:35 P.M.

Wally Wolfson was an attractive, blond boy of a little more than average height and about average build. Poliomyelitis had left him unable to walk without leg braces and crutches, although he could stand with support and pull himself up readily with his arms and shoulders. He was a little past two when he contracted polio and, since leaving the hospital, he had regularly received physical treatments in a nearby city and daily massage and infrared treatments, given by his mother, twice a day. Ordinarily, around the house, he either crawled very adeptly on his hands and knees or was carried. Outdoors, he used a small express wagon to get about, putting one knee in it and pushing with the other leg. His health was excellent except for his disability.

Wally lived with his father, mother, and younger sister, Maud, in the small town of Manchester, in Midwest County. Mr. Wolfson, a veteran of World War II, had become an independent carpenter after working for some time with a contractor in Capitol City. Mrs. Wolfson's sister, her husband, and four children lived in the house next door. The cousins were 13, 8, 6, and 2 years of age, and all were nearly constant playmates of Wally and his sister. The father's two younger brothers were often visitors in the home. Wally's paternal grandparents lived on a nearby farm. The pet of the family was a hunting dog.

The Wolfsons owned a two-story, white, frame house and had done much to improve it. The rooms consisted of a living room and kitchen on the first floor and two bedrooms upstairs. There was a pump in the yard and an outdoor toilet. Manchester had no city water.

Bobby Bryant: M, 7-4, II
March 26, 1949: 8:35 A.M.–9:42 P.M.

Bobby Bryant was living a restricted, yet busy and interesting life. He suffered from a congenital heart defect, diagnosed as Eisenmenger's Complex. Because of an opening in the interventricular septum, some of his blood, after returning to the heart, entered the peripheral circulation without first going through his lungs. This gave his skin a bluish color. Bobby was smaller than the average seven-year-old. He had to forego any strenuous activities and rest several hours each day. It was not possible for him to attend school.

The family included Bobby's father, mother, two brothers, and his father's older sister. Mr. Bryant was a professional man whose work kept him away from home much of the time. Bobby's mother was active socially in a group made up of her husband's colleagues and their wives, although her main interest was to make a comfortable home for the family. The brothers, Kenny, an 11-year-old "All-American boy," and Jack, an active 3-year-old, spent much of their time with other children. Aunt Alice, who had come to live with them all when Bobby had shown a desire to learn, was the widow of a missionary and herself a former school teacher. Having the required background for tutoring Bobby, as well as the understanding and love that his problems required, she had happily accepted Bobby as her particular charge.

The Bryants lived in an attractive, white, two-story, frame house in University City, population about 24,000.

INDEX